I Should Have Gone To College

An Origin Story

Jason A. Rosman

This is a work of nonfiction. In order to disguise the identities of some of the people depicted, I have changed their names. Any resemblance to anyone alive or dead that is not in this book is a coincidence and unintentional.

I Should Have Gone To College

An Origin Story

(DBA) Rosman Publishing

E-Book ISBN- 978-0-9998503-1-2

Print ISBN- 978-0-9998503-0-5

FIRST EDITION

Dedicated to my dad, the coolest man I know

Contents

Prologue

This is not a story of war although you may think it is. I prefer to think of it more as a story of a simple unremarkable man in remarkable situations wondering time and time again what the hell was he doing there. Most military books these days are from the viewpoint of elite soldiers. They are usually written by special ops guys like Navy SEALs or Delta Force. These men are very humble when they say anyone can be like them. They are also lying because it is simply not true. These men are the peak of fitness and born with a lot of physical and mental gifts that I could only wish for. I was far from an elite soldier and my perspectives are much different because I was very different.

Imagine yourself between the ages of eighteen-twenty-two. Where were you in life and what kind of responsibility was placed upon your shoulders? When reading this book, it's important to remember the characters were this age, and they were all just normal people put in extraordinary positions having to make life and death decisions with no time to think about them.

I began writing this book in Houston, Texas, in December, 2015. I continued working on it during some of my travels and can proudly say that I have written countless pages in countries such as Brazil, Ireland, Sweden, Montenegro, Turkey, Bulgaria, and Poland. There are so many more countries I could name but it would get tiring. I've written these pages during my stay at crowded youth hostels and cheap hotels. I've written pages in planes, trains, cars, and even jotted down ideas on my phone on a horseback ride in Athens.

Many people view their early twenties as the high point of their lives. I don't agree. I view this time as a stepping stone to bigger and better things, but what I experienced during this time shaped my path to the future. In the following pages, you will be exposed to this portion of my life – however, I consider it a book about how we respond to life's entirety.

Many people will not be mentioned by name because I was unable to locate them and some would surely not consent. Some of the men have given full permission to use their names, but I have chosen to give them a nickname instead, something that I feel suits them best. Regardless, I have a great memory and these stories are not from any journal entries or tape recordings. There is no dramatization, but only the truth as I could see it. To give a fuller perspective of certain events of which I wasn't an immediate witness, I have asked some of my friends who were. Unfortunately, this is a true story.

Happy reading, and remember:

The end is the beginning.

I Should Have Gone To College

An Origin Story

Introduction

I stood in the relative safety of the vehicle hangar bay with mortars landing dangerously close to our little base. By this time, being mortared was quite common. We were about a one hundred-yard sprint from where we slept at night, waiting for the sound of the mortar attack to stop. My heart was pounding waiting for our moment to run. I had no protective gear on and looked to the man next to me. He was one of my best friends and was known as the Big Guy.

The mortar attack stopped and the big doors that closed the hangar bay opened. As soon as they opened, the Big Guy and I looked at each other and started a full sprint towards our sleeping area. After a few steps outside, the mortar attack resumed. Not exactly sure where they were landing but we were definitely running under fire, I wondered if shrapnel from mortar fire hit the taller man like I was told lighting always did.

I've always wondered what being normal felt like. What do normal people do on a typical day? What do they find funny? What motivates them? I do have lots of experience in what not being normal feels like. Laughing when it's not appropriate is probably a big one and always saying the most ridiculous things to people because I find it funny is probably not what normal people do. Just to reiterate something, I am not the Big Guy who was running next to me during the mortar attack. He is on the far side of normal too. On the physical scale, I am the complete opposite of him. To describe the difference between the two of us would probably be what the audience felt like when they watched *Twins,* with Arnold Schwarzenegger and Danny DeVito.

I think it is only fair to introduce myself considering you will be reading this book for a while. How to describe myself? I am at the time of putting pen to paper thirty-years old Physically, I am 5’3”, one hundred seventy-five pounds and balding, which I am not too happy about. I go long periods of time being unemployed. I have a wicked sense of humor and my body feels way older than it should be. I am a very calm person on the outside but inside I feel like every second wasted, I am getting closer to death and want to make up the time. I want to do many exciting things in life and constantly feel trapped.

Before joining the military, I was the typical upper-middle class kid who grew up in suburbia in Orange County, California. I always had a car and never had to rely on public transportation, if any even existed. I played high school soccer and never had to struggle financially because my parents had well-paying jobs. I had never been camping or even shot a gun before. I was as far as possible from the traditional person who would enlist in the Marines. Everybody has a right to serve their country. From the back woods of Texas or the gate-guarded community where I lived, with a house so big that one of the rooms I may have entered no more than twice in my life, we all have the same right to serve. Some people acted shocked when I said I wanted to join, coming from an upper-middle-class existence like that, but I have never cared what anyone else thought. I wanted to do something different and didn’t care that all my friends in high school would be going to college.

My name is Jason Rosman, and this is my origin story.

Where to start is the hardest part. Boot camp is the obvious place but that would be boring. You can watch YouTube videos and probably have seen *Full Metal Jacket*, so I guess I can skip that part and go right to the end of infantry school when we were told what unit we would be going to.

Struggling on our last hump before graduation (yes, hiking in the Marines is called “humping” like we are camels in the middle of the of the desert), a high-ranking officer was walking next to us and would ask each of us our last name. He then looked on a printed sheet of paper and would tell us our unit. It is remarkable to look back and see that my whole future was in this stranger's pocket and that destiny could have sent me to any number of places.

My unit would be 2nd Battalion, 4th Marines, located in the 62 Area of Camp Pendleton, not far from where I was currently training. Most people would be going there it seemed, but a few would get unlucky and go to Hell, also known as 29 Palms, which was a hot, rocky middle-of-nowhere desert. I would be staying next to the beach on the border between San Diego and Orange County. There would be no place in all the military that I could be closer to home. From door to door I would be only thirty-five minutes from my barracks room to my parents' house. How lucky was I? I could have been sent to Hawaii, the Mojave Desert, or somewhere in North Carolina. Where the hell is North Carolina? Does anyone even know?

For whatever reason, maybe a week later while still in infantry school, I was in a Humvee with a Marine who was already in for a few years. I think he got in trouble and they sent him to infantry school to help out. Naturally, he asked me what unit I was going to and I told him 2/4. He responded by saying that unit sucked shit and that the 1st Marines, stationed in Camp Horno, were the best.

Being still very new to the Marines, I got scared and wondered what made the 1st Marines so good and my future unit so shit. I got in a bad mood and was bummed out not wanting my career to get off on a bad note with a bad unit. Little did I know, all Marines think that their unit is the best and think all other units are shit. This Marine, who had never been in 2/4, was just being an arrogant bastard and wanted to scare me. Being a gullible eighteen-year old, I believed him. He was also an asshole, which was apparently common in my new profession.

This Marine, whom I would never see again, would somehow end up joining 2/4 and would die five months later.

My assigned unit had an interesting history. I won't get into all the details because a book could be written just about this topic. During WWII, our regiment, the 4th Marines, was forced to surrender during the Battle of Corregidor and the Japanese seized the unit battle flag.

The four battalions of the regiment would never again be allowed to re-form under a single command element. Instead, the 4th Marines were broken apart and sent from one regiment to another in a constant state of turmoil. Every few years they would move again, always under threat of being deactivated forever.

In present times, even though we were the 2nd Battalion of the 4th Marines, we were actually part of the 5th Marines and were considered the bastard child of the regiment. This is where the "Magnificent Bastard" unit nickname came from. Other battalions of the 5th Marines, like 1/5, 2/5 and 3/5, didn't have to explain what regiment they were in because it was straightforward. On the other hand, my unit was like the son who had to explain why his last name was different than his remarried mom's. I would have to say that I was with 2nd Battalion, 4th Marines, part of the 5th Marines.

All this history wouldn't matter as the buses slowly left the School of Infantry towards the 62 Area. Training was over and the real Marine Corps was about to begin.

Arriving at the 62 Area, I figured things would be different now that I was done with boot camp and SOI, perhaps more civilized. How wrong I was. After a short ride, I got off the bus with dozens of other baby-faced Marines and was greeted by Marines standing in the catwalks on the upper levels of the barracks, whistling at us like we were fresh meat. It was now their chance to make our lives miserable when not that long before, they were in the same position.

Since there were so many new guys checking in at once, we were herded around like sheep to do the whole check-in process without having any idea where anything was or which units we would be attached to.

One Marine checking in with us was a sergeant originally from a different unit that fought in the invasion of Iraq. His uniform had so many ribbons on it, it made my jaw drop. He had like eight compared to my one. Waiting in line to check in, he would tell us all war stories of the fighting he went through the previous year. Still so new to the Marines, I couldn't fathom what he was talking about or even imagine myself going through what he did.

This sergeant would end up becoming one of the three squad leaders in my platoon.

Meeting My Squad

My life as the new guy or boot truly began after I was situated and given a room. My barracks room was supposed to be for two men but our unit had so many new people that we were now forced to have three. Since there were only two beds, I volunteered to take the extra cot because I lived close to home and those men didn't.

I knew one of the Marines, Chris "Tommy" Thompson, vaguely from boot camp and infantry school. From St. Louis, Missouri, Tommy was a few inches taller than me and looked twelve-years old with a baby face mostly covered by large glasses. The other Marine was an East Coaster from New York and I had no idea who he was.

Random Marines wearing regular clothes with no rank insignia would come into my room and start yelling at me because I wouldn't address them by their rank even though it was impossible to know. The pushups and sit-ups I was forced to do never seemed to end. I just wanted to get some sleep. The first few nights were absolute hell wondering how we were supposed to fight alongside these guys if we wanted to kill them more than anyone we may meet on the battlefield.

Even though I was assigned to Golf Company, I still didn't have an assigned platoon. It was just a bunch of guys who acted like a team leader one day and then the next, we would have someone else telling us what to do. I wasn't the only one confused because every new guy was getting treated exactly like I was.

Behind our camp, there was a small firing range that we used to zero in our weapons. Zeroing in a weapon is getting your individual weapon sighted in just for you. Even if you use the same type of rifle, people's zeros will be different. You can take an M-16 right out of the box and it would still need to be zeroed. That is the reason why you always use your own rifle. The perfect shot you think you would get with someone else's rifle would actually be a little off.

On the walk to the firing range, there was this one Marine who wouldn't stop yelling. He was kind of a small guy walking us in a single file line constantly making us scream, "Yes, lance corporal." I wasn't sure exactly why he was yelling all the time because what we were doing was pretty simple. We literally were just walking in a straight line following the guy in front of us. But there he went again yelling for no reason. "When someone speaks to you, you will respond quickly and loudly and address them by rank," he said, "Do you understand?"

"Yes, LANCE CORPORAL," we all shouted back in unison.

A few days later I was assigned to a squad and would finally get some kind of normalcy in my life. Being that in a little over a month we would be going to Iraq, I wanted to meet my squad so I could start learning from them as much as I could. I was assigned to 2nd platoon, 2nd squad, 2nd fire-team.

My team leader was Corporal Shepherd from Los Angeles. He was about average height with an athletic build. He didn't seem like the yelling type of guy but you didn't necessarily have to yell to be an asshole. From the start, he made my life difficult. Even though he was an asshole to me, he seemed like a good guy overall. To be friends with your team leader at this stage was an impossibility. I was nothing more than an annoying boot to him and nothing I ever did pleased him. If I did something perfect, he would find some excuse as to why it wasn't.

The next guy in my team was the guy who was yelling at us for no reason while we were walking to the firing range to zero in our weapons. His name was Lance Corporal Cantu from Corpus Christi, Texas. He was short but still taller than me and didn't seem like he was the athletic or weightlifting type. He didn't have the sort of body that screamed, "I hit the weight room every day." He was in no way out of shape being he was a Marine but I'm sure if he didn't drink as much as he did, he would have looked more ripped. He had a little bit of a cowboy accent which I found to be funny having only heard a Texan accent on TV before.

Lance Corporal Marenger was the machine gunner in our team. He was from Tampa Bay, Florida, and seemed like a solid guy. He was very tall, skinny, and wore these thick rimmed glasses that made him look like the nerd he wasn't. He had a very sarcastic personality but not in a negative way and was a good guy to have around.

I rounded out our four-man team.

Some of the other members of the squad were quite interesting as well. Our radioman, Private First Class Drinkwater was very intelligent and for this reason was given the radio. The radio is a complicated piece of equipment and you better have a smart person using it. He was also an incredible artist.

Although his last name may have been of English origin, he was far from English. His was 100% Italian. His family story is quite typical of the times and what makes our country so interesting. His original family name (which I don't remember) was so Italian, it might as well have been Ravioli.

When his ancestor came into Ellis Island, being that in the old days political correctness wasn't a known term, the immigration officer decided to give him an English-sounding name. So instead of letting him keep a beautiful Italian last name, the immigration officer said, "You are now Drinkwater."

Brian Lenhart was a native of Maryland and along with our radioman the smartest in our squad. He was of average height and build for an eighteen-year old. An extremely thoughtful and handsome guy, he was one of the few East Coast Marines that would come to our unit in the west, and I'm happy he did. He was the youngest in our company and only three months younger than me. Because of his excellence, he was given the important role of point man in our squad. He was a model Marine and great person. I wished I had his intelligence and work ethic.

Then there was the Big Guy. Well, he was just big. Everything about him was big and whenever he would enter a room, people would always stop and stare. He grew up in a one-horse town called Comanche, Texas. So small was this town, they didn't even have a McDonald's. A country boy who didn't grow up on a farm, he sure did have incredible country boy strength. At times seeing him, I would curse the heavens wondering why I couldn't be as naturally strong as him. He was also a very creative person and could build something out of nothing. I wish I had this type of intelligence.

The leader of this band of characters would fall onto the big broad shoulders of our squad leader, Sergeant America. I call him this because I was happy he was fighting on our side, the American side. He was massive and only a little smaller than the Big Guy. Everyone I spoke to told me that Sergeant America really knew what he was doing and I was lucky to have him as a squad leader.

I was confident in our squad because we had a good balance of everything. We had guys who were incredibly strong and others who were incredibly intelligent. With my capacity to eat and only think about food, how could we go wrong?

My dad told me one weekend while I was home to learn everything I could from my team and squad leader. They had all the experience and had been to combat before. He said to soak up everything they taught me like a sponge. Taking my dad's advice, I asked my new team leader about his experiences in Iraq and that I wanted to learn everything I could. His response was troubling to say the least.

"I have never been to combat before and nobody in our squad has," he said, "In fact, maybe only two or three people in our whole company have seen combat."

My mouth dropped as I couldn't believe I would be going to combat with men who had zero experience in the real thing. My confidence immediately dropped knowing that the real-world perspective I wanted wouldn't be coming from anyone in my company.

We would all be getting our real-world experience at the same time.

Types of Bases

From my vast four years spent in the military, I learned there are three types of bases you can expect to find in a modern combat zone. Now as best as I can describe it, there are massive bases that serve thousands of troops in transition to other parts of Iraq as well as people who are stationed there for their entire deployment.

The Al Asad Airbase was an example of this great type of base. These bases are bigger than the eye can see, with landing strips, gyms, many cafeterias, and even fast food chains. Yes, I said fast food chains, like Burger King and McDonald's. These bases have movie theaters, swimming pools, and great overall facilities. They have hot water showers and even post-exchanges (PX), where among the snacks and other various items, condoms were also sold. The cafeteria food was the best I had ever tasted with steak and lobster every Wednesday. Every day there was also a hot food line and a grill. There was a potato bar, salad bar, and refrigerators longer than the eye could see, with almost every kind of drink available, including non-alcoholic beer. Let's refer to this base by my official name:

"Awesome Fucking Base."

Next on the list is a big step down but still not the worst type of base. These can be tent cities of various sizes with a little more resources or just small bases with no luxuries. Since a headquarters unit was probably stationed there, they may have laundry services and hot water. With that being said, they are still roughing it and it is far from easy. The food they have could be tray rations, which are basically community-sized MREs that the cooks would prepare by heating. I spent a lot of time in a place like this and it isn't pleasant. I call this type of a base:

"Pretty Shitty Base."

Last on the list is where the fun really begins. This is not what you would call a base in any way shape or form. This is a house or some structure that is taken over, surrounded by barbed wire and now is called a base or better known as a forward operating base (FOB). It could be a house or even something made by bulldozers by putting in big concrete walls to create a compound with protection from enemy fire. Electricity no, generator maybe. Running water, not a chance. Showers with bottled water, maybe. Baby wipes, definitely.

Since everybody always wonders how we go to the bathroom in this type of place, I will tell you. We built wooden port-o-johns with buckets underneath. Some poor low-ranking Marine would then at the end of the day get the pleasure of taking the bucket, pour gas in it, light the gas on fire, and with a big stick, stir the shit until it essentially turned into dust. If he was smart, he would wear a gas mask; if he was dumb, he wouldn't. I refer to this type of base as:

"I Should Have Gone to College Base."

After thirty days of not showering, we got word that we were going to the "Pretty Shitty Base" to finally shower. I had never been to this base, so of course I was excited. The most important thing was getting our clothes washed and getting cleaned.

This base was much bigger than the current base we were staying at. That wasn't saying much because our base, nicknamed the Playboy Mansion, was just a house. At the "Pretty Shitty Base" it was at least big enough where you could run laps inside the perimeter and get a good workout in. There were very few modern-day conveniences and sand was everywhere. I knew the command element of the battalion was here, but that was all I really knew. There were large tents everywhere, where the Marines did everything, from sleeping to taking showers.

I am truly convinced there is some general somewhere in Washington D.C. who decides how long a Marine can go without showering before they have to try and get you one. Our first time in Iraq, it was so hot that if we didn't shower regularly, we would have all gotten seriously sick and not been able to continue with our mission. I am convinced that because this time we were in Iraq during the winter and it was cold, that general who went home every day and showered and slept in his nice comfy bed probably thought that they could push us between thirty to sixty days without a shower. He probably thought we didn't sweat much because it was cold. I will never be a general so I will never be able to confirm this, but I do have my suspicions.

Since we were the infantry platoon coming from a different FOB, we had the priority on the showers and laundry. I had never taken a field shower before but with us smelling like chemical weapons after thirty days of not showering and being dirty from constant patrolling, we needed one badly.

Getting into a massive green tent with probably room for ten people to shower felt great. As the hot water came out of the showerhead, I felt a huge relief come over me. Looking down, I could see dirt coming off me into the drain not sure whether I should sing like I always did in the shower or keep it all in. Ten minutes later my shower was done and I felt like some rich guy taking a shower at the Ritz Carlton. It is amazing how a little shower can make you feel so much better. Oh, the simple things in life you learn to treasure.

Excited to be walking around after a hot shower and wearing clean clothes, it was now time to get a haircut. Normally you get a haircut then take a shower, but the Marine Corps normally did things I didn't understand. The Marines have a fascination with haircuts that I am still grappling with ten years later. No electricity, no running water, not an excuse for a Marine not to have a haircut.

Good hygiene was not a top priority when it came to haircuts. There would be one electric shaver and we would each take turns sitting in the chair. If you were lucky and the Marine in your platoon had some skill, maybe you were able to get a little shave on the back and side of your head to conform to the minimum regulations.

Usually you can tell the motivation level of a Marine by how long his hair is. If it's a high and tight, that means he is really motivated. The low regulation which I had, basically meant you had no motivation and would be getting out of the Marines as soon as you could. Naturally, if you were a young Marine, it didn't matter your motivation level because you would be forced to have a high and tight regardless. When you had seniority like I did, being this was my third deployment, you could choose your style.

One of the Marines developed horrible lesions on the back of his head from getting haircuts from the same clippers as everyone else. These little whiteheads were disgusting and there was nothing he could do. He even had surgery at one point and they came back. I was lucky that this didn't happen to me.

Sitting around the "Pretty Shitty Base" with other Marines from our company, we got a friendly surprise by seeing the sergeant major of our battalion. He was quite an impressive man or so it seemed to me. He was like a real superman. Over forty, he could still score a perfect three hundred on the yearly physical fitness test (PFT), which is no easy task. He also had jump wings and a scuba bubble which are pretty awesome things to have. He was highly decorated and well respected and his fatherly talk to our group was really cool.

"Men," he said, speaking in a relaxed tone, "I started out in this radio regiment and did my time there and it sucked, so I moved on to another unit. I then went to this unit, did my time there, and it sucked so I moved on again."

He continued telling his Marine life story and how every unit he was in seemed to suck. Being a barely twenty-one-year old Marine getting out of the military in a few long months, I couldn't help but wonder what would make a man continually reenlist in the military if every stop in his career was as he put it, "shit."

"Rosman," I heard a voice say. It was the sergeant major. I wasn't necessarily afraid of the man (or maybe I was), but he apparently had not received the memo that my last name was actually Bond, not Rosman. I then made the mistake of turning around and running to him and saying, "Yes, sergeant major."

"Rosman, I noticed you had a little mustache growing there."

"Well, yes sergeant major, it's my lucky mustache; it keeps me safe from bullets and IEDs." I wasn't being facetious either. I really did believe that. It's a combat thing -- you would really need to be there to understand how a few whiskers can make you feel protected.

He then "nicely" told me that if I shave my mustache it would grow much thicker, which was code word for "shave your mustache now or I'll whoop your ass." I thought, would he possibly know if I did or did not shave it? I stayed at another base and neither he nor any of the other high command ever ventured there.

Still to this day I can only grow a few whiskers on both sides and nothing in the middle, so I was really proud of the few whiskers I had at that time. Since I didn't have a mirror of any kind, I imagined I looked really rugged and cool. In reality, I most likely looked like what I was: an underfed and undersexed twenty-one-year old with a shitty mustache.

"Aye aye, sergeant major," I said, acknowledging his order that I would shave my mustache as soon as I could get a razor.

The sergeant major would be dead in the next few weeks.

First Field Day

I just wanted to get a good night's sleep. But it was a Thursday, and this wasn't going to happen. Thursday is field day, which means every nook and cranny of your room from top to bottom needs to be cleaned. This is a long night for everyone and it is generally understood that nobody will be able to leave the base on Thursdays. Even though the guys with seniority had to clean their rooms, it came with no stress, and a clean toilet meant a clean toilet. Because it was a long night, it was always an opportunity for all the senior Marines to get as drunk as possible and constantly fuck with us.

Keep in mind that we didn't have to clean a massive house or anything. All we had to clean was one shared room and a bathroom. The rooms were very basic, with two beds, two closets and a storage locker in the back. That was it. Since we had three men instead of two, it should have taken thirty minutes to properly clean.

Three hours later we got our first inspection. We failed within the first ten seconds. I wasn't sure what dirt they were looking at, but apparently their vision was better than mine. An hour later, my team leader walked in and failed me immediately. Another hour later, he walked back in and failed me again without even looking in my room.

Not wanting to take a piss on the toilet I had just cleaned for two hours, I ran across the road to the gym to use their bathroom. I wanted to go to sleep and would run into a gym to piss if that was what I needed to get done.

With my immaculately cleaned toilet, I knew that there was no way anyone could fail me. Of that I was certain. Entering my room at that moment was someone about my height who I had never seen even in passing before. He was wearing athletic clothing, so again I didn't know his rank. After speaking to him for a few seconds, he went on a tirade.

"Why aren't you addressing me by my rank?"

"I don't know your rank, you're not wearing your rank," I nervously stuttered.

His eyes started bulging out of his head when he started screaming at the top of his lungs, "You should've asked!"

He turned away from me and sprinted towards my bathroom and did a baseball slide headfirst under my toilet.

"Come here. You see this dirt?" as he showed me his finger.

There was no dirt on his finger. How could there be? I just spent two hours cleaning that toilet, including that same exact spot he put his finger on.

"You failed," as he stood up and walked out of my room. This guy would end up being one of the squad leaders in my platoon.

Since Tommy was in 3rd platoon and the East Coaster was in 4th, this meant that in addition to people from my platoon inspecting me, they also had their own inspections of our room. It was a never-ending cycle of strange people I had never met walking in and out of my room, putting their finger onto some imaginary spot and saying we failed because they found dirt. The drunker they became, the dirtier our room somehow was. At around 0200 my roommates were deemed to have a clean room and could go to sleep. On the other hand, I still had not passed and was still cleaning until 0500 when I decided enough was enough and fell asleep on the cot.

Why I wanted to join the Marines

I wanted to be a Marine for as long as I could remember. The only thing that could've changed my mind was if I had the chance to play sports at either the pro or collegiate level. At the age of ten, I saw a black and white film called *The D.I.*, and from that moment on I knew I had found my calling. *The D.I.* was a straightforward film about a struggling recruit and the drill instructor who never gave up on him. This movie is generally considered what *Full Metal Jacket* is, but thirty years earlier. Still to this day I can recite almost every line of that movie. The Marines seemed like something so challenging, yet once completing the training it would be the greatest satisfaction you could ever have.

I love and admire all the branches in our nation's military, but something about the Marines seemed different. The Marines always seemed to have the most pride in just simply being Marines. Even their commercials were different. The Army commercials that I saw all seemed to be speaking about the benefits of being in the Army after getting out of the service. How could a commercial talk about the benefits of getting out when the people watching the commercials weren't even in yet?

The Marine Corps commercials were much different. They offered you a challenge. No promise or guarantees. Not in one commercial did they ever mention the benefits after leaving the service. The Marine's message was simple. *Maybe you could be one of us. The Few, The Proud, The Marines.* Holy shit, I was hooked. Action, adventure, a challenge, and probably getting to bang lots of chicks with that awesome uniform they wore. What more could a teenager want?

It must have been fate when at 16, I saw a military recruiting station in the same complex where I was going to driving school. During one of my breaks, I walked straight past the Air Force and Army recruiters' doors into the Marine recruiting office.

"How can I help you?" the recruiter asked.

I was a little nervous, being that this was the first active duty Marine I had ever spoken to, and he was absolutely huge with muscles bulging out of his forearms. You must be pretty serious about lifting weights to have muscles bulging out of your forearms.

"I am at the driving school on the second story and want to join the Marines after I graduate high school."

"Aren't you a little small to join the Marines?"

"Probably, but if you're mentally tough you can make it through anything."

I grabbed a couple brochures and left his office thinking what an asshole he was. Little did I know, in a little over two years, I would have more medals on my chest than he would have in ten years of service in the Marines. That was the first asshole of many I would meet in my career.

In the next few months I would turn seventeen and with my parents' signature join the Marines in the delayed entry program. Essentially this means that you have joined the military and are just waiting to graduate high school or you are waiting for a date to ship out to boot camp. Twice a week, I would go to the recruiting office to go running and do calisthenics with other people in the program, who were known as "poolees."

Mark Doddridge was one guy in the program with me. He was about two years older than me and seemed like the coolest person in the world. He was an arrogant California dude yet somebody you would want to be friends with. His military occupational specialty, or MOS, was military police, the same as our shared recruiter. Being that I had never tried smoking a cigarette before, when he did pull-ups with one in his mouth, it only added to how cool I thought he was. He didn't seem to care about anything, which made me think even more highly of him.

Sleeping with Fat Chicks

To sleep with her or not to sleep with her: That is the question. In times of uncertainty, evoking the great work of William Shakespeare always seems appropriate.

I needed some kind of enjoyment. My life was a real hell getting treated like shit from the moment I arrived to my unit. I was beginning to question if the Marines were the team that I always hoped they were. At night, I needed to get away from everyone and would drive to Burger King and just stay there for hours at a time.

I was relieved when a day or two later at the chow hall, I ran into David Portillo, an old friend from my poolee days. He'd just gotten back from Iraq with the 3rd Battalion 5th Marines and was about a year ahead of me in terms of his contract. He invited me out that night with some friends from his unit. They lived in the same barracks as me but across the basketball court.

It felt good getting away from my unit because I was tired of getting picked on and just wanted to have some fun. Besides Portillo, the people going out with me that night were Diego Quintana and Greg Rund. Rund was an interesting character and was actually a freshman in high school during the Columbine High School shooting massacre. We all agreed to go to a nightclub about an hour away and had to figure out transportation.

My old friend Doddridge showed up in his MP car to say hi and I asked him to play a joke on one of the 3/5 Marines. The joke would be for Doddridge to walk into this Marine's room and say he was responding to a report of shots being fired in the air. I asked my new friends who we should do this to and they all said simultaneously, "Simms."

Doddridge walked straight into the room with this guy still in his boxers, and with a straight face, never losing his bearing, started berating and interrogating him about the suspicious gunfire. Simms had a look of absolute terror, almost like someone had walked in and caught him masturbating. His face went completely white as Doddridge started yelling at him.

All of us were crouching under Simm's window watching Doddridge in action, trying not to laugh, but it was just too hard. Simms started crying when Doddridge told him he would be placed in handcuffs and arrested.

"I didn't do anything, I swear," he cried out.

"I know dude, I'm just fucking with you," Doddridge said with a grin on his face.

We all busted into his room, not being able to contain our laughter any longer. Simm's face went from turning pale to an angry red color.

"You mean I'm not going to jail?"

"No dude, you're fine," Doddridge said in his typical deep bro voice.

Doddridge said goodbye to me and got into his police car and left. Still to this day whenever I think of someone who can hold their bearing in any situation, Doddridge's name and face are the first I think about.

I was quite excited when we finally got into the car and made our way towards the club. I was only eighteen-years old and looking back, I don't think I had ever been to a club before. Portillo would be meeting us there later and I was quiet in the car because I was with the two guys that I had just met an hour earlier.

Suddenly the car broke down. I don't remember if there was a flat tire or the engine gave out, but we were forced to pull over. The pickup truck behind us pulled over to give us assistance and it was decided that we would just leave the car on the side of the road. Somehow, the three of us ended up in the bed of this truck. It was absolutely freezing going seventy miles per hour on the freeway in February as I hoped not to die during our journey because that would have really sucked dying amongst people I didn't know.

The driver decided to pull over at a gas station because he didn't feel it was safe with three people lying down in the bed like that. He dropped us off and took off. We now were stranded far from base, not sure if we should try and return or somehow get a ride from someone else to continue to the club.

Rund, whom I would soon learn was very fast and persuasive talking to people, was able to without even offering money, convince a complete stranger to drive us a little out of his way to the club we were going to. Thanks to his smooth talking, it seemed like in only a few minutes we were back in another car continuing towards our objective. Marines are goal-oriented people. Whether it is in combat or making it to a nightclub, Marines will find a way.

Now in the car with this kind stranger; we found out he was of Middle Eastern origin. Rund, who was now drunk, started becoming rude insulting the driver and the Arab people more and more. I wasn't sure if he had already been to Iraq, but being drunk also led him to be a mean and disrespectful asshole. He kept drinking in this poor stranger's car and screamed while he threw his beer bottle out the car window.

Now I wished I could just disappear into the seat. I regretted even coming. Dealing with a drunk disrespectful asshole I didn't know, wasn't my idea of a good time. I got a text from Portillo telling me that he was canceling and wouldn't be showing up. I was stuck far away from base without my own car with all these people I didn't know and the only friend that I had wouldn't be coming. I would just need to tough it out. Finally arriving at the club, I thanked the poor stranger and apologized for Rund's behavior as the scared driver sped away.

Being that I was under twenty-one, I got the famous X mark on my hand, signifying to the bar and most importantly the girls at the club that I wasn't able to buy or drink alcohol. This meant that I would be having a boring night out, pretending to enjoy myself while everyone else would be having a great time. My new friend Quintana, who was over twenty-one, started slowly feeding me drinks. Being the wise eighteen-year old I was, I put my wallet with my all-important military ID in my sock, thinking that if I got caught drinking maybe they would take it from me. I put my hand in my pocket so no bouncer would see the X while I drank.

I suddenly felt a big paw on my shoulder and turned around. It was a bouncer from the club. He caught Quintana slipping me drinks and was trying to kick us out. Next to us, Rund was being kicked out at the exact same time. Quintana kept telling the bouncer that we didn't know that guy, that he had nothing to do with anything. Frustrated, the bouncer finally told Quintana, "Look, that guy is being kicked out for something entirely different. It has nothing to do with you guys." I still have no idea what Rund did.

Now all three of us were back on the street with no way home and we were too far away to take a taxi unless it was an absolute last resort; it would've cost a few hundred dollars easily. Rund quickly disappeared up the street and I saw him talking to two women. He then motioned for us towards the car and told us that they agreed to drive us back to base for the small fee of $50 each. We agreed and jumped into the car. Being that I was drunk and it was dark, I never really saw what the women looked like. I was sitting in the back-middle seat with Quintana to my left and Rund to my right.

I hastily gave them directions the best I could remember and immediately fell asleep as the car started to drive away. I remember waking up here and there during the drive and noticed that Rund was hitting on the girl in the passenger seat. I thought that he had no chance with her. How much can you get to know a person speaking to them from the back seat? I fell back asleep and awoke again, but this time with the passenger seat head rest between my arms. Rund and the woman were making out with each other. Fuck, this guy was good. They asked me final directions to the base and I fell asleep one last time.

Rund woke me up as we approached our barracks and uttered this sentence that after eleven years is as crystal clear now as it was then:

"Jason, do you think we can go to your room and you can kick your roommates out while you and me fuck these two girls?"

"Of course I can," I responded excitedly. I was about to get laid and started celebrating in my head.

I remembered that I still had no idea what these women actually looked like because I was drunk, it was dark, I was in the back seat with their heads facing away from me, and I was asleep most of the time. I leaned forward to get a look at both women. I put my head back on the seat and looked again for verification. They were absolutely fat. I don't mean like you put on a couple pounds your first year of college fat. I mean like four hundred pounds each fat. They were so fat that if the police asked me to draw a sketch of the two of them, all I would've needed to do was draw one big circle for their faces. They were so fat they didn't even have facial features.

I looked to my left shoulder and saw Devil Jason winking at me, telling me to go ahead and do it. Fat chicks need loving too. But these women were more than just fat; they could potentially break my ribcage. I looked to my right shoulder and saw Angel Jason. Angel Jason told me not to do it, to have some respect for myself. I was still young and had my whole life ahead of me. Each shoulder presented an excellent argument and it was now time to decide as we started entering the barracks parking lot. The decision was made.

"Sorry Rund, gotta go." I listened to the angel on my right shoulder. I opened the door and ran as fast as I could, leaving the two fat chicks, Rund, and Quintana behind. I opened my barracks room door as my two awake roommates whom I barely knew told me that earlier in the night some military policeman knocked on our door and busted in with his gun drawn asking for me. By this time, Doddridge knew where I lived because I had told him my exact room number, and I guess he felt like scaring the shit out of my roommates. I was too tired to explain all this to them as I immediately laid down in my cot and fell asleep.

Greg Rund would die in Fallujah, Iraq, nine months later.

The next day I woke up in time for breakfast, but I couldn't find my wallet, which is where I kept my military ID. Losing your ID is quite a serious offense and usually gets you a write up that goes on your record.

Being new, there was no way of getting out of this one. Senior Marines might get a slap on the wrist but not yelled at because they are most likely friends with their sergeants.

I missed breakfast and was looking everywhere for my wallet, trying to decide when to tell someone I lost my ID. Now being sent on a working party (what they are called in prison too), I heard a corporal call out, "Is there a Rosman here?"

"Yes corporal, that's me."

"Go to the command post. They found your wallet, and the MPs are looking for you."

I went to the command post and the commander gave me my wallet. Fortunately, someone turned it in with all my cash, credit cards, and military ID. He never mentioned why the MPs were looking for me. I left relieved that I wouldn't get in trouble for losing it, and also that I was now able to go to the chow hall without having to pay cash.

Later that day, I called Doddridge and asked him why the hell the MPs were looking for me. I could tell he had a smirk on his face when he told me that on the night of my check-in to Golf Company, he wanted to find and surprise me. He knew that I was in the 62 Area but didn't know what company or battalion I was in. The 62 Area isn't a small area where you would just randomly find one unit without knowing where it was. No matter what rank you have, an MP still has complete authority over you. If the MP was a private and he pulled over a captain, the MP would be in control, not the captain. For this reason, most military police are hated by other Marines. They have a reputation of thinking that their badge gives them ultimate authority (which it does), and they also hand out speeding tickets and fines to other Marines. Usually Marines look out for each other, but because of their job description they always seem to be the bad guys.

My first night at 0200, Doddridge started going to all the commands he could find and started asking for me. Don't forget that our battalion that day probably just got two hundred new guys; it was chaotic, organizing everything. Each person needed rooms and had to start the intake process. Doddridge busting into a duty hut at 0200 asking specifically which room Rosman was in was next to an impossible task assuming he even found my company. He went around for like an hour going all over the camp asking for me. He even started yelling at officers who oversaw the guard shifts for each battalion.

"You need to have accountability at all time for your Marines," he yelled to a lieutenant. The lieutenant got nervous and started fumbling around looking through random paperwork. Word soon got around camp that the MPs were looking for this mysterious guy named Rosman.

In all actuality, it was just my good friend doing what good friends do, and that is fuck with you. Of course, no one else in the 62 Area knew this. When you're new and are being constantly treated like shit, you don't want to give any of the senior guys more of an excuse to make your life even more difficult. You wanted to be as unnoticeable as possible, even ghostlike.

I wasn't being very ghostly at the given moment.

The next week or so, I linked back up with my new friend Quintana and I wanted to get the scoop on what happened with the fat chicks that night. He told me that Rund had no problem having sex with his girl but had trouble finding someone to sleep with her friend. After arriving at his barracks at like 0300, he put his girl in his room and started knocking on doors.

"Hey man, can you sleep with this girl?"

They took one look at her and shut the door. Apparently, he knocked on ten doors before one guy who could barely open his eyes said,

"Fuck it, I'll bang her."

Even at 0300, if you bang on enough doors with Marines inside, eventually one will have sex with a massive four hundred-pound fat chick.

Goodbye United States

Just as fast as I arrived to my unit, it seemed like it was time to leave. We all gathered on the parade deck with all of our equipment and said our goodbyes to our families. It was an exciting time because it seemed like one big adventure to me. I would be going to a strange foreign land and play the hero helping local people live and thrive in their new lives. I still had no idea what I was doing and didn't even know the names of everyone in my platoon.

We said our goodbyes and were driven by bus to March Air Force Base where we waited six hours for our airplane to fly us to Kuwait. The jet we would fly on wasn't a military aircraft but a civilian company contracted by the government. I had never heard of this particular company before but it was a normal flight with meal service and an entertainment system. What wasn't normal was that everyone was dressed the same and we had our rifles with us.

As the plane lifted off taking us towards our destination, the thought of any of us getting killed or wounded never crossed my mind. I thought the upcoming deployment would be a mix of fun and hard work, but violence I wasn't expecting.

Kuwait

While in Kuwait preparing for Iraq, we had a lot of time to dedicate to training. We had physical training in the morning to help us acclimate to the new environment and would constantly train for the upcoming convoy ride we would take into Iraq.

We would train for hours a day on convoy maneuvers. Every situation we prepared for and would practice simulated attacks. We would all sit in our assigned platoon 7-ton truck and one of the vehicles would be hit by an IED. We would then need to dismount and attack the target or gather the wounded. We would then all get back in the vehicles and do another practice run.

The squad leader of 1st squad, who was one of the only men with actual combat experience in the company, spent considerable time training us for riot control situations. It was physically exhausting training having to learn to use batons and hold off the other Marines pretending to be rioters. We would have to learn to drill almost like we were in a parade but with full riot gear, listening to commands while the whole group would all pivot in the same direction preventing the rioters from snatching one of us when they changed directions. The more we practiced the better we became but it was still hard to imagine really doing this against an angry mob. Along with the convoy training, this riot control training was what I remember most.

In addition to the training and preparation, we also had endless amounts of classes that would mostly cover the rules of war and the rules of engagement. It was during these classes we were assured that we would be loved by the Iraqi people and would probably be given flowers upon our arrival. I even heard someone say that the only reason we had weapons was because it was the rules but we wouldn't be needing them. This was very reassuring to me because I didn't want to be in a situation where I would need to use my weapon in Iraq. If I could go the whole deployment only having to help the local people that would have been a job well done. We needed to bring security to these people and rebuild their police and military forces so they could defend themselves and have the rule of law handled by their own populous. We were repeatedly told over and over that the Iraqi people were not our enemy and we were there simply to help them.

Standing Guard

Standing on post has to be the most difficult and boring thing one can possibly do in the military. Post is the term for standing guard. You can be the biggest badass in the world but everybody is always guarding something. Even though standing post is in itself a very easy job, it is actually one of the most frustrating and requires the most discipline. The job entails that you just stand in your fortified guard position and look out in your assigned sector for any suspicious activity. When standing guard, it is very easy to fall asleep and this is the biggest sin you can make in all the military. There is no way to be forgiven for falling asleep on guard duty. Looking at your watch as your eyes get heavier and heavier praying that the minutes move faster so your relief can appear, only makes the time tick away even slower.

The newer you are in the military the more you get to guard. I've guarded the other Marines while they were sleeping which is called fire watch. I've guarded Claymore mines which got stolen (not my fault). I've stood many posts on top of roofs in Iraq. All these needed guarding and are definitely understandable, but the next one doesn't need a guard, but there is a Marine Corps saying that I made up that goes*: If there isn't something to guard, the Marines will find something for you to guard.* Yes, I have even guarded a port-o-john. That's right I said it, instead of letting us go to sleep, we had to do a roving guard shift on a row of port-o-johns. Why? I have no idea. These shitters were obviously used by many people before us, but we were given strict instructions to ensure that after every Marine left the shitter, we were to inspect it with a flashlight to ensure there were no new writings on the inside. What writing you may ask?

Things like, *call Fred for a good time*. They were always very funny sexual drawings. So, you had a young Marine trained to kill that had to look inside the port-o-john with a flashlight after each person left to ensure that there were no new writings inside.

Standing guard all alone next to this row of shitters, I stared into the vast flat Kuwaiti desert and suddenly felt very alone. Even though it was dark, the lights scattered throughout the base revealed just how desolate we were as I stared into what looked like infinity. Not even one hill to break up the landscape and it seemed as barren as photos of the moon.

I was also nervous because in the morning our whole company would be getting in a huge convoy and driving to Iraq. I was hoping that once in Iraq, this strange organization which I joined just seven months prior would start to make more sense to me. I looked into the Kuwait desert and again at the row of port-o-johns.

"This wasn't in the brochure before I signed up," I thought to myself with a solemn shrug.

Lance Corporal Cantu

Everywhere I went, Lance Corporal Cantu would go with me and vice versa. He would help me in my patrolling skills and constantly watch me like a mother hen. I definitely needed the guidance and extra practice because I really didn't know anything. Lance Corporal Cantu already had been deployed once before but to Okinawa, Japan. During the invasion of Iraq, our battalion was the only one in the 5th Marines who didn't get to fight.

While the war was getting ready to begin, my future battalion was stuck in Okinawa. With the war starting, the men in the battalion had high hopes that they would be sent to the war to fight. Unfortunately, this wasn't the case. They were extended for an additional period in Okinawa and missed all the fighting. Cantu joined 2/4 and was sent to Okinawa during this extension.

To make it even more humiliating, on everybody's return home, the regiment held a parade. Every battalion in the regiment which had been to Iraq wore their desert uniforms while 2/4 suffered the double humiliation of not getting to fight in Iraq and also being forced to wear their jungle uniforms in front of everyone.

Lance Corporal Cantu was second in command of our team, so if our team leader went down it would be his role. Him taking up more responsibility was part of the job. What made this man so incredible wasn't how much weight he could carry or how fast he could run but rather how he would never doze off during a guard shift.

The End of Kuwait and Entering Iraq

The drive was long leaving Kuwait for Iraq. The only interesting parts of the drive was the beginning when the over one hundred vehicles turned on their engines at the same time, sending the sound of thunder rumbling through the desert and when we were on the freeways and finally got to look at something that wasn't just endless sand. Looking at the horrified Kuwaitis as a massive military convoy drove by them was the only entertainment we had during the trip.

During the never-ending convoy ride from Kuwait to Iraq, Cantu never once fell asleep. In the friendly lines of Kuwait, sitting in the back of an open 7-ton truck we had our rifle muzzles facing down. We couldn't have our weapons facing outboard towards civilian Kuwaiti vehicles. We were guests in their country and weren't at war with them. It was boring sitting under the desert heat with all your gear with no room and it was easy to fall asleep. There was no danger because we were in Kuwait and everybody dozed off. Lance Corporal Cantu wouldn't even close his eyes. There was nothing wrong with sleeping in the back of the vehicle and it was allowed even though it never was mentioned. Wanting to teach me discipline, every time I closed my eyes and drifted for a second, I would receive an elbow to the ribcage. Who was this freak of nature? There was nobody who could stay awake like him.

Not knowing much about the Middle East, I was under the impression that is was just one sand field. From my vantage point in Kuwait, this was the absolute truth. I had no reason to think Iraq would be any different.

"In five minutes we enter Iraq," Sergeant America yelled at us breaking the boring monotony of the ride we had been on for three days.

This is about to get real I thought to myself. I looked back and wondered if the little training I had would be sufficient for the vast undertaking I would soon encounter. I slowly relaxed and got my breathing under control and would need to remember to take everything one step at a time and look towards Cantu and Corporal Shepherd and copy whatever they were doing.

"Weapons out," Sergeant America yelled as the rest of us in the 7-ton gave a motivated scream of excitement.

This is it, this was our Super Bowl where we finally would get to play in the biggest game of our lives. There was a generation of Marines who could have spent a full twenty year career in the military and not even gotten close to seeing action. I needed only seven months to go into my first combat zone.

Lifting my weapon from the downward position it was facing, I now put it on the side of the vehicle facing outward. I pulled the bolt back and it immediately sent a bullet into the chamber. Condition 1 of the weapon. I was locked and loaded ready for action. Now, I wouldn't be able to even close my eyes for a split second not that I would've but if I did, Lance Corporal Cantu would've been waiting with an elbow shot to my ribs.

The terrain was the exact same as Kuwait and I prayed it would soon change. Even though this part of Iraq, the border region with Kuwait was one big desert, the majority of the country was far from this. I saw this with my own eyes as the countryside slowly began to change from desert to beautiful rolling hills and farmland. There was water and the terrain was beautiful enough that in theory, there could be great tourism one day if the infrastructure was better.

Ramadi

On the drive into the city, I saw it was much more developed than I had in my mind. It had good sized buildings everywhere and wasn't anything like a big farming village that I had imagined. I thought that Bagdad was the only big city in Iraq but I was wrong. This city on the banks of the Euphrates River had a population of four hundred thousand people. I hoped they would all be friendly but I had no way to be sure. I entered the city with nothing but goodwill and hope, willing to do whatever I could to make the lives of the people here better. Would I leave feeling the same way?

I would soon have my answer.

Ramadi was the capital of the Al Anbar province and the headquarters of the old Baath Party loyal to Saddam Hussein. The majority of the people here were from the same Sunni branch of Islam as the recently disposed of dictator.

Our convoy first entered another outpost named the Snake Pit to drop off some vehicles that were part of our battalion's Fox Company. This would be where Fox Company would stay during the deployment. After ten minutes sitting in the vehicles, the convoy continued and we started driving to a different outpost which we would call home and be sharing with Echo Company.

The Combat Outpost

After a fifteen-minute drive, we arrived to the Combat Outpost which would be our home for the next seven months. The outpost was small but not too cramped at first glance. There were a lot of unfinished structures that were under construction when we arrived and we would need to live in cramped quarters until they were completed. The building that was being used as the mess hall had no roof on it and our first meal eaten at night would be under the rain. Near the back of the outpost there was a big building that would be used to station all the vehicles. The big doors could shut in case of any mortar attacks. This building would also be where the command element of our company would stay and house all the officers. The little aid station where the corpsman would work would be located in a room next to all the vehicles. This little base would fall under my category as a "Pretty Shitty Base".

As soon as the vehicles stopped, our gunnery sergeant (Gunny) started frantically yelling at us to get our gear off all the vehicles. Even though we would be here for seven months, he wanted to do this quickly to start organizing everything immediately. The set of rooms where my squad would sleep were still unfinished, so we had to share one of the big rooms with the rest of our platoon. A room meant for fifteen people now had thirty in it trying to find room to get organized. This would be a very uncomfortable first night.

My unit would be replacing Army National Guard soldiers and they were there for the transition. They would be responsible for taking our unit leaders around the city and showing them all the important and any dangerous parts of the city. As part of the handover of power, they would also need to introduce our leaders to all the important contacts and people of power in Ramadi to continue to forge those relationships.

From what I heard, the National Guard soldiers told all of our leaders that the city wasn't dangerous at all. They didn't do any patrolling on foot and would go everywhere by vehicle. All the contacts and police chiefs throughout the city they had complete trust and confidence in.

I don't know anything about the National Guard except for the fact that they wear Army uniforms and they aren't Marines. They didn't seem like a motivated bunch because there wasn't one sandbag in the whole compound. Sandbags and military are like Brazil and beautiful women; they go perfect together. I am not sure what the condition of the outpost was before the arrival of the National Guard, but it seemed to me that they were not very proactive in the maintenance or improvement of the base.

Besides the locals who were contracted by us to finish all the building, we also had a lot of work to do ourselves to turn this strange place into our home. It seemed like every free second we had was devoted to filling sandbags. We fortified all the structures and the watchtowers. In case the outpost was overrun, we even dug and fortified long foxholes so we could fight until the last man. During one of the mortar attacks, one of them landed inside the base and the fragments destroyed a port-o-john while someone was inside taking a poop. He was injured bad enough that he had to be sent home. In response to this attack, even the port-o-johns had to be sandbagged. Even though I am writing about all the improvements in just a few paragraphs, it may seem like the work didn't take that long to finish. This would be incorrect. The work on the outpost would never be complete and was always an ongoing process of maintenance and improvement.

The man responsible for the planning was as usual our Gunny. I don't know if he had a list of things to do written down or he just found ways for us to get as little sleep as possible. Working parties which I thought I would do just in Camp Pendleton were as common at the Combat Outpost as back home in California.

The structures completed first by the contractors were the buildings where we would all sleep. Fortunately, we only lived in the cramped quarters for two nights before our rooms were completed. In our building, there were three rooms. The main room would house the majority of 4th platoon. In the small room attached, the team leaders for my squad would sleep. Walking through their room, there was another door where the rest of my squad would sleep. In the room where I slept, we had eight men. The rest of our platoon would sleep in another house across the dirt road from us. Sergeant America would share a small room in the other building with the other two squad leaders.

The Gunny

Our Gunny was a scary and intimidating presence. He was born in the Philippines and had a face so tough it looked like sandpaper. When he spoke, his voice cut through you like a sharp knife. He came to Golf Company straight from being a drill instructor and it showed. I was afraid of this man from the moment he spoke to us for the first time.

After we held a formation on the basketball courts next our barracks in Camp Pendleton, we held a small company school circle and we were introduced to our new Gunny. He would be my first Gunny ever, but a new Gunny to the more senior Marines. Since we were no longer in boot camp I was under the impression that the screaming I was used to would be a thing of the past. Wow was I wrong. I quickly learned that just because somebody finished being a drill instructor, that didn't mean the drill instructor attitude had left them. The Marines I worked with who came from the recruiting side, they never yelled or seemed angry. They seemed like normal people you could bring out in public. The ex-drill instructors would always yell like we were still recruits and they still had their raspy drill instructor voice from screaming like psychopaths all the time.

"Listen motherfuckers." Listen was the only thing I understood that wasn't profanity in his heavily accented tirade. Not one word was intelligible from his thick accent besides, fuck, cunt, bitch, pussy, and motherfucker.

The Gunny was the face of our company and if you didn't know that, after a five-minute ass chewing you would wet yourself and never forget it. His role was to manage the day-to-day activities of the company and get all the platoons the things they needed to function. The platoon sergeant has the same function as a gunny but on the platoon level. The gunny is the boss of the four platoon sergeants and would do their job but on the company level.

Besides his heavy accent, he was also a colorful character. He would say things to us that still make me smile all these years later. Colorful sayings that on the surface do not make any real sense but if you look deep into the meaning you might understand.

"Men, I'll suck your dick, but if you cum in my mouth, I'll fuck you in the ass."

This was the most colorful thing I have ever heard someone say, while we all looked at each other and shrugged our shoulders.

"If you want to play dick, I got a big cock." Again, another colorful analogy.

Finally, "If you lose one of my checker pieces, I'll fuck you in the ass." I don't think this was an analogy, but more of a threat.

Wow, we had a badass for a Gunny. Even though his knees creaked like he was eighty-years old, he was still out there for every patrol and every raid. Even after he was injured by a grenade, he still never went home and instead recovered at the Combat Outpost, toughing it out and finishing the deployment.

He was a great man that I will never forget. I am honored to have served with him.

The First Patrol

The first patrol I didn't go on because it was only for essential personnel. The majority of my platoon would just be hanging out with our platoon sergeant while all the squad and team leaders would be going out with the National Guard soldiers learning about the area of operations (AO). Everyone that wasn't allowed to go on the patrol was bummed out wanting to get a taste of any action or at least walk outside and say we had been on a combat patrol. I would get my chance two nights later.

I was nervous that's for sure. I suddenly felt like all the training I had was very useless. I was excited but more than anything, just wanted to get my first patrol over with as soon as possible. Even though night makes for a safer patrol because only we had night vision goggles (NVG), it complicated everything else. Your vision is skewed and you can't see as far in front of you. The perspective you have always differs at night from the same street during the day. The streets are darker and seem narrower and it always feels like it takes longer walking at night.

I pulled the bolt back on my weapon and the familiar sound of the bullet entered the chamber as I walked past the front gate. I took my first tense step into the unknown not exactly sure what I was supposed to be doing. I needed to relax and control my breathing because my legs felt very heavy from all the pressure I felt. One foot in front of another I kept telling myself as I looked to make sure I was copying everything that Lance Corporal Cantu was doing.

I was very happy we saw no action on the first patrol. I'm not sure if I would've had it in me to fire. I was so busy worrying about not losing sight of the guy in front of me that it never really crossed my mind that there was a chance we could take enemy fire. Even though I have never asked any of my friends how they felt during the first patrol, I can't imagine I was the only one who felt like this. For all the training and expertise that Sergeant America had, he had as much experience in the real thing as I did. I imagine he felt the stress of being responsible for twelve men for the first time in a combat zone.

We walked for what seemed like forever but that little patrol we did wouldn't even classify as a patrol in the coming months it was so short. Because of our unfamiliarity with the area and the darkness it felt like it took forever. We halted and did a security check. We all found a covered position and just sat there for what seemed like an eternity. Staring into the darkness, you start getting tired and when you get tired your mind plays tricks on you. From my position, I was staring into a bunch of bushes sensing my team leader's angry eyes burning into my back. I could sense this because he always seemed angry at me. I didn't ever want to shoot Corporal Shepherd so that was a good thing I guess.

Our squad leader gave us the signal to stand up and we started the walk back towards the Combat Outpost. Just like that my first patrol was over. We entered the outpost and did our gear check. Every piece of serialized gear would need to be checked by our team leader and then given the thumbs up to Sergeant America. Your serialized gear is all your equipment given to you by the government that has a serial number on it. My serialized gear was my fighting knife known as the Ka-bar, an M-16, night vision goggles, PEQ 2 laser that could only be seen when using your night vision, and an AT-4 which was a rocket launcher.

Out of nowhere, my team leader started accusing me of falling asleep when we were on our security halt. First of all, he was behind me and it was dark outside. If you see a guy sleeping you're supposed to wake him up so he could do his job and not just let him continue. If I was asleep why didn't he immediately go and beat my ass which was his right? Falling asleep under any situation like that is inexcusable.

Trying to get me better at my job was definitely why he always fucked with me and I respected him for that. To accuse someone of going to sleep during a patrol with no evidence was beyond bullshit and for the first time, it crossed my mind to shoot him.

The Routine

I wish I could say that every day there was some kind of shooting or excitement going on. Modern war as it is fought today is far from the battles of yesteryear. In those battles, there was a fortified enemy entrenched on a beach or a mountain and the Marines would invade and fight to the death. The casualties during WWII are simply not possible nowadays. Our military is much more advanced than the enemies we fight and if they were entrenched, we would just send our jets who would drop bunker busting bombs.

In Iraq, we acted more like police officers walking around making sure the streets were safe. Beach landings, which makes the Marines unique among the other services were as far from our minds as possible. The last time the Marines made a beach landing under fire was during the Korean War in the 1950s. Besides the uniforms we were wearing, our jobs were something the Army would typically do, not Marines.

The architectural highlight of the city would have to be the Saddam Mosque. Looking at the mosque there was nothing out of place and was perfectly taken care of. The call to prayer would happen every day at the same time and would almost be soothing. If the people here took as good of care of their city as they did for this mosque, it would be the most perfect and cleanest city in the world. This beautiful structure I walked by almost daily, I would never get to go inside because we weren't Muslim and you can't just walk into a religious structure with rifles and machine guns.

The most important street in the city was Route Michigan. This street was massive and was the main artery of the city. The morning patrol's first responsibility was to always clear this street of potential IEDs. It was common to bring engineer Marines with us with their metal detectors to help us with this mission. All major transportation through the city went through Route Michigan and it was vital for us that this road was clear of any obstacles.

Once everything was settled, we started to have a rotation with the other platoons. It was a four-day rotation because of the four platoons in our company. For my platoon, day one would be day patrols. Day two would be night patrols. Day three would be our quick reaction force (QRF) and rest time. Day four would be base security. This order could change at any time if our whole company had to go on a raid. If there was a big battle, we would all respond regardless of what day you were on.

The Government Center and Agricultural Center were two important strategic parts of the city. Both these locations were used to set up security and gave us a more full-time presence in the center of the city. We also were frequently stationed in the Government Center and from there, we would occasionally spend the night and run our patrols. Instead of going back to the Combat Outpost when our patrol window was over, we would wait for relief from one of the other platoons. Since I had such a low rank, I never knew why one week we would randomly seem to do this, then not do it again for a month.

During all this time, patrolling almost every day, my skills definitely got better. I had a little more confidence and just like anything in life, if you do it enough you get used to it. The rigorous patrols we would go on you actually got used to. When you're young and stupid like I was, you can take anything. If I had to do that now, I would say no thanks even before my body quit on me.

There was even a period where we were all worried about not getting our Combat Action Ribbon. You actually need to be in combat to receive one and not just in a combat zone. Going all the way to Iraq and coming home without one would've felt like a catastrophe for us.

The reason why we covet the Combat Action Ribbon more than any other is because it shows everyone else that we have accomplished something important. There is no greater honor as a Marine than seeing combat and this ribbon reflects that. If you were a low-ranking Marine like I was and you have a Combat Action Ribbon and someone with a higher rank doesn't have one, even though you still need to follow their orders, you have something over them. There are no amount of training exercises or rank that gets you the equivalent respect of the Combat Action Ribbon in the Marines.

Since I never planned the routes, I never knew in detail where we would go. From my perspective, when we left the base we would always turn right. To the right was the city and our AO seemed to go on forever. We could drive in vehicles for thirty minutes at a time and still be inside it. I had no idea where it actually ended and I'm not sure anybody truly did. Looking back, I am truly convinced that in one eight-hour patrol block, you couldn't walk to the end of the AO and back in time.

Once leaving the front gate we also had another option. We could go straight, which we did only a few times. Going straight was like entering a different world. To the right was all city, straight ahead was nothing but rows and rows of palm groves. It was strange how right next to each other the places could be so different. The palm groves were perfectly in order and walking to the end of it, there was a railroad track where no trains ever passed. We would never cross over the railroad tracks. Echo Company would always turn left out of the front gate.

First Action

In this type of combat, you never know when you will get attacked or when a sniper will shoot at you. We were a bunch of Americans in military uniforms walking around with big guns, there was no hiding for us. Our movements were always known and if we wanted to be stealthy it was almost impossible in this type of urban environment.

In the palm groves at night, it was deathly quiet. It was just us out there within view of the Combat Outpost when I heard a ping sound in the distance and looked up not really sure what it was.

Boom! The explosion landed one hundred fifty meters in front of us as we all turned and started sprinting away as fast as we could.

That ping sound was the sound of insurgents shooting mortars at the Combat Outpost. They were horrible shots but somehow got close to us unintentionally. There was nothing we could do as the insurgents were too far away and we had no chance of finding them. I learned later that the insurgents were actually quite intelligent in their tactics and you need to give respect to your enemy even when their methods were not what I would call honorable.

In order to get the local populous to start hating us, the insurgents whoever they were, devised a plan where we would respond to their fire and our return fire would kill innocent people and destroy property. On Camp Ramadi, which was a huge Army base on the other side of the city, they had all the artillery and the big guns. Whenever the insurgents would shoot a mortar at us, they did so from a back of a pickup truck. Normally you dig a mortar pit and start firing from there. Firing from a back of a pickup truck was horribly inaccurate but it drew the counter battery from Camp Ramadi.

The radar systems would see the launch and would respond to where the fire came from immediately. The second the insurgents fired the mortar they drove safely away from the incoming fire headed in their direction. Our artillery which was aimed at the insurgents would never hit them and would land and create horrible collateral damage.

Over time, the people of Ramadi grew tired of their streets being destroyed and innocent people getting killed. It was decided that all counter battery fire would be suspended as to not further inflame the people we were trying to help.

Insurgents 1 Marines 0

The Damn Kids

I was always the last man on the patrols and this along with the point man was the most stressful position. Even though I wouldn't be the one setting the pace on the patrols or know exactly where we were going at all times, my responsibility was huge. Turning around every four steps and walking backward looking for anything suspicious for a few steps than doing it all over again, is a stress that unless you were the last man on patrol, you could never truly understand.

Whenever anyone else turned around during the patrol which was every eight steps, they had the satisfaction of seeing one of us knowing that there was somebody friendly behind them. When I turned around it was either emptiness or people not from my unit staring at me. Months and months of patrolling like this slowly affect your mind and then there were those damn kids.

These kids would always shout pro Saddam chants and dance as we would walk by them. I wasn't sure what was wrong with them because from what I saw since I arrived in Iraq, we did everything we could to help these people. None of us came there with bad intentions and being greeted by pro-Saddam chants was annoying to say the least.

Another reason why being the last man on patrol sucked was because these same kids would always throw rocks at me. Everyone else on the patrol was fine but it was only me getting hit by rocks every day. The kids were smart because they wouldn't throw rocks at the other Marines because the Marine behind him would just snatch the kid and probably give him a couple punches to the head. Since I was the last guy, they knew there wasn't anything I could do about it.

Even though I had a helmet and gear on, it still hurt getting clunked on the head and back with rocks on almost a daily basis. Trust me when I tell you that at times, I was close to throwing a grenade at them but the thought of me going to prison prevented it. One time out of nowhere, I lost control and turned around and found a burst of speed that I didn't think I had being weighed down by all my gear. I almost was able to catch one of the kids, but they were just too fast. All of the sudden, I was on a different street than the rest of my squad and got my senses back. I needed to forget the kids and run back or I would run the risk of being shot or kidnapped.

Kids 1 Jason 0

Finishing February and March, there wasn't that much violence and I was beginning to think that maybe the intelligence we got was correct. The only injury that I remember happening was to a member of 4th platoon who was critically injured by a bicycle bomb. He lost an eye and took horrible shrapnel to the head and shoulder.

Since each platoon had their own shift, the only time we would see the other platoons would be inside the now completed cafeteria. Since Marines are taught to put all the emotional pain away for a later date, losing someone to a horrible injury was usually kept quiet. Having a guy get horribly wounded is a big deal but is never big enough where the platoon loses their motivation or discipline. The men in the platoon have a job to do and it never stops regardless if someone is killed or wounded.

First Raids

When we went on missions that involved using the vehicles, Lance Corporal Marenger was always one of the drivers. Since the machine gun he carried would always need to be manned, it was me who got to carry his weapon while mine was kept in his vehicle.

Since I didn't have much experience with the squad automatic weapon (SAW), I needed refreshers so if I was in a situation that involved shooting, I would be smoother with the weapon. In times of fear, you always instinctively revert back to your training and I didn't have that much training with the SAW. My biggest fear would be running out of ammunition and struggling to reload. Doing this is fairly straightforward but under stress, making specific precise movements is difficult. In my free time, I would borrow his weapon and with the help of Ozzie, another Marine in my squad, I would practice barrel changing procedures and reloading. After training with Ozzie, I had the confidence that if something happened to Marenger, I could replace him as the machine gunner in our team.

On one of our first raids, I was the one carrying our team's machine gun. Our whole company would be involved in the raid but it was my team who would be the assault element. Simply speaking, I would be the first one through the door. If you got the sinking feeling in your stomach when reading this, that's OK because I got it too when I was told I would be the first one breaching the door.

The intelligence I wasn't too thrilled with either. I never was. At times, it felt like the intelligence department was forced to do something and would give us incomplete rushed intel. I got the feeling they were under pressure from their bosses and just gave them the 20% complete intel they had so their bosses would get off their back.

On one hand we were told to expect shooting, but on the other hand we were told we needed to knock on the door. Why would we knock on the door to tell the bad guys we were coming and lose the element of surprise? Maybe that's great for everyone else, but not for me. I would be the first one through the fucking door and I needed the element of surprise so I wouldn't get shot in the head ten times.

Up to this point I had never shot my weapon and I was hoping I wouldn't need to that night. Entering a hostile house through the front door is how the first man always dies. They know where you're coming in from and you don't know where they are hiding.

We went by vehicle to the house and stopped a hundred meters away from the target. We jumped off the 7-tons and ran as fast as we could. Fortunately carrying the machine gun, I was able to let someone else hold my rocket launcher.

Running with full gear and the SAW, I arrived at the front door. The front of the house was strange because they had two front doors next to each other and we weren't sure which was the main front door. My team leader started pounding on the door to the left while I had my finger on the trigger ready to enter and start firing if necessary.

After what felt like a few minutes, a door opened. We picked the wrong door as the door behind me opened. I turned around and looked face to face with the man who opened it. He looked like he was sleeping and we definitely woke him. I froze for a second because I was expecting shooting, not to be greeted by a man with his eyes half closed. He was unarmed and I rushed past him lifting my machine gun as I entered his house. It was empty, not one guy could be found. The rest of my squad and others came inside as we immediately started searching every single inch of the house.

We found nothing.

After searching, we all got back in the vehicles and returned to the Combat Outpost. It was always frustrating getting excited for something and it always turned into a massive letdown. Even when we would do something and it resulted in an arrest, we would never receive confirmation as to what they did wrong. Later than that, if these guys went to court or were found guilty of a crime, we never had the sense of satisfaction from something being completely finished. It would have felt good to be told something like,

"The guys that were arrested from your raid were the leaders of a terrorist cell and are now in jail." We almost never received any positive news like that.

The Battle of Ramadi

On April 6, 2004, the Battle of Ramadi had begun and 2nd platoon was on the sidelines.

By this time, Tommy and I had become excellent friends. Whenever we had free time at the base we would always joke around and usually eat together when our schedules aligned. Whenever I would see his squad returning from patrols, I would always check to see that he wasn't hurt.

As was always the case, my platoon replaced his on post and they immediately went into day operations. While standing around the front gate, Tommy's squad ran into an Echo Company patrol and they all stood around speaking for a bit.

Moments before stepping off, there was a phone call in the guard shack and Tommy's squad leader ran to pick it up and told the squad that it was the same intel they always received about them being potentially attacked.

Leaving the base and turning right onto Route Michigan checking for IEDs which every platoon always did, 1st and 3rd squads split off and they started satellite patrolling near Canal Street, another important artery for the city.

With Tommy at the end of 3rd squad, he got the standard treatment from Iraqi kids throwing rocks at him and chanting Saddam's name. Angered, Tommy and TJ both at the end of the patrol turned around and started sprinting full speed trying to catch up to some of the kids to start beating the shit out of them. Unfortunately, those damn kids were too quick and chasing after them left Tommy a good hundred yards away from the rest of his squad.

As soon as Tommy almost made it back to his squad, he heard the sound of a rocket and saw it coming towards him hitting a tree and spinning towards a power line then exploding. Both men hit the ground shielding themselves as the insurgents opened up with machine gun and AK-47 fire ambushing his squad.

Lunchbox, another Marine in his squad was immediately shot in the arm looked up at Tommy and said, "Purple Heart and Combat Action Ribbon all in one day, ain't that some shit." Tommy couldn't hold in his laughter from what Lunchbox had just said when in the front of the squad another Marine screamed, "Contact Front."

Looking down an alley, Tommy saw a man twenty-five meters away poking his head out and all of the sudden the insurgent shot a full magazine of AK-47 fire towards him completely missing. Every instinct in Tommy's body told him to shoot back but he was momentarily frozen because he never had shot his weapon towards another human being before. What also caused him to momentarily freeze was that the man shooting at him was dressed as an Iraqi policeman and they were supposed to be the good guys.

Lifting his weapon up to fire, being the first time he would ever shoot anyone, Tommy thought to himself, "Please be right."

We were taught so thoroughly the rules of war and didn't want to get into trouble that it was in our subconscious to never make a mistake. On countless patrols, we saw Iraqi policeman with weapons and would walk by them, because cops have guns. Having an Iraqi policeman shooting at you was unexpected.

Tommy shot the guy two times dead center in the chest giving him his first kill.

With his squad reacting and on the defensive, surrounded by dozens of enemy shooters on one street and dozens more on the cross street, how could so many insurgents gather at that one point and know that the patrol would walk by there?

Tommy believes that the interpreters Golf Company used, sabotaged them and gave away their patrol information so they could be ambushed. That is the only way he thinks it was possible. It was never a smart idea to trust them anyways because I doubted anybody could even validate the truthfulness or the screening process of the interpreters before they were given to us.

Needing to take the initiative during the battle, Tommy and two other Marines stayed back while the rest of the squad was forced into heavy fighting crossing a cemetery. Dying in a cemetery would be an ironic way to go out.

Every weapon in the insurgents' arsenal opened up while Tommy was shooting in every possible direction. His eight mags were quickly disappearing as he started shooting every car that turned down the road, first taking out the driver then the passenger. It looked like the cars were picking up and dropping off fighters moving them to different ambush sites trying to confuse the Marines.

1st platoon was QRF, wasn't able to immediately help because they got ambushed, leaving the two platoons completely cut off from each other. Tommy's squad was spread apart and they were cut off from their 1st squad who were trapped. 1st squad had entered into a building and made a Casualty Collection Point (CCP) blocks away which may have well been miles away because of the intense fighting. 2nd squad never got into the fight because they arrived earlier in the day to the Government Center and were under orders to hold it at all costs. The insurgents wanted to take over control of the building and was the reason for the ambushes in the surrounding areas.

2nd squad listened in horror as they heard all hell breaking loose on the radio around a mile away but could do nothing. They heard screams from their fellow Marines but would not be allowed to leave and join the fight. During this day of fighting, the Government Center was never attacked with not one bullet being sent in its direction.

During all of our patrols in an effort to win the "hearts and minds" of the Iraqi people, we would be forced to do certain things that tough Marines wouldn't be associated with. Every time we would walk by Iraqis, we were under orders to smile and wave at them. We were supposed to only use our right hand because using your left hand was seen as disrespectful in the Arabic culture.

The insurgents seeing how nice the Marines were for months on end waving and trying to rebuild the city's infrastructure, decided that we must be cowards and would make for an easy victory once they attacked us.

Instead of picking up a history book and learning that Marines always have a will to fight whether at a bar or battlefield, the insurgents underestimated the will of the Marines and were taken by surprise by the tenacity of everyone involved, rendering the Government Center safe.

Triple Canopy who were the private contractors guarding the Government Center on a full-time basis, heard all the chaos through the radio and the calls that more ammo was needed. Riding in their armored Suburban, they threw ammo crates to the Marines giving them the vital resources they desperately needed.

Lunchbox whose arm wound wasn't serious, now suffered the bad luck of being shot again trying to cross the cemetery. This time it was no laughing matter as the bullet entered through his stomach. He was in critical condition by the time the MEDEVAC arrived.

Over the radio, Tommy's squad heard that two Marines from 1st squad had been killed in action.

The gunfire seemed far away but was still close enough that I could tell it was intense. Nothing so far in our deployment had we seen anything like this. Nobody was attacking our base but we were prepared. We weren't speaking to each other like normal on post, but were stone faced ready for battle. Our brothers were fighting stranded in the city without air support of any kind. We just had each other.

I knew something was seriously wrong when a helicopter landed at the Combat Outpost. There was no landing pad for a HELO because this was too small of a base for that. The landing would need to be absolutely perfect or the pilot could easily crash. When seeing the massive helicopter landing near me, I knew that something major was going on and it wasn't just a couple skirmishes here or there.

During the course of that day I cannot relate to the fighting that went on in that city because I wasn't part of it. We had our job and we did it. I was very scared from all the uncertainty. We wanted to fight and get some action like the rest of our company and on our six hour break from guard duty, we had too much adrenaline to sleep and begged our superiors to go out. We were rebuffed saying that we still needed to protect the Combat Outpost. We continued to beg and even asked if the cooks could fill in on guard duty for us.

Marines are very competitive and stupid to a large extent. It may seem strange to outsiders, but even though we Marines are on the same team, we are very competitive against one another. It wasn't our fault that the combat happened during our guard shift day, but we didn't want the other platoons having anything on us. Standing guard is easy and having the other platoons see combat while we were the only ones not to, was a bitter pill to swallow. Automatically, the other platoons would think they are better than ours because they've seen more action than us. It's crazy I know, but all the Marines I know are crazy.

Inside the garage area where we all were gathered begging to fight, an Army fighting vehicle called a Bradley, came inside at blazing speed. I had never seen one of these vehicles up close before and we had no Army units in the Combat Outpost. The situation must have been dire for an Army vehicle to come to our base.

The man on top of the vehicle was missing his arm screaming while the medics were helping him off the vehicle. I had never seen anything like that in my life. The blood, the suffering, the carnage from arm to bone. I got scared and didn't know what to do. Most of my squad turned around not wanting to lose their psyche or just from the trauma they were witnessing. I continued to stare at the poor soldier fixated on what

I was seeing until he disappeared in the medical room for life-saving treatment.

"2nd platoon, you're going outside the lines to provide cover for the other platoons as they return to base." I don't remember who said it after so many years but it doesn't really matter. All that mattered was that we were going outside the lines to help our brothers and if we were lucky, we would see combat. We were 2nd platoon and we had a point to prove. Don't fuck with us would be our message we wanted to send and we wanted to send it through every city street.

My hands were shaking as I tried to get the magazine into the magazine well of my rifle. The magazine fell to the ground as I picked it up and tried once more. I dropped it again as it bounced off the floor. I looked around hoping nobody would notice but was relieved because everybody else was worrying about themselves.

"Jason," I told myself, "Relax and remember your training. Calm down and take it step by step and breathe. Your brothers need you right now and you need to perform."

I calmed down and inserted the magazine. Step one done. Step two, get the rifle in condition 1 by racking the bolt back. Step three, get my gear on. Step four, walk out of friendly lines and kick some ass.

We departed friendly lines, turned right, and walked three hundred yards down the road. We found some bushes to hide in and got some cover as we provided watch while the other platoons returned to base. Was it glamorous what we did? Of course not, but it was something that had to be done. We returned to base within twenty minutes with no action for 2nd platoon and no messages sent to the city. We weren't done for the day because we had to finish our guard duty. Remember, a Marine always has guard duty.

Our second guard shift was set to begin.

On April 7, the Battle of Ramadi continued. Exhausted from standing guard from midnight to 0600, we had time to get extra mags of ammo and fill up on water. By 0615 we were hitting the streets not knowing what the future would hold, how our lives would change, how we would look at the world differently, and how we would look at the mission in Iraq. Thirteen years later, I think about this day, every day.

This day motivates me to explore the world and it motivates me to look for the good in it when there might not be much. It also motivates me to realize how precious life is and not care about jobs that I am not passionate about when I feel there is still so much for me to see and learn about in this world we live in. These events that I experienced in my life were the best and worst things to have ever happened to me. The best in the sense that I do not take things too seriously because let us be honest, after seeing what I've seen, is anything really that serious anymore? I am well-traveled, kind-hearted, always laughing, and always planning my next adventure.

These events have made me for the worst because I can't stop thinking in the short term. Three months seems like a long time for me. I lose interest in jobs but I know that if I quit, I will always start at the bottom of a new company never getting ahead and never getting the salary I want. I feel trapped, like I am drowning and need to escape my surroundings. I feel most at ease being anonymous, nobody knowing who I am wandering around different countries filling a void in my life so deep that I don't think it could ever be filled.

April 7, started calm, but by the time the day ended, lives would be changed and our own pages in Marine Corps history would be written.

Leaving for patrol on the 7th, our typical teams were a little different than normal. One of the team leaders was sick leaving Sergeant America to change up the teams. As was usually the case, we had engineer Marines with us to help us clear Route Michigan of any suspected IEDs. I was in a three-man team that day with someone who was in the Marines a little longer than me who was put in charge.

Walking through the desolate city, you could hear a pin drop. The eerie silence left my hairs standing on the back of my neck. My adrenaline was racing and heart was pumping. No action yet, but it wasn't looking like we would return to base without something happening. No kids playing, no taxis on the road, no shops opened, increased the tension in the squad. Remembering my training, I constantly reminded myself to breathe and stay calm and if anything happened, to just squeeze the trigger and shoot back. We trained so often in tactics and different scenarios, I felt that sometimes people overcomplicated things and just needed to remember to shoot back.

Every few steps I would ask myself, if something were to happen right this second, where would I run and seek cover from? Another five steps, OK, I would sprint to that corner and get a good support position where I am not exposed and I can get a good field of fire.

A man approached me out of nowhere and told me a few words which still haunt me to this day and simply put the whole Iraq war in perspective for me.

"Do you know why they don't like you?" he asked me about a foot in front of me in perfect English. "It's because, like me you guys are Christian and they think you are dirty dogs."

I didn't know what to say, first off, I hadn't really spoken English to an Iraqi before and second, I was shocked at what occurred. Looking back, I find it amusing that he didn't say the reason we were hated so much was the fact that we invaded and occupied their country, or that hundreds of thousands of innocent people were unfortunately killed, or the ensuing chaos that was brought to the country and not the stability that we promised. Those were not the reasons for the hatred. Just the fact we were Christians and nothing else. Being that I am Jewish, his sentence wasn't exactly accurate but I wasn't going to let some Iraqi guy know my religion. If he thought I was Christian, so be it and I would celebrate Christmas and even get baptized if I had to.

Fifteen minutes later we turned the corner and we saw a man wearing a red headdress. Apparently, people wearing that on their head that day were on the, be on the lookout list (BOLO). "Catch that guy," screamed our squad leader. I started running, weighed down by an AT-4, rifle, and forty pounds of gear. I took off like a bat out of hell and was running as fast as I could, but had no chance of catching a man that far in front of us who was wearing only robes as weights on his body. Turning around another corner, he was gone. I was out of breath hunched over trying to get the air back in my lungs, thinking that we didn't get paid enough for this shit.

The rest of the squad caught up about a minute later and we regrouped and reformed our squad formation.

Incominggggg!

An explosion hit right between our patrol sending smoke everywhere. I wasn't sure if it was an RPG or a mortar. Whatever it was, it was explosive and I'm not sure why nobody was killed or wounded in that instance, but on any other day our whole squad could have been taken out.

We thought that the fire came from the house to my left and we attacked. From nowhere, I had leadership ability and not sure where it came from. Well that's a lie. I had a will to live and my mind was very clear and focused.

I screamed, "Let's clear this house and push those motherfuckers out the back. I'll be on the side and when they make a break for it, I'll blow their fucking heads off."

"Let's do it," said Sergeant America.

I tried to donkey kick the fence surrounding the house and slipped on the ground. Five of the guys had their guns ready to blow the gate off and judging by their faces, they didn't look like they wanted to wait to fire any longer.

"Oh shit," I thought as I crawled out of the way while the team opened up with their weapons and opened the gate. As they entered the house, I went into the side of the outer wall and looked around and was surrounded by what looked like a waist-high maze of coal. I jumped over one of the maze layers and focused my weapon on the back of the house praying that whoever shot at us would soon jump out and be greeted by one of my bullets.

Waiting patiently controlling my breathing, the house directly to my left looked like it had a strange person staring at me from afar. The thought of Norman Bates in *Psycho,* dressed as his mother quickly entered my mind. Was it my mind playing tricks on me or was somebody actually there? Oh the joys of combat.

A hail of machine gun fire erupted all around the street in my direction. With my rifle and AT-4, I ran and leaped and somehow rolled over another part of the coal maze. If I could have been an ant hiding in the ground, now would have been the time. The sound was deafening only outdone by my beating heart. The sheer terror of the situation caused me to nearly forget my training.

"Stay down hidden from sight," the logical part of my brain told me. The other part of my brain, the side where courage and character must come from told me, "Get up, stop being a pussy, you're a United States Marine and you've been waiting for this moment for your whole life."

I slowly rose looking for the enemy shooters. I couldn't see anything or anyone. I guess the video games aren't very realistic, the bad guys actually hide in real life. The street got eerily quiet until an unknown voice yelled, "Corpsman up."

The "Corpsman up" call means that there is an injured Marine and the "Docs" as we call them spring into action under heavy fire if need be to attend to the injured Marine. I looked up trying to see where the injured Marine was so I could assist in any way possible. No luck, the chaos was too much and the injured Marine must have been in another part of the street far from me.

"Get inside the house," another unknown voice yelled. I started running like Usain Bolt in the Olympics stopping at the door entrance looking for the wounded Marine. Still no luck. Well if I go to the second story, maybe I will be able to see where they are from a higher vantage point. Running inside and finding the stairway, I sprinted upstairs and went to a balcony overlooking the street.

Still nothing. Then I saw the injured Marine being helped into the house. Without anyone that I could see, I decided to shoot at a far wall on the street to my left side. Whatever bullets shot in any direction would keep the enemy shooters down, giving the injured man cover to get inside.

The bullets erupted out of my weapon with a certain intensity that I had never felt in training. My rifle seemed to know the dire situation we were in and responded. My magazine emptied in what felt like a few seconds.

"I'm out, shit I need to change magazines."

Remembering how I struggled to insert a mag the day before in the safety of the Combat Outpost, I needed to calmly walk myself through the steps of this combat reload. Take the new magazine out of the pouch and bring it towards my weapon. Take the empty mag out of the magazine well and insert the new one. Press the bolt release button and close the bolt cover. Put the empty magazine in my pants pocket.

Unlike the day before when I dropped my magazine twice, this time I did it under pressure with no errors. I was locked and loaded ready for anything else in front of me.

I saw someone run out of another building to my left and was running on the other side of the street in front of me. Holy shit, that guy has a gun. For a split second, I wasn't sure what to do because I never had the opportunity to shoot a human being before. My training kicked in and without hesitation I aimed in and I started shooting at the bastard across the street. Pop, pop, pop, breathe, relax, pop!

He went down like a ton of bricks. A myriad of feelings rushed through my body. First, I felt sadness for shooting and killing another human being. Second, I felt a sense of being in a real-life video game seeing that bullets actually do hurt people. Third, even after everything that happened the day before, I felt that this was actually happening to me. This was a very unique experience killing someone and within the same split second how I could have so many emotions.

"Fuck yeah," I thought, thinking about my friends from high school probably partying in college at the same time I just shot a dude in the neck.

Holy shit, what a rush! Back home you go to jail for doing shit like this. I had never felt so free in my life. The rules became very simple and straightforward to me. Remember your training, use your best judgment, and for Christ sake, shoot and keep shooting that glorious weapon in your hand.

I went down to see who was injured. Although all Marines are equal, I was hoping I didn't know him. Walking downstairs, I immediately recognized him. Fuck, it was my mentor Lance Corporal Cantu. He was laying on the floor being looked over by our corpsman and Sergeant America. His ankle was mangled and I wasn't sure if he got shot or took shrapnel from an RPG. All I knew was that he needed major-medical attention on his ankle.

With chaotic fighting everywhere, the QRF finally arrived with more Marines to bring to the fight and a Humvee to take Cantu back to the Combat Outpost. Cantu's ammo was dispersed to the squad after he was MEDEVACED to start the long process of going from hospital to hospital on the journey home. I wouldn't see him for another two months.

Before leaving the house, our squad reorganized and we departed. Leaving the front door, every corner was treacherous and every alley could be deadly. In a city of four hundred thousand angry people, we were outmanned, outgunned, but never out of the fight. We had no air power because that was probably all in Fallujah, so we just had our squad weapons with us. The safest spot in the city would be a roof and by this time our whole battalion was in the city fighting in a repeat of April 6, the day before. From our experiences, we knew that we needed to flood the city with Marines and hit the enemy hard and with no mercy. Those sons of bitches took our handouts and greeted our smiles and handwaves with fake smiles of appreciation.

Today 2nd platoon was in the fight and fighting we sure as hell did. On another rooftop, we let hell rain over the city. Firing at every moving target we could see, some of the shots were from far distance, some weren't. We were given orders because of the fighting the day before that if fighting erupted on April 7, we could shoot anybody in the street at our own discretion.

I looked at this from two vantage points. If you are on the street during hellacious battles you are one of two things or maybe even both. One, you are a fighter and dare test your fighting abilities against angry Marines. Two, you are an idiot who thinks having gunfights in your city are a source of entertainment and you want to watch it. Either way, my platoon, 2nd platoon would blow your head off.

Spanish

I can honestly say that I saved the life of a family of four by speaking Spanish in Iraq. In one of the many houses we entered on April 7, this turned out to be the strangest experience of my life. As usually the case, when we entered a home, we always would go to the rooftop to get optimal coverage of the city below us. Getting to the high ground has been a fundamental part of war since the beginning of time. Unlike traditional roofs in the United States, roofs in Iraq are completely different. There is a staircase leading to the roof and they are completely flat. You can walk on the whole roof and throw a huge party up there if you wanted.

To prevent you from falling off the roof, each house had the roof surrounded by a wall. Being that I am short, I would always have a problem looking over the wall to the city around us. Great for being hidden from shooters and bullets, but not so good if I wanted to shoot back. Usually, I would find something to stand on like a brick to give me a few inches of height. In this house, I had no luck. I was sent back down to watch the family and if anyone walked into the front door after us.

This job although boring and not glamorous is very important. My job was to put the whole family in one room and guard them and the front door. They aren't allowed to use the telephone because they could let enemy fighters know our location. They aren't allowed to leave for the same reason. It's not as easy as it sounds. The gunfire outside, the screaming of the crying kids in a language you don't understand, make things absolutely chaotic.

With all this chaos and me going downstairs to tell the Marines below that they could go to the roof because I would watch the family, I was suddenly surrounded by a family of four with the husband, wife, and the two kids. The man was a huge human being who towered over me not only in height but in just simple all-around mass. He never missed a meal I can promise you that.

Once the rest of the Marines started going upstairs, the man started yelling at me in Spanish.

"Hijo de puta," he yelled at me as we looked at each other.

My first thought was, "It's a shame they speak Arabic instead of Spanish here, but why is he swearing at me in Spanish?" Was it my imagination or did this guy just call me a son of a bitch in Spanish?

I asked him, "¿Donde aprendiste español?" (Where did you learn Spanish?)

He responded, "Estudiaba en España cuando era un estudiante." (I studied in Spain when I was a student).

Incredible! I thought Saddam was this horrible person, I never realized that even in Iraq people could leave the country to learn and study abroad. Studying abroad was something I would want to do one day and this guy did it. I guess I had a lot to learn about the world.

Unlike the fluidity I have in Spanish today, my ability then was very limited. Just some of the basics I remembered in high school and swear words. Guarding the family, the man wanted to leave the house to see his uncle. I was under strict orders to let nobody out of the house at any cost.

"Quiero ir para ver a mi tio." (I want to go and see my uncle)

"No puedes." (You can't.)

"Quiero ver a mi tio." (I want to see my uncle)

"No puedes." (You can't)

"Quiero ver a mi tio." (I want to see my uncle)

I finally had enough.

"Lo siento, no puedes, pero por favor vea la tele o eche una siesta, voy a dejar tu familia en paz, solo quedarte aquí en esta habitación y que no use el teléfono. Cuando salgamos de aquí, puedes llamar e ir donde quieres."

(I am sorry, you can't, but please watch television or take a nap. I will leave your family in peace, just stay here in this room and don't use the phone. When we leave here, you can call and go where you want)

"Quiero ir a ver mi tio." (I want to go and see my uncle)

I usually was chosen more than most to guard whatever family was in the house because I had a good nature about me. I didn't look angry all the time like most of the Marines and I smiled a lot. Since I wasn't this huge monster of a man like the Big Guy, my small stature and personality put most families at ease.

I became extremely angry that my smile and friendly personality with my young John Travolta look alike face wasn't helping. I finally had enough and yelled at him in Spanish,

"Si sales de esta casa voy a matarte." (If you leave this house, I will kill you)

Sometimes being nice doesn't work so I tried the other route. Threatening someone's life while you are holding an M-16 rifle and an anti-tank rocket seems to do the trick. It is a shame that in the civilian world when you are in the customer service industry and somebody treats you like shit, you just need to smile and nod your head and take it like a bitch. This was not that time. I had a large gun, an anti-tank rocket, and eighteen years-worth of testosterone.

What did I do to deserve this? Even though we barged into his house randomly without permission, I was trying to be nice and respectful because I meant no ill will towards this man or his family. It was so stressful and loud because of the intense fighting outside, plus the sound of the screaming kids in my face. The mother with her stare, I could tell was imagining me dying. The father for all I know wanted to tell the insurgents exactly where we were so he could help get us killed. This was crazy what I was experiencing and was harder than anything anyone experienced on the roof above. Before today, the idea of real combat seemed fun but in reality, it wasn't. For the first time in my military career, this thought briefly crossed my mind.

I should have gone to college.

I was fortunate the man got the message and his family stayed in the house. If they would have taken a half step outside, an eighteen-year old kid from Orange County would need to decide whether to pull the trigger on an unarmed man a foot in front of his wife and two kids. My friends from high school were having the time of their lives in college and on the other hand, I was making decisions whether to blow the head off of a man in front of me. Amazing how life's decisions make for some interesting choices.

If he would have stepped out that door even an inch, my mind was already made up. I would have squeezed the trigger and killed him.

Thank goodness I paid attention in Spanish class.

The Fighting Continues

The shooting never stopped as we entered another house and we again went straight to the roof. I was enjoying the feeling of no bullets heading our direction while we were laying large amounts of destruction below us. Lenhart made the most amazing kill shot I had ever seen. With no scope, he must have hit a guy over five-hundred meters away. That is about five football fields. That is the longest the M-16 is accurate to without a scope. What a shooter, what a shot, what a fucking Marine!

"Holy shit!" I screamed, "Lenhart that's the most incredible thing I have ever seen and I'm so hungry, I wish we could order Domino's pizza right now."

Marines think only about three things: Sleeping, eating, and sex. Combat doesn't change that.

Since I always was on rear security on patrols, I somehow always got rear security on the roof too. After that excitement, I turned around and got bored while all my buddies were shooting and I was looking at another part of the city by myself with nothing to shoot at.

Certain things bug me about that day that I still can't shake all these years later. The image is so fresh in my mind that I wish I could just forget it sometimes. While staring into a part of the city by myself, a woman left her house and started to hang her clothes outside on a clothing line. There was fighting all day before, and there was fighting all day today. What the fuck was wrong with this lady? I understand the clothes need to dry but come on lady you people can't be that stupid, can you?

I have the right to blow this woman's head off. She is in a designated combat zone in the street not in her house. What am I supposed to do? Everyone else is looking at another part of the city engaging and observing targets. Meanwhile, I get to stare at a middle-aged lady putting her clothes on the clothing wire.

I control my breathing, stare into my sights and focus my weapon dead center onto her chest. I felt like a sniper for the first time in my life. I was in a hidden position and I was watching every detail and movement of her body. How her muscles moved as she bent down and picked up her clothing. I noticed the clothes she was wearing, the way she grabbed the sheets and hung each and every one of them with such care and precision. My eyes were laser focused and I could see the sweat on her forehead on this miserably hot day. I kept asking myself,

"Should I shoot her, or shouldn't I?"

I took my weapon off safe and moved the selector switch into the fire position. I cracked my neck as I put my tip of my index finger on the trigger. Could I kill a woman with no weapon on her while she was hanging up her clothes? The answer was yes, she could have been a spotter or a million other things, and I was allowed too.

I aim in as I slowly pull the trigger back and at the last second with the trigger pulled halfway, I changed my mind and adjusted my firing position. I placed a well-aimed shot one foot from her head passing through one of the hanging sheets. I hoped that she would be terrified and run into the house which would mean that I made a good decision for saving her life and she would be out of danger into the safety of her home.

The woman turned her head and looked into the bullet hole a foot from her. She never looked up and continued finishing hanging her laundry. This fucking country. If I did this back home, the city would be locking their doors and hiding before I would even pull the trigger. She didn't even care and continued with her day. We must have opened up a hornets nest and these people must be pretty tough to try and continue their daily lives through all this turmoil. Maybe I was just an ignorant eighteen-year old kid with too much responsibility and wasn't ready for the real world.

Or maybe, I just wasn't ready for Iraq.

Why didn't I shoot her? That is a question I ask myself all the time and I always come back with the same answer. It wasn't worth living my life with regret over something I didn't have to do. Why was that lady hanging up her clothes in the middle of such chaos? That is a question that I will never be able to answer. What I can answer, is who I am as a person. Even though I was allowed to shoot her because we had orders because of the heavy fighting from the day before and at the present time, doesn't mean I should shoot her. I didn't find her to be a threat to me and I didn't have it inside me to kill an unarmed woman. I am a lot of things, but I could never at the end of the day dishonor my moral code or my family name doing something like that. I made a choice with no information. She could have been an enemy spotter or even someone who shot at us, or she may have just been an innocent woman trying to live her life as normal as possible. There was no right or wrong shooting her or not. I know I made the right choice because even after all these years, I've never regretted my decision.

I got bored and turned back around to see what the other Marines were doing. We saw a man on his motorcycle about five hundred yards away and the whole squad opened up with everything we had. Bullets sputtered and hit in every direction but him. The harder we tried the more we missed.

"Let him go," said our squad leader, "That must be the luckiest man in the world right now." Another hour on the rooftop we stayed while the rest of the battalion which included Fox, Echo, and Weapons were fighting their own battles in the city.

We again moved to the streets staying low while bullets buzzed by us as I saw my first dead body up close. The dead man was wearing a white man dress where it clearly showed where our machine gunner shot him at least six times. Because of the white color of the dead man's outfit, you could see each circular blood pattern from each bullet.

Running by him, time seemed to stand still as I felt paralyzed looking at the dead man. It still didn't feel real the idea of seeing a dead guy just lying there in the middle of the road. If this wasn't combat, this would be a big deal and everybody would have stopped and checked on the guy and called for help. We all ran by this man like he never existed.

Dying of thirst from five hours of fighting, I was out of water as was the rest of our squad. Going inside another house, the kind Iraqi man inside started boiling water for us without hesitation.

What a lifesaver. Because of the chaos, I didn't even realize how thirsty and tired I was. Staying so laser focused for such a long time is very draining on the body and I was starting to feel its affects. With my camelbak now full of fresh boiled water, I quickly guzzled what I could and headed to the roof. The squad was running low on ammo yet I was surprised at how much ammo I still had left. Surprisingly, I did remember my training and was very selective with what and when I used my bullets. I handed out two full mags of ammunition, one to my team leader and another to the Big Guy.

Back on the roof, things had quieted down a bit and we could finally catch our breath and hydrate. Looking down below, a man on his bicycle was going past us on the street. I screamed, "Sergeant, there is a man approaching us on his bicycle, can I shoot him?"

"Is he armed?" he asked back.

"No, but he could be an enemy spotter."

"Shit you're right, shoot him."

That little hesitation caused the bike rider to get out of my view. I would've had the easiest shot in the history of warfare. A man riding his bike a few miles per hour ten feet from our position while we were twenty feet above him. It wouldn't get any easier that.

"Fuck," I thought to myself. Of all the times for my squad leader to have a heart, why now, why this time?

My chance vanished as the bike rider disappeared around the corner. After another hour on the roof, the city began to quiet. The enemy must have lost their will to fight. I don't blame them though because after the beating they took the last two days, I wouldn't want to fight much more either.

Leaving the house, we walked a few blocks and rejoined with our 1st squad. No longer satellite patrolling, we were walking down the street when Brooklyn the man in front of me got shot in the arm.

"Damn, I've been shot," he screamed.

I couldn't control my laughter. The way he yelled with his New York accent was too overwhelming for me to handle. Brooklyn had a stunning resemblance to the actor, Mario Van Peebles and his personality was very similar to his role in the movie, *Heartbreak Ridge.*

The injury didn't seem too severe because we kept continuing the patrol. After getting my laughter under control, we continued our patrol back to the Combat Outpost. Rounding another corner, we linked up with what looked like Weapons Company. They were all vehicle mounted with massive guns attached to the back. They had the Mark 19 which is an automatic grenade launcher and also 50 Caliber machine guns. I suddenly felt much safer knowing we had such powerful weapons at our disposal and got the feeling that I might make it out alive on this very intense day in my life.

A taxi appeared from behind us which was the biggest mistake of the driver's life. We had so much time to prepare; I remember stretching before the whole firing line opened up on the poor taxi. It seemed like every weapon in our arsenal opened up on that dumb bastard. Not wanting to miss out on the fun, I decided to join in and put around ten rounds aiming in on the driver's face. The taxi was riddled with hundreds of bullets in only a few seconds.

My AT-4 was still hanging off my back and I had yet an opportunity to fire that thing in action. Being that the insurgents had no tanks, I always found it interesting that I carried an anti-tank rocket on my back with the key word here being anti-tank.

My squad leader asked me for my rocket and the next set of events were some of the most interesting moments I have ever seen. My squad leader took the rocket and fired it into the corner. As the rocket was about to launch, I covered my ears only imagining how loud it would be. Training with rocket paint ball rounds didn't prepare me for this.

The rocket thundered towards the target and hit the man dead center. I stood in awe and was frozen still from the carnage that was in front of me. There was nothing left to look at but particles of human flesh and bones etched into the wall behind. I imagined what Nagasaki and Hiroshima looked like when the atom bombs dropped, leaving only shadows of their victims. The only thing left of the man were his sandals which were still standing in place as if a man was still standing in them. We were always taught to leave one dog tag around our neck and the other one in our boot. They told us this because the boots usually survive any explosion, so if you can't be identified, they have the dog tag from the boot. The sandals the Iraqi was wearing had no dog tag in them. I highly doubt he was ever identified to his next of kin.

I guess we should rename that weapon the AH-4 (Anti-Human rocket)!

Walking back to Combat Outpost with Weapons Company in their vehicles as overwatch, we finally made it back to friendly lines. I never was so tired in my life and felt like a part of me was left in the city. We did our customary gear check of all serialized gear then walked back into our room to drop our gear off. Our whole platoon regrouped in front of our little house where we received heartbreaking news.

One of the members of our platoon was killed in action. He was from 1st squad and his death was heartbreaking. Although I barely knew the man, I couldn't control my emotions. I hid my face into my hands and started crying uncontrollably. There wasn't a dry eye in our platoon and even his squad leader who was in the invasion of Iraq and knew people who died, had tears dripping from his eyes.

Their squad of course knew what had happened to him, but this brief just confirmed that he had perished. My squad had no idea this had happened and we were just told about it for the very first time. Walking back into our rooms at around 1600, I collapsed in exhaustion from the day. Our whole squad was lying down, some in their beds and some on the ground too tired to make it. I fell asleep on the floor so tired that I dreamed about sleep.

We were then woken up by a complete stranger telling us that the sergeant major of our battalion was coming through. I don't think any of us cared, we were too tired from nine hours of fighting to give a shit. It was probably some asshole who only cared about his career and promotions who honestly didn't even fight. If I had more experience in the Marines and self-confidence, I would have punched him right in the face. He wanted us to clean our room and make it presentable for the sergeant major.

I will give you a little background on our sergeant major. He was former Force Recon with jump wings, scuba bubble, expert shooter, and a total badass. He carried an M-14 not an M-16 like the rest of us. Everybody respected this man. He was a Marines Marine, a fighting man who didn't hide in some office drinking coffee when the shit went down. He left his headquarters every chance he could and literally chased down insurgents. He was and still is to this day a badass motherfucker.

Eleven years later, he was one of the five sergeants major who was nominated to be the Sergeant Major of the Marine Corps, which is the highest enlisted position in all the Corps. He didn't get it. Even the Marine Corps is too political of an organization to let a warrior like him be number one leading Marines. He has recently retired and lives near Waco, Texas.

Waking up from my deep sleep, everyone else in my squad probably didn't hear the call that the sergeant major was on his way. Hearing someone enter our room, I lifted my head out of my haze and saw the sergeant major. What a sight it must have been. Seven Marines, all teenagers some sleeping on the ground too exhausted to make it to their beds. Lifting my head up with drool all over my face, all I could muster out of my mouth with all my energy was a mumbled barely audible, "Good afternoon sergeant major." He looked at me, then our room and back at me. He smiled and nodded his head. I finally felt like I made it as a Marine. I felt I was acknowledged warrior to warrior and was allowed to rest and didn't need to worry about some bullshit if our room was clean or not. I passed back out not even waiting for the sergeant major to leave.

Both sides took heavy casualties during the fighting. Thirteen Marines from 2/4 were killed between the 6th and 7th of April. The casualties were in the dozens. Many of the men didn't just go down because of being shot or injured by grenades, but from heat exhaustion. The fighting was intense and unfortunately death and injuries are a part of war. We Marines know this and if we are to go down, we sure as hell will take a lot more of them with us. It was estimated that we killed around four hundred fifty enemy insurgents, a number that I wish was much higher. I felt we wasted a lot of hard earned American tax dollars by shooting bullets that didn't hit more of them.

One of the Marines killed in Echo Company on April 6, was the Big Guy's drill instructor not six months before. The loss was unbearable. The drill instructor becomes a father figure to you as a recruit and they are people you will never forget because of the importance they have in your life. Because I was also in boot camp with the Big Guy, I also knew his drill instructor. We were in different platoons but in the same boot camp company, so his drill instructor chewed my ass a few times too. I was deeply saddened not only for his death but also the way my best friend the Big Guy must have been feeling.

Getting up and going to the chow hall, I could tell the stress had already set in. We were shell shocked and on edge. Sitting inside eating, everybody was eerily quiet not having the will to speak. There really wasn't much to talk about. How's your day going didn't seem like an appropriate question to ask anyone.

There were large freezers inside the cafeteria that would slam down when somebody would open the freezer door and let it fall back down without slowly bringing them down. Every time somebody forgot to do this the freezer door would slam down making a huge bang sound.

Bang! Everybody hit the ground as someone else forgot to close the freezer softly. Bang! Somebody did it again.

"Slowly close the fucking freezer door," somebody shouted.

Everybody laughed and breathed a sigh of relief as we finished our spaghetti and meatballs. We weren't in Italy, but damn that prison quality food they served us sure as hell tasted like it came from Naples. Oh the joys of combat.

Later that night we were briefed for the next mission the following morning. I know what you guys are thinking. How much did we get paid for all this work that we did? The answer is around $1500 a month. That's right, *overworked and underpaid*, I believe is the expression.

The mission was to be as follows. The whole battalion would get up before dawn and head to our individual objectives. We were to clear every single house on every single street in our zone. This mission was named, "County Fair". How cute I thought, thinking back to the county fairs that I had been to and seen on TV. Roller coasters and popcorn, chasing girls with your friends, were what county fairs were supposed to be. I guess this was a different kind of county fair.

We awoke still tired from the previous days of fighting and gathered our gear. We each packed nine mags worth of ammo instead of the customary six expecting intense house to house fighting. I felt more mature and knew what I was doing. My team leader finally got off my back and I felt like I belonged. He stopped treating me like dog shit and I thought that he may actually be a cool dude instead of an asshole.

The cooks were put in charge of base security while the whole Combat Outpost vanished into the night towards the objective. Walking for what seemed like ages, we arrived and our company hid under a small hill under whatever cover we could find waiting for the sunrise. I wanted to sleep so bad still tired from everything that had just transpired. I stayed awake not wanting to let my teammates down as I prayed for the sun to hurry up and rise as my eyelids got heavier and heavier under the weight of the last three days.

The glorious sun in all her beauty finally rose over the battle-scarred city of Ramadi. Day three would soon begin with hundreds of Marines going door to door begging for the city to explode in battle. My squad got in formation and we started entering houses. The streets were still empty as we pushed from house to house. At each and every house we went inside, we flipped everything over. We pulled every mattress, every blanket, and left nothing unturned. We were looking for bomb making materials and weapons of any kind.

In full gear with a rifle and another AT-4 slung over my back, it became agonizing to lift countless mattresses and blankets over and over. My shoulders and back started to tire and ache after twenty minutes. Being that we probably had another five to six hours, I knew I was in for another long day.

Our battalion Humvees with attached megaphones were taunting the city challenging them in Arabic to stop hiding and be men and fight the Marines. There were only a few scenarios left. All the fighters left the city, they were all too much of pussies to fight, or the other option, they were all dead.

Five hours of searching house after house, street after street, we found absolutely nothing. Our platoon was completely exhausted and disappointed that we didn't find anything noteworthy in the houses nor did anyone fight us. Another punishing day in the hot Ramadi sun was over.

We returned to the Combat Outpost exhausted. From what I saw, the County Fair turned up nothing. Upon entering the base, we did our customary gear check. Removing our flak jackets in our room, my undershirt was drenched in sweat like I had been swimming in a pool. In the chaos of the last three days it was hard to believe that one of the members of our team was no longer with us. There was only his sea bag and an empty bed. Since space was tight, we now used his bed as storage for our weapons and gear freeing up space for us.

I could only imagine how 1st squad felt. They also had a missing bed. The man in our squad would be in a hospital somewhere far away waiting for our return in California. They would be missing their man forever. Our platoon was exhausted and deeply saddened.

The feeling had finally set in that our platoon had man one killed. His name was Christopher Mabry from a small town in Mississippi. He was only nineteen-years old. From the little time that I knew him, he was a very thoughtful and caring person and seemed like a great guy. His life was lost much too soon and his death devastated the men in our platoon closest to him. After these last few days of battle, it became apparent that we weren't invincible and could die at any moment.

Our platoon went to the chow hall where the whole company ate in silence. It must have been the combination of hunger and exhaustion but nobody said a word. The mood was too solemn for that. I don't remember what we ate, most likely spaghetti and meatballs again with some vegetables. Normally I couldn't wait to eat, but tonight I couldn't even taste the food.

I started feeling like the character in the album, *The Wall* by Pink Floyd, who after each traumatic event in his life would have another metaphorical brick built over him hardening him to what was happening in his life.

It all started feeling like a brick in the wall to me.

The Battle of Ramadi was finally over and the first of many bricks was put in my wall. 2nd Battalion 4th Marines had 13 men killed during the battle with dozens wounded. There were an estimated 450 enemy insurgents killed during the battle. While Fallujah was getting all the media coverage around the globe, there was one little battalion of Marines who held the city with no air power of any kind. The insurgents failed to take control of the capital of the Anbar province. Their will to fight was broken over the three-day battle. They picked the wrong city with the wrong group of Marines I guess.

Insurgents 1 Marines 1

Trying to Get Back to Normal

Two days later I got to call home using the satellite phone. Excited isn't the right word I should use to describe the moment but I don't know any word better than that. I learned early on that regardless of the time back home because of the time difference, I should call home whenever I could get the chance. Being that I could die at any time in this city, I knew that my parents wouldn't care, in fact, they would be thrilled to receive a call even at 0300.

"Are you alright son, we have been watching the news?"

"Yes thankfully, I am ok, I can't really tell you who was killed or injured until their families are notified."

"Did you kill anyone?"

"Yes, I killed somebody. We fought very well, the Marines who fought in Iwo Jima would be very proud of us, I can promise you that."

Hearing my dad's voice was such a good feeling as tears rushed to my eyes. I found it hard to speak because of all the emotion. After another ten minutes of chatting I hung up the phone and handed it to another Marine who was excited to call his family.

A Family's Wait

A few years later I heard the ordeal that my family went through. I knew the situation we were in because I was there. It is always harder for the families a world away without any communication with their sons. They may have the rumor mill or maybe a support network or two.

The worst is hearing that your son's unit is locked in heavy fighting by way of the news.

My father who every morning would leave the house by 6:30am to make it to work by 8am in Los Angeles, was driving listening to music. It was the same routine as usual until he got a phone call from my stepmom.

"Sergio, have you heard what happened in Ramadi?"

My dad immediately turned the music down and listened in.

"Thirteen Marines have been killed in Ramadi, they are all from 2/4. It's all over the news."

My dad immediately had the fear of God put into him wondering if his son was OK. At work instead of watching soccer all day, he was hooked on the news looking for any information about us. He even called my recruiter asking him what happens if something happened to me. Would he receive a phone call or a knock on the door or something like that? The recruiter told him that if something were to happen to me, it could take up to three days to be notified. If you hear nothing in that time frame, then everything is ok.

They were also worried because we lived in a gate guarded community and if someone came informing them of my death, the gate guard would possibly notify them before that the Marines were here. The three-day agonizing countdown started waiting to hear if their son was injured or killed in the fighting. Imagine their relief when I called at 3am and they answered the phone. How fast those three days went by for me must have seemed like a lifetime for them. As I said earlier, not knowing is always the hardest part for the families.

I also thought we were allowed to call home because of the heavy fighting and the command wanted us to let our families know that we made it through the battle. It took me a few years to realize that the call didn't exactly happen for that reason. The date of that call was around Easter Sunday and being near the holiday, that was the main reason for the call. I didn't have a calendar and the days all seemed the same to me so I lost track of time. I also had no idea when Easter actually ever was because I'm not Christian, which was probably the reason I didn't know it was Easter.

I still don't know when Easter is.

Standing More Guard

At the Combat Outpost, Cantu and I stood guard together on post one. Post one was the base entrance. Our job was to try and keep track of hundreds of cars driving by looking for anything suspicious and operating the big arm letting vehicles in and out. Standing guard with someone, you really get to know them. There isn't enough action not to speak to one another and it was me basically nodding my head listening to this guy telling me story after story of all the women he slept with and how he started drinking at the age of thirteen. I think he was lying about a good amount of the stuff he was telling me. If you could pull women as easy as he made it sound, why would you give that up to be in a real shithole like we were currently in?

After the injury to his ankle on April 7, the guard shifts had to be reorganized. I was moved to guard the secondary entrance on the side of the Combat Outpost with you guessed it, the Big Guy. I learned that the Big Guy didn't like being bored and would pass the time taking gunpowder from bullets and lighting it on fire. Standing on post was so boring looking for countless hours at the same spot, that sometimes you would just do whatever it took to keep your sanity. Standing on post at night wasn't any better. It wasn't quite as hot but the silence would eat away at your soul.

During our guard shift, sometimes you just needed to sleep. I wasn't sure if there were any regulations against sleeping on post as long as one man was awake and vigilant and I wasn't about to ask. If the Big Guy wanted to sleep, I couldn't really stop him as he outweighed me by over one hundred pounds. Our squad leader or lieutenant, would come in and check in on us every once in a while to see if we were awake or not. I told the Big Guy that he should take a power nap. I would rather have him sleep for a quick twenty minutes on the floor and wake up and be alert than be falling in and out of sleep for the rest of our shift. I told him that we needed a go-to conversation. Anytime we would wake up, we would immediately start talking so the person checking in on us would think that we were both awake. I decided we would talk about NASCAR because I thought people from Texas liked that sort of stuff.

Our post was elevated and you needed to use a ladder to get up to us. It would be impossible for anyone to walk up to our position without making noise. As long as one of us was awake there would be no need to worry. The Big Guy was asleep next to me while I continued being vigilant looking out into the quiet street in front.

I heard a noise below that could only be coming from somebody climbing up the ladder. I kicked the Big Guy in his leg as he did his shimmy and opened his big eyes not sure where he was for a few seconds. The Big Guy jumped up and looked like a baby cow learning to walk for the first time and almost on command in his thick Texan accent which I barely understood said, "I love NASCAR, I love the way they drive fast."

Our lieutenant entered our post and looked at both of us. He was a native of Virginia and son of a Marine officer. He was tall, skinny, and wore glasses. He seemed like a great guy and was extremely intelligent and I felt lucky he was our platoon commander.

"You guys like NASCAR?" he asked us.

We both looked at each other, "Yes sir, we love it."

The lieutenant started climbing back down the ladder. "You guys have a great night," as he disappeared out of our sight.

"Hey Big Guy, do you know anything about NASCAR?"

"Not a thing, what about you?"

"I also don't know anything about NASCAR."

"Why did we pick this topic to talk about then?" I asked him.

The Big Guy got flustered, "Ahhh, I don't know."

"Ok, so do you like soccer?"

"No."

"Do you like football, baseball or basketball?"

"I don't like any sports," the big Texan responded.

Who would've thought a guy from Texas didn't like sports, not even football.

"Big Guy, you need to help me out here. What do you like, so we have something to talk about the next time you wake up from a power nap and we don't look like idiots in front of the lieutenant?"

The Big Guy smiled with his cute little gap between his top teeth and said, "Tacos, I love tacos."

Putting my hand on my forehead, I was in disbelief as I was contemplating how I could respond to something as ridiculous as the words that came out of his mouth. If this was the circus, the Big Guy and I would've been hired in the freak show exhibit.

"It's 0300 Big Guy, I need to lay down for twenty minutes. Fuck it, tacos it is."

I laid down and immediately fell asleep.

Eight years later, well after I was finished with my military career, our lieutenant was hit by an IED in Afghanistan and was terribly injured. I spoke to him over the phone and told me he was in the hospital for a couple of months and would probably be for a couple more. The doctors told him that if he was lucky, 50% would be the new 100% for him in terms of recovery. Since our last conversation that day, he completely disappeared off the face of the Earth and I nor anyone else knows where he is or what has happened to him.

Uneasiness

There was now a huge sense of uneasiness amongst us all. The battle was over but the patrols would still need to continue as normal. The next few days came and went in the same fashion as always. Night patrols, day patrols, base security, QRF, which meant more working parties. The city was once again lively as though it seemed nothing had transpired the previous week. On patrols, we would still always smile and wave to the people to try and win their hearts and minds because we were instructed by Sergeant America to continue this previous policy as if the past battle never even happened.

"Is that a fucking joke?" someone in our squad griped.

"Guys, we know this is bullshit but remember our mission is to improve the lives of the people in this town and let's not forget that."

Our squad nodded our heads in fake agreement knowing that our squad leader didn't actually believe any of that bullshit he was telling us but was just passing down these orders from a higher authority.

We had a mission to do and that would never stop. The problem was still the same. We had no idea what the bad guys ever looked like. They were too smart to walk around with weapons and would just stockpile them and shoot at us, drop the weapon, then go to another stockpile. They knew we wouldn't shoot unarmed people and they took advantage of this.

It was hard to process how it seemed overnight an entire city could seemingly turn against us. I'm sure we did some things wrong that may have angered some people and turned them against us, but there is no way that all the good we were trying to do could have been all for nothing. I still believe even in my more cynical moods, that we still had the support of the majority of the people in the city. I know that if all four hundred thousand people took up arms against us during the Battle of Ramadi, we would have lost a lot more than thirteen Marines.

Before the big battle, we arrived full of hope to improve the lives of the people here. No matter what we were told, after the battle we knew it would now be about survival. We would do our jobs with the same passion because that's what Marines do, but the difference was that we wouldn't assume the Iraqis in this city were our friends anymore.

The Day our Staff Sergeant Lost his Nipple

Sitting on top of the agricultural center on another scorching day, we were there for hours looking into the city and hoping to see something.

Unfortunately, that meant a lot of looking and not a lot of seeing. There was never anything that I actually saw on a normal day that I would deem suspicious. What stands out is how scary and funny something can be at the same time.

From the little time I knew him, our staff sergeant who was our platoon sergeant seemed like a cool guy. He reminded me of the character, Ichabod Crane from the short story, *The Legend of Sleepy Hollow*. He never yelled and was easy to talk to. I didn't know anything about him or where he came from, but since he was our platoon sergeant, I guess he was an infantry Marine. The fact that he didn't seem like a crazed psychopath really made me think highly of him.

He always reminded me of someone who was too big for their own body, like it was meant for somebody else. Our platoon sergeant was very tall, skinny, and didn't look very athletic. I would bet that he never played sports because he just didn't have that look about him. He was the type of guy that was so uncoordinated he would trip over himself walking, which he did many times.

Sitting on a chair looking into the city below trying as hard as I could to stay awake, a sniper took a shot at us.

Crack!

The bullet ended the quiet of the last few hours as the bullet shattered the sound barrier and made contact somewhere on our lookout position. Our staff sergeant who was sitting in a chair a bit to my right, fell straight backwards on the ground. I thought he was shot. We all hit the ground at the same time, when I heard a horrible scream come out of his mouth.

"I lost my nipple."

Another Marine in my squad was also on the ground not moving. I thought he had been shot too because for some reason he decided not to speak and just laid there.

"Are you ok?" I yelled to him. He finally moved and I realized he was fine. He just had the wind knocked out of him by the fear of what just happened and how quickly he fell to the ground. I was worried about him being shot and also the staff sergeant screaming about his damn nipple.

With all of us laying on the ground, we all looked at each other not sure if he had really been shot, but if he was, how would he know that he lost his nipple with all his gear on? It turned out it was just his camelbak. When he was sitting in his chair, the sniper bullet hit the cement right in front of him and somehow the force of him falling backwards knocked the nipple off his drinking system.

Once we realized what he was talking about with our whole squad laying on the ground under sniper fire, we couldn't hold our laughter in. What a sight it must have been, a bunch of guys in such a dangerous situation just laughing like nothing was wrong. Laughing is a great way to relieve stress, and let us be honest, the sniper could see us but we sure as hell couldn't see him. If you aren't laughing and you think about how dire your situation really is, you can get depressed very quickly.

Our staff sergeant's nipple was safe, we just needed to find the sniper or get off the roof.

The Worst Shots in the World

On one-night patrol, we entered a large apartment complex to set up a lookout position. It was hard work walking up ten flights of stairs with all of our equipment on. Bending over catching my breath, I walked to my position on the roof. From this high vantage point, which seemed like the highest in the city, it almost looked peaceful and beautiful below.

Sergeant America now had a completely unrecognizable weapon that looked like it came from a video game. During the deployment, he slowly modified his weapon well beyond putting a scope on it. He changed out the barrel to where it was now only eleven inches long, making his modified barrel even shorter than an M-4. He switched out the buttstock and replaced it with one that could collapse if he wanted, just like the M-4. Instead of using the typical thirty round-magazine, he was now using a banana clip like they did on the AK-47, that could hold fifty rounds. His weapon was like something out of an Arnold

Schwarzenegger movie where such a big guy was holding a gun way too small for him. It seemed unfair to me that I carried a rifle and the AT-4 on my back, which when I walked uphill, would bounce off the ground.

With nothing going on in the city below, we were getting anxious and tired on the rooftop. Sitting around is always nice but makes time go by really slow and you start counting the minutes until you start the patrol back home. I then spotted something on the streets approaching from my left. It was two men with a wheelbarrow walking below us. This was very unusual to be doing at 0200 and I told my team leader to check it out. After looking, he told Sergeant America who told our radioman to call it in to headquarters.

"Headquarters, we have two men walking with a wheelbarrow, it looks very suspicious."

The response on the radio which was one of the most awesome things I have ever heard, was simple yet effective.

"Light em up."

For the first time in our deployment we would have the first shot on an unsuspecting enemy. We had so much time to prepare, I remember stretching before we initiated the attack.

"Light em up," came the order from Sergeant America to our squad.

Sergeant America with his modified super weapon was going to take the first shot.

Click! His weapon jammed.

"Shit," he screamed.

We all opened up and fired towards the two men with the wheelbarrow. We had twelve guys shooting at these men with all the time in the world to aim in. The men in the city below, as soon as the fire rained down upon them, ditched the wheelbarrow and took off into the alley next to them. The Marines with their reputation as the world's best marksmen didn't hit absolutely anything. All of us missed, with not one drop of blood spilled from the men below. It was a shameful display of shooting.

I learned that sometimes people just say things to make themselves feel important and build themselves up. We had twelve Marines with all the same training with time to aim in on an unsuspecting target. We all missed terribly. Missing turned out to be a good thing because those guys were actually not jihadist but just stupid. A squad of Marines somewhere else in the city moved towards the wheelbarrow and its contents were nothing close to having any bomb making material in it. It was just flour or something as unimportant as that. Those men pushing the wheelbarrow were lucky that we were all horrible shots. They would've been killed over flour because their activity was very suspicious of people who were planting IEDs.

We ran back down all the flights of stairs full of excitement past now awake Iraqis looking at us. We all flexed our muscles as we ran by them, not sure exactly why, but probably because we were all dumb teenagers.

Marines may be great marksmen by reputation, but on this night, we were the world's worst.

The Market

Walking through the center market was always nerve racking. Lots of people, lots of potential threats, and we were always outnumbered. Being the last man on patrol was even more difficult in a crowded market. I had to constantly look behind me to the point where I would almost walk backward the whole time. The problem is that you lose your balance very easily and can't see in the natural direction you are supposed to walk. More importantly, it is easy to get separated from your squad because they walk in their normal direction and normal speed, while I was busy protecting the rear of the squad.

If the majority of the people in Ramadi did hate us, the perfect time to show it would have been in the market. Irritated that we were in their city probably, but truly hated us, I felt it couldn't have been too many because we all could've been swarmed and killed. Somebody could have easily walked behind me and stabbed me with a knife and I wouldn't have ever seen it coming. We were thirteen guys walking down the tight marketplace streets surrounded by hundreds of people. Besides the excitement of the marketplace from all the noise and people, in reality, I always hated going through there because too many things could go wrong. On this particular day, the market was crowded, unusually crowded and I had a bad feeling walking through it.

My uniform blouse had ridden above my pants revealing my last name. Since I was the last man in the patrol, I had no one behind me that was my friend. Somebody in the crowd behind me who could read English yelled out my name.

"Rosman," I heard my name as my life flashed before my eyes thinking I would be shot or stabbed at any second.

I thought I was a dead man.

I had never been so afraid in my life. I turned around expecting the end to come and was greeted by about fifty Iraqis staring me down like they wanted to slit my throat and parade me around town. Their eyes had fire in them as they probed me up and down. I stared back at them for a split second and if they could've read my mind, it would've said one thing and one thing only.

I should have gone to college.

More Raids

There was never any shortage of action at the Combat Outpost. This didn't mean that we were getting shot at or having epic battles every day but because of the size of the city there was always something we were doing. As a young kid thinking about what the military was, I imagined I would have all this cool equipment and go on all these secret dangerous missions. I would be the ultimate badass, no one would dare fight me because I could take care of them with hand to hand combat if I wanted to.

Fast forward thirteen years and I am now in the military the farthest I could essentially be from what I imagined as a young kid. Yes, I was in the Marine Corps infantry which is still difficult to make, but still very far from Special Forces going on secret missions that I can never talk about. The closest thing I did in the military where I felt like some kind of cool elite soldier was when we went on raids.

In my mind, a raid was a mission where there is a high priority target and you do a lighting quick strike and attack the house. You kick in the front door and there will be a few chaotic seconds of intense fighting then it's over. Collect all the intelligence in the house and quickly disappear into the night.

At the Combat Outpost, we did a big raid about twice a month. These night missions were difficult because if you were on day patrols, instead of getting sleep at night, you had to do a raid which took forever. We would get briefed on the mission and our company would practice inside the Combat Outpost to simulate the roads and what we could expect.

Every scenario was replayed over and over again and the amount of detail you needed to remember was staggering. You had to know the main plan, secondary plan, and even the tertiary plan. If you got lost, you would need to know the rally point to get picked up and if that one didn't work, you would need to know where the secondary pickup point was. Memorization was crucial because our Gunny could pepper you with questions at any time to see if you understood the mission. Letting our Gunny down would equate to a verbal thrashing that could never be understood because of his thick Filipino accent. He was such a scary individual that it was better to just pay attention and not incur his wrath.

On one raid that was deemed high priority, we were told that Army Special Forces would be responsible for breaching the door while the Marines would provide a cordon around them. Nobody is allowed in or out once we set the perimeter. I was never able to confirm what Special Forces they were, but I know they weren't Delta Force. They were probably Army Rangers or Green Berets. The mission was too high risk and they didn't want Marines doing it because they thought we weren't up to the task, so they gave it to the "cool guys."

I had never seen or worked with Special Forces before so I was excited. I heard that they had all the cool gear and were "high speed".

They were the guys that I dreamed about becoming before I realized how bad at soldiering I really was. I was motivated for this mission even though I would lose even more sleep. I didn't want to let the Special Forces down.

The night was dark but the mood was light, everybody was joking sitting next to their gear waiting to mount up on the vehicles. I did another check of my gear and ensured that my NVGs had batteries in them and that I had an extra pair in case they were needed. I checked that my camelbak and two canteens were full of water, because not having water was just as bad as not having bullets for your gun in this heat.

"Mount up," the order came and we all jumped into the back of the 7-tons. The adrenaline hit me as the loud roar of the engines were all started in unison. It was loud but almost relaxing as we drove towards the front gate of the Combat Outpost. Everybody was serious now, you could see it on our faces. The look of professionals who were used to performing under extreme stress where it almost became routine.

We drove towards the objective and fifteen minutes later, the vehicles came to a quick halt. We jumped out of the 7-tons and started sprinting in full gear towards the house. Instead of one of the platoons being the assault element, we all just took our places around the block surrounding the house. My squad was positioned right outside the wall of the target house and I actually saw the Special Forces in action.

Taking a knee behind some cover I saw the men arrive in their Humvees. They didn't look particularly special to me except their flak jackets looked better and lighter. They didn't have any special weapons and I don't think they even had big beards which I thought Special Forces guys had. They didn't look any more capable than Sergeant America for example.

Still in awe that I was in the presence of the Special Forces, I looked around to see if I could do anything to feel cool. I looked up and noticed that I was visible because I was kneeling below a streetlamp.

"If I was Special Forces what would I do?" I thought to myself.

First thing is that Special Forces work in the darkness. I looked up and realized that to protect myself I needed to get out of the light and not present a silhouette of myself. I reached up with the muzzle of my rifle and knocked out the streetlamp.

The bulb shattered and I was surrounded by darkness. I then somehow felt cool, like I was Special Forces or something and started walking around the vicinity I was in and started smashing all the lights. Soon with all my excitement, the whole block was in complete and utter darkness.

These Special Forces I was watching must have been the reserve team because they really sucked. They drove their Humvee up to the perimeter wall and instead of checking to see if the front gate was open, they just started having guys jump over the wall. One of the soldiers with his NVGs which connects to the helmet, had it lifted above his head. When he tried jumping over the wall, his NVGs got stuck in the power lines. It was like watching the movie, *The Naked Gun,* with one funny parodied scene after another. The other men were trying to help this guy not get electrocuted as they untangled him.

Their team was finally able to get to the front door of the house and instead of knocking or taking a shotgun to blow the hinges off to breach it, decided to use an ax. I was in awe of the absolute ineptitude of these men. Taking a little ax to a thick front door is not what I imagined Special Forces did. The guy kept chopping and chopping and the door just wouldn't open. It seemed like a good five minutes I stood there watching this one guy try and chop it down. Whatever element of surprise they were going for was lost a long time before.

The door was finally breached and the "not so" Special Forces entered the home. There were no gunshots which never happened by the way. I must have taken part in ten raids and not once did we shoot our weapons. The soldiers came out with their detainees and drove away. The total time it took from insertion to extraction was about twenty minutes. All we did was stand there and watch. I didn't care that much because I discovered something awesome. Whenever I would go anywhere from now on when it was dark and we stopped, I would destroy the streetlamp above me.

I had never destroyed public property before, but hell I was in Iraq, and it made me feel like a cool Special Forces guy.

After the raid, I randomly started talking to a Marine staying for the night at the Combat Outpost. He was in intel and I was curious as to how the intelligence gathering process worked. From my perspective, even though my rank prevented me from seeing this, I imagined that our commanders received intel and formed their plans based on the intel they received. The infantry is the hammer and the target is the nail.

The plan is formulated and the infantry searches and destroys the target with no hesitation. This is how it should work because everyone should do their job. I did my job and knew the job of the machine gunner in case he was killed. Intel provides the intel and the infantry fights.

The problem is that intel is wrong regularly and puts the infantryman at risk unnecessarily. I have never met a Marine who trusted intel. In fact, I guarantee that no Marine in history has ever trusted them.

My conversation talking to the intel Marine gave me insight into the intelligence gathering process and I was a little disappointed at how careless and amateur it all seemed.

He told me how we had informants all over the city that would get paid to give intel about IEDs and terrorist cells. From there, they would interrogate subjects the same way you see cop shows on TV. They would play the good cop bad cop routine, where one interrogator would be mean then the next one will be kind and understanding with you. Anyone who has seen the show, *Law and Order* understands.

The Marine didn't seem too concerned or care when I told him that his intelligence sucked and nobody trusted the crap information we were given. Every raid we went on, we were given intel and told to expect heavy fighting and it never happened.

Later on, I found out the truth about how intelligence was gathered most of the time. Iraqis would simply lie about people they didn't like knowing that we would respond with a raid of their house. Who knows why they didn't like each other but it wasn't because they were insurgents.

The majority of our raids were done because an Iraqi had a personal issue with another Iraqi and our intel believed them when they reported them as insurgents. That is why most raids turned up nothing.

Too Much Stress

Of all the night patrols we went on, most which ended without incident, one sticks out to me and I still cannot close my eyes and forget about it. Night patrols were much easier than day patrols but they followed a similar pattern. We definitely walked much less at night because there was little to see. We would spend most of our time on different roofs throughout the night.

If we have a patrol block of eight hours, it is impossible and illogical to actually walk and patrol for that long. This isn't a traditional World War II mission of hitting the beach and fight to the death. We would walk around, hit our checkpoints, and look out for suspicious activity. Because the enemy, whoever they were, didn't have night vision goggles, the chance of getting into a firefight at night was almost zero. We owned the night and our NVGs were a matter of mission security. If a pair of NVGs were lost on patrol, the whole company would be awoken to walk the city in a combat zone to retrieve the goggles. That is how crucial the NVGs were to having superiority over the enemy.

The organization of the patrols were generally organized like this. Our captain had specific objectives that he wanted accomplished and relayed this information to our lieutenant. Our lieutenant then told our three squad leaders and between them, they planned the execution of the mission. A mission doesn't have to be a specific target house or anything like that but in this case, mission being more like theme of the night. They could want our patrols concentrating more on one area of the city over another.

Discussed between the squad leaders were other important details. Our squads would all be patrolling near each other but never with each other. This satellite patrolling technique was used by the British during the 80s fighting in Northern Ireland. We would need to know the location of the other squads at all times to know where our help would come from and in what direction not to shoot at to avoid friendly fire.

As with every night patrol it is a bit awkward and stressful to knock on a stranger's door at 0200. Being that we have the guns and the power, the Iraqi homeowner has no power or control over the situation.

Put yourselves in their shoes. It's 0200 and you hear a knock on the door. It will either be one of two things at that time of night. Either the jihadists are coming to kill you and your family which is a very possible outcome or it's the Americans who are knocking on your door. Answering the door and letting the Marines in, even though they don't have a choice can be seen by the jihadists as working with the Americans and could be a death sentence for them.

It was through this fear that the jihadist in the city of Ramadi controlled the population. They were outnumbered no doubt, but the insurgents used fear as their most powerful weapon and when you have this, you can have an incredible hold on the population and give you complete control over them.

Knock knock, it was more of a bang. That was the sound of Marines who were tired and angry at 0200 demanding that whoever lived in this house open up their door.

Bang bang, we kept knocking. Five minutes later, a man opened up the door half asleep. I looked into his eyes and saw true fear as he opened the door not knowing who it was on the other side.

"Move we're coming in," one of the Marines said as we rushed into his house.

Because of the time of night, we weren't in the mood to hear any of his complaints or deal with his reasons why we shouldn't have been there. Considering this happened on every night patrol on the roughly two to three houses we would randomly choose to go into, we were used to the complaints by now.

Something about this house was different on the inside and something inside the house still leaves me with regret all these years later. Being the low rank I was, I had no authority in the matter but if I did, I would've turned around and kept walking until I found another house to enter.

This was a typical Iraqi house, quite large with very little furnishings mostly carpets and cushions. The houses are very well made and look like they can survive for hundreds of years. On the roof, the house had the typical square roof that was perfect for ambushes or barbecues. I prefer barbecues but this was Iraq, let us be honest.

Inside there seemed to be more people than normal. Let us say that eight is a typical sized Iraqi family living in a house. It is hard to understand the family dynamic because nobody spoke Arabic. This house had so many people in it, we were trying not to step on them while we were walking through to the roof.

I counted around thirty people in the house. It was absolutely terrifying having to listen to scared woman running to cover their faces with their headdresses and children crying looking to find their parents. It kept getting worse and worse and I felt like I was in a nightmare where I keep telling myself to wake up but I just kept on sleeping.

Making my way to the roof, I was relieved to get away from the chaos downstairs. At least I could get fresh air on top and be left alone from all those people downstairs.

Wrong! Upon entering the roof in the pitch dark, I almost stepped on an infant's head.

"Jesus fucking Christ," I muttered as I nearly crushed this poor baby's skull. It just would never end and the nightmare continued. On top of the roof there was easily another fifteen people, mostly little babies sleeping. Now at 0230 speaking no Arabic, we were tired and in bad moods and had to tell people in a language they didn't understand to pack their things, hurry up and go downstairs, so they could all be guarded by one Marine. This took time and patience which we didn't have, especially the latter.

"Hurry the fuck up," one of the guys said, "If we have to be awake, so do you."

We hurried everyone downstairs then took our positions on the roof. Sitting down catching my breath, I slowly played back what just happened. We entered a house like we always did late at night and go to the roof. Normally there is no issue and we let the family sleep and have one Marine guard them. We go to the roof for security until we are done then we leave.

This time we did everything the same. What were the odds that in this house of one in a million, this one would have over thirty people in it. I may have been too young and stupid to know any better, but the thought of this now really irks me. We could have easily given thirty more people an excuse to hate us. For what reason? Were we too lazy to go to another house? I don't know.

Sitting on that roof catching my breath with my undershirt dripping in sweat from the 90-degree Iraqi night, I started to feel the stress of the deployment getting to me. This was no longer fun and exciting like it had been before. This was starting to take its effect on me. Morality slowly goes out the window in war. No matter how strong and moral you are, your soul slowly starts being eaten away.

I am a very moral person. Even though our squad didn't do anything wrong, nobody was hurt or killed, I just felt bad about what we did to all those poor people in that house. Iraq had changed me, not for better or worse necessarily; I was just tired, tired of not sleeping, tired of always being the last man on patrol, and that same damn Pink Floyd song kept playing in the back of my head.

Another brick was put in my wall.

The Day I Pooped my Pants

Shitting yourself is never a good thing, I think we can all agree about that. Normally from what I've read, usually things like this happen when you're scared. An example of this is getting shot at and your body just kind of lets everything loose. What isn't normal is this happening the other way around. Yes, shitting yourself then hearing gunshots is not the way it is supposed to work.

Getting the taste of chicken outside of friendly lines was always a treat. It was something different from the base and lets you speak to the locals and get to know them. Just like anywhere in life, people desire change and get tired of the same thing over and over again. Everybody knew that eating the chicken was risky not for fear of being poisoned, but rather just getting undercooked food that our Westernized stomachs weren't used to. Every person that I remember would gladly give money so they could eat chicken and there was a period of time when there was a sickness going around base. I was one of the guys who got sick and actually puked when our first sergeant was talking to our company in the vehicle hangar bay. I was given an IV and bed rest for two days.

My squad was now changed around a bit because there was only two people left in my team temporarily. Lance Corporal Cantu was of course long gone and Corporal Shepherd was back in the United States because of a death in his family. Before he went back home, he asked everyone in the squad if they wanted him to buy them something so he could bring it back to them in a week after returning to Iraq.

The answer was the exact same out of everyone's mouth, "Porn."

Now I had Marenger, who was second in command as my team leader. On another night patrol, tragedy struck. While leaving our observation post and getting formed up starting to walk to our next objective, all of the sudden I had to go to the bathroom. Normally when you have to go, you can hold it for a few hours. This was not that moment. I instantly got cold and was sweating at the same time. As soon as the sensation hit me, I told my team leader, "I have to go to bathroom," as the words trembled out of my mouth. In less than a second from the sensation of having to go, to telling my team leader I had to go, I shit myself.

Ashamed is not the word I would use at this point because nobody had yet to find out. I immediately began thinking of ways how I could get away with this even though I knew it would be tough. These were my options. I was in the middle of a combat zone at 0200 a few miles away from base with no change of clothes. My options were just one. Tough it out for the rest of the patrol with a full load of runny shit in my pants. Fortunately, I was always the last man in the patrol and if the wind was right, nobody would be able to smell anything, or so I hoped.

Suddenly with the luck I had, I heard the sounds of bullet fire. Pop pop, as fast as I heard it was as fast as it disappeared. The bullets were close but not near us. Since I never had a radio, I had no idea what was going on. In response to the bullet fire, we started running. Normally running with full gear is a challenge, but now running with full gear with pants full of runny shit was excruciatingly difficult. When we hit a wall and started to climb it, one of the guys asked, “What smells like shit?”

I needed to say something quick or someone would suspect it was me. I said the first thing that came to my mind.

“It smells horrible, I think there’s a sewer around here somewhere,” hoping that the situation we were in would soon let him forget about the horrible stench.

Upon returning to base, my plan was to go as fast as possible to drop my gear off and sprint to the shower hoping that nobody would find out about the massive amount of shit in my pants. My plan didn’t work.

When we entered friendly lines, we did our gear check. It didn’t matter if you had to pee or shit, nothing came before your gear check and getting the all clear from the sergeant. It became obvious that I wouldn’t be able to hide the shit in my pants anymore. The smell was overwhelming and as soon as my gear was inspected I heard someone ask,

“Rosman, did you shit yourself?”

I wanted to die or disappear, whatever was faster and least painful. I said, “Yes I did, it must have been the chicken but I’m feeling fine now.” We all walked back to our room that we all shared where my squad shook their heads and gave me some dirty looks (no pun intended). I gathered my towel and hygiene gear and headed to the showers outside a little walk away.

In turns out that shitting myself was not just a unique experience for me. Very few people feel comfortable talking about it but turns out that I was far from the only person this happened too. Whenever I tell this to any of my friends, it turns out that they also shit themselves at least once in Iraq.

While showering the shame and shit off my body, I couldn't help but crack a small smile. My name is Jason Rosman, I am eighteen-years old and I just shit myself.

A few days later, I randomly found out why we were running and where those gunshots came from. One of the Marines from 1st squad was in a building and slipped and lost control of his SAW. When he fell down the stairs, he somehow pulled the trigger shooting himself in the ankle. His injuries were severe enough that he needed to be sent home and would eventually be medically discharged from the military.

Staff Sergeant Psychopath and Captain Casualty

Having great leadership is so important and can never be stressed enough. Quality leadership means Marines have less to worry about and can concentrate on what is most important. Great leadership means the men will never second guess their leaders and trust them to make the right decisions in battle. Good leaders take care of their Marines even before they need it.

In combat, fighting the enemy is the only thing that matters. Marines shouldn't have to worry about going back to the base and dealing with any other stressors that would take away from their success on the battlefield.

Marines in combat are simple creatures and don't require much. They want to come back to base and have a decent shower and meal. On their down time, they want to hang out in their room and watch movies all day with their squad mates. These seem like very small requirements to keep young men who are in heavy sustained combat operations happy.

I am happy to say Golf Company had extraordinary leadership from top to bottom but unfortunately, I couldn't say the same for our brothers in Echo Company.

Staff Sergeant Psychopath was universally the most hated Marine I have ever met. What can I honestly say about this guy. Whenever I think about him, I think about pure evil. He was a real fucking asshole. He was a platoon sergeant in Echo Company and on paper, he was the world's best Marine. He was not only an expert marksman, but he shot a perfect score every time. Not only was this guy in shape, he scored a perfect three hundred on his PFT every time. He was a black belt martial arts instructor too. His knowledge was impeccable. You could probably ask him to recite page twenty-three of the weapons guide book and he could recite it word for word. This guy was a perfect machine.

He was tall and had short dirty blond hair. He was well built but not in the typical bodybuilder fashion. He looked to me like a poster boy Aryan soldier you would see in a German propaganda film in WWII. His eyes were the scariest thing about him and looking at them from a distance it looked like he had no soul.

Sometimes looking at a mugshot of someone you make observations with no evidence. Things like, "that guy looks guilty," or "he looks like a murderer." There is no validity to a way someone looks in regards to a certain crime, but we always make assumptions like that.

When seeing his photo in his dress blues or even in person, to me he always had the look of someone who tortured animals. No soul, no heart, and no compassion. Pure evil.

The cafeteria was where everyone had their first encounters with the psychopath.

In a building in the military upon entering, you are supposed to remove your cover. This wasn't what I would call a real structure because we were in an outpost in the middle of a combat zone and were running in and out with guns.

As soon as you would cross the threshold of the cafeteria, he would scream at the top of his lungs, "Take your fucking cover off."

His red devil eyes would bulge out of his head as he yelled from one guy to another. People would look at each other confused. I had a rifle and a rocket while others had blood on their uniforms and he's yelling at us like a madman to take our cover off. Looking back at it, this "perfect" Marine was wrong.

In garrison, which means at a base, when entering indoors you take your cover off. The exception to this is when you are "under arms" which could also mean a duty belt not just a weapon. At the Combat Outpost, we were as far away from garrison as possible and even if we were, carrying a rifle and rocket launcher is enough to be considered "under arms".

Echo Company's captain was horrible too and was given the nickname, Captain Casualty by his men. He seemed incompetent and took stupid unnecessary risks getting his Marines needlessly hurt and killed. The Marines' workload was so intense barely getting any rest that individual Marines would start losing control and have emotional breakdowns.

They would get back from a grueling patrol and after trying to relax, would be constantly given more duties taking away from their rest. With so many of the casualties and killed coming from Echo, their ranks were already thin without having to be run to the ground.

Echo Company had it terrible. While our captain would later win the award for the best company commander in all the Marine Corps, Captain Casualty would be relieved of duty. While our crazy Gunny, although nobody understood his English, got us showers, guys from Echo Company would ask to use ours. While the morale in our company was always high, Echo Company struggled to have any. There were horrible rumors going around too.

Supposedly, Echo Company patrols were being sent into known ambushes so when they called for help, the people responding would be in a position to earn medals of valor. I think I should repeat this, Echo

Company patrols were being sent into known ambushes so when they called for help the people responding would be in a position to earn medals of valor. I should correct myself about the whole rumor thing as well. This has been told to me by many members of Echo Company over the years. Year after year I am told the same thing.

Just because they were in another company than me doesn't mean I didn't know them. I went to boot camp and infantry school with many of the men in Echo Company. These men who I am still in contact with today, tell me the same stories year after year. Never once, have I spoken to any man who doesn't hate Staff Sergeant Psychopath and Captain Casualty.

When I first arrived to 2/4, I never gave it any thought as to why I was sent to Golf Company. When I arrived from infantry school, essentially the whole graduating class came to 2/4 with me. There was a rumor going around because Fox Company was a boat company, that they had all the best swimmers. I knew this couldn't be true because one of the guys I knew who came to Fox, was the worst swimmer we had. I suck at swimming but I was like Michael Phelps compared to him.

I soon figured it out. In the military, you are not a person but rather a number or letter. Fox Company got all the guys whose first letter of their last name fell in the first third of the alphabet. Echo Company got all the guys in the middle of the alphabet, while Golf Company got all the men from the end. It was no coincidence that we had guys with names like Rosman, Tapia, and Thompson in my company. I was blessed that my last name wasn't Martinez or anything similar that fell in the middle of the alphabet or I would have been in Echo Company.

Echo Company having their company commander relieved of duty is the worst humiliation possible. A captain having his company taken from him is normally a ticket out of the Marines. That is how bad it got for them.

Let us not forget about Staff Sergeant Psychopath, he was moved to be the platoon sergeant of sniper platoon. This is not a bad position to have, but to be moved from one company to another during a combat deployment is akin to being fired. There is nothing worse that can happen to a Marine in a leadership position.

I have spoken to many of my friends who were in Echo Company and the biggest regret they have in Iraq is that when they had the opportunity, they didn't shoot and kill Staff Sergeant Psychopath and Captain Casualty. Trust me, it is easy to do and get away with it. If there is a firefight and chaos in every direction, they will assume that an insurgent did it. It is not like the United States, and I doubt any investigator would have gone to the most dangerous city in the world when every Marine in Echo Company would have said the same story and backed each other up.

Their leadership was so bad, that besides all the other things that I mentioned before if that wasn't bad enough, they even had platoon formations outside friendly lines. Staff Sergeant Psychopath would routinely play what we Marines call "fuck fuck games" with his men.

"Fuck fuck games" are always done in boot camp to fuck with you. They could be anything from making everybody throw all their belongings in the middle of the squad bay and then the drill instructors will run around and kick everyone's stuff around. Since everyone's stuff is the same you would never get all of your stuff back. Another "fuck fuck game" commonly played would be to take all of our locks and lock them all to each other. Instead of going to bed, we now would need to try and find our identical locks connected to eighty others.

Once you become Marines this type of treatment is supposed to stop. Once you get to combat and start fighting insurgents, this type of treatment should most definitely stop.

Staff Sergeant Psychopath didn't stop and the dumb games he played as a drill instructor carried into a combat zone. Outside of friendly lines he would force his men to jump in and out of the 7-tons over and over again to simply fuck with them.

One grenade or RPG could have killed all of them. These men should be ashamed of themselves. Would you like to know what happened to Staff Sergeant Psychopath and the captain? You are probably thinking that their careers were forever negatively affected by this and they were processed out of the Marines not being permitted to reenlist. Unfortunately, you would be wrong. Staff Sergeant Psychopath continued his military career and is currently a sergeant major. Captain Casualty has also continued his career and the last time I saw him ten years after this deployment was still in uniform and a much higher rank.

It felt like sometimes other Marines were more dangerous than the insurgents we were fighting.

Corporal Shepherd Returns

The Marine Corps sets itself up in a way that everyone should know the job of the person above them. I would never be a team leader in my first deployment because that was more than one job ahead of me. My job would be the machine gunner if Marenger went down. I had complete confidence also that if Sergeant America was killed, the team leader replacing him as squad leader would have just as much success.

Marenger did a great job for the short time he was a team leader and I felt that he would have no trouble if he needed to take over that position permanently. His leadership style was a little different from Corporal Shepherd's and I liked it more because he left me alone. I just did my job and that was it. He never fucked with me and I felt I grew as a Marine because I had more freedom to think on my own and make decisions.

When Corporal Shepherd returned, he was greeted warmly by everyone and they all hoped he brought them the porn magazines he promised to buy everyone. The look of glee on everyone's face as their magazine was given to them was like Christmas had come early.

Back on patrol, Shepherd knew I had changed a little. Instead of just waiting for him to tell me what to do, I was actually doing it a second before. I'm pretty sure he didn't like losing control over me as it seemed was the case in the week he was gone.

"Corporal Shepherd, we've been kneeling in this same spot for like twenty minutes, don't you think we should move positions?"

"Rosman, shut the fuck up, I don't want you thinking for yourself."

I laughed when two minutes later he told our team to stand up and change positions.

A Lesson Learned

Some valuable lessons in life I have learned from the Marines. When applied in the civilian world with a little modification, they can actually be very valuable lessons that you can take with you in any situation. I notice how different my attitude is when faced with certain tasks or challenges that other people may stress over. What may be stressful to them, is not stressful at all to me because of a certain mental mind frame that I carry with me that I've learned throughout the years. Maybe it's the constant nightmares that plague my sleep that makes me never forget. The feeling of failure, the feeling of forgetting something, and the feeling of letting myself and my friends down when I'm needed most. These nightmares are the ones that hurt me the most.

An example of how different I act is when at a job my reaction is completely different to everyone else when a supervisor yells, "The boss is coming."

I don't freak out like everyone else. I just nod my head in fake panic and pretend that I am as worried as everyone else is. The big boss was no ordinary boss, but the founder of the company and a billionaire. I happened to work at the Costco warehouse across from the world headquarters in Issaquah, Washington. Getting visits at the warehouse from across the street was an everyday occurrence and was nothing new. I could be wrong, but I think the owner of the company after so many years was actually semi-retired and had someone else as the CEO. He still had the power being the founder and majority shareholder, but I guess he just liked to walk through the warehouse every day and get a hot dog.

I never understood why people act crazy and freak out when the big boss comes through. People start panicking and run around like chickens with their heads chopped off. On the other hand, I work at the exact same speed as if nothing changed because I know something that I learned many years before.

Failing to prepare is preparing to fail.

If you do your job imagining that the CEO of the company will walk through at any time, and when he does, why would you need to panic and freak out? If you work at a normal pace that is expected and do your job to the best of your ability why should you worry? If you could perform better when the big boss walks through, as an employee who receives a paycheck and benefits, shouldn't you perform at this level when he isn't touring the warehouse? That is the attitude I have and it rubs people the wrong way. It looks like I don't care because I don't panic under these in all actuality non-stressful life events. I laughed when I was the new guy and I didn't even drop a bead of sweat when everyone else was sprinting trying not to bump into customers while trying to improve a job that was already done.

Being that the CEO probably understands the business considering he started the company from nothing, he knows what is right and wrong with his company. There is a difference between real world expectations and a closed room no customers present inspection. It is a tragic waste of time and resources trying to make a warehouse where there are thousands of daily customers look like the place never had a foot step inside it before. The CEO knows this because he wants the place to have customers. He didn't become a billionaire by having empty warehouses all over the country. Where did I learn this lesson about always being prepared?

Laying in a rack in the ready QRF room at the Combat Outpost with boots unlaced but ready for action in less than thirty seconds, this was the time where we could get some rest while also being on standby. A room with a platoon full of men with all their gear and weapons at the foot of the rack, and this was a time of rest for us.

"Rosman," I head the familiar voice of Sergeant America.

"Fuck." It wasn't that I was scared of my squad leader, well that's a lie, I was terrified of him. He literally could have killed me in three seconds with his bare hands if he wanted. There would have been no point to even fight back because I would have died a more painful death.

Just close your eyes and in three seconds you would be dead and it would all be over.

"Let me see your rifle."

He undid my rifle and took a quick look inside. My heart pounded not knowing what he would say, yet knowing exactly what he would say. I was in the Marines long enough at this point to know what they always say. Sergeant America didn't really say exactly what I thought he would say or exactly in those generic terms. He definitely couldn't have predicted what he said next would have a profound effect on my life.

"Rosman, see Lenhart over there? See how we are sitting around not doing much. See how he is cleaning his rifle. He isn't doing anything special that will pass him on a weapons inspection before a parade. He is just doing basic maintenance and if we get called out, he can lube the inside of the weapon and be ready in fifteen seconds. That is why Lenhart is a better Marine than you."

Sergeant America didn't yell because he never did, but I died a little on the inside. Letting your squad leader down seemed worse to me than dying. The thing was, he was completely right. Lenhart was a better Marine than me. Lenhart was stronger than me, he was smarter than me, and he was better looking than me. Sergeant America wasn't talking about any of those things I mentioned as I turned my head and saw Lenhart cleaning his rifle being perfect as always. Lenhart was better than me because he wasn't lazy.

He understood that just because you may have finished an eight-hour patrol in the scorching heat, doesn't mean you earned anything. In this instance, we were just sitting in the ready room doing nothing but resting or sleeping and I should've finished my most important job. Cleaning my weapon to a certain standard that was expected of me and I failed. Some memories fade over time, while some stay with you forever, a reminder of your past and errors you made that you try to never repeat.

Thank you, Sergeant America and Lenhart for teaching me that lesson.

Death and Casualties

There were no more battles quite like the Battle of Ramadi, but there were definitely firefights. Our platoon was one of the luckier ones I guess because it seemed like we missed most of the action. Our company from all the casualties we took actually needed to have combat replacements sent in to us. Some of the men were experienced Marines that weren't allowed to get out of the service and were forced to stay in by a process called stop loss. The other guys we got came straight from the infantry school. One day you would be eating with someone and the next day you would never see that person again.

Marines are in-the-moment people. They don't have time or care to think about how what they are doing today will have some impact ten years down the road. It isn't our job and our job is too hard and complicated to worry about the unknowns in the future.

Although the job is always difficult, at times it breaks down to something very simple. That man over there is shooting at me and I need to eliminate the threat so my friends and I can live. That is about as simple as possible. Survival is our most basic primitive instinct and that's what combat is.

How can you rationalize it when one of us gets killed? Stuck in the middle of a strange foreign country trying to help people who openly hate you and then dying at eighteen or nineteen is hard to justify.

When one of us dies, the speech is always the same. He was a good man, beloved by his friends, and a strong Marine. He died for the greater good and his sacrifice will be felt for years to come.

Time after time, those speeches became tiring because they almost seemed rehearsed. How do they know that the sacrifices will be worth it in the future? What evidence do they have for these claims?

Between Marines, all we cared about was if we died, we died fighting. Charging forward in the heat of battle with everything on the line, leaving nothing behind is the most honorable death imaginable.

The worst death was to be killed by an IED. Just walking or driving along, then boom!

You're dead.

Even though Echo Company took the majority of the casualties, Golf Company couldn't escape either and we had our share of tragedies too.

1st platoon suffered a terrible tragedy and it hit our company hard. While on patrol, their platoon stopped by a school to give out school supplies. The Marines surrounded by kids, had an RPG shot at them. There was terrible carnage all around with dead kids and missing body parts everywhere. We lost a good Marine too.

Even though I didn't know Lance Corporal Bolding, I could tell he was very much beloved by the reaction of his friends when we were told of his death. How could these insurgents shoot an RPG with kids around? I will never understand the mind of someone who can do that.

If you want to talk about tough, Lance Corporal Bolding was one tough guy. He survived long enough to be flown back to Germany, where his family could see him before he passed away. He was one in a long line of proud Texans to give their life wearing the uniform of the Marine Corps.

War sucks and that's really all there's left to say.

Getting Shot

After spending the afternoon at the Agriculture Center standing watch over the city, I never thought that my life would change forever. It always seems major life events happen randomly. Whether you meet your future wife or girlfriend, it seems to just happen for no reason. Why not the day before or after? I could've been shot on any day but for some reason, it happened to me on Monday, June 14, 2004.

Walking down the street towards the Combat Outpost in our usual patrol formation, the roads were clear which was never a good sign. Usually the locals know when an attack was going to happen and this was no different. I thought I heard a noise but it happened too fast to be sure. I felt an incredible pain in my back which could only be described as a baseball bat hitting me. My first thought that crossed my mind was the stupid fucking kids had hit me with a big boulder. Being shot was so far from my mind that I literally thought it was a rock before a bullet could hit me.

Still staggering forward, I couldn't see anything wrong with me or why all of the sudden I felt very tired and out of breath. I looked down and saw my right wrist gashed open and I could see my tendon shaking.

"Holy shit, I've been shot."

I slumped to the ground wrapped around my AT-4 with heavy gunfire all around me. The following seconds were pure chaos as Doc Grimes and Drinkwater under heavy fire, ran to my position and helped me stand up. We turned and ran to the nearest house where the Doc unloaded a pistol mag into the door frame around the handle. The Big Guy football tackled the door down allowing our entrance. I took off my flak jacket and Doc Grimes cut open my blouse not sure what we would find. What we found was absolutely horrifying, I had a huge exit wound the size of a half dollar coin in my right chest. The Big Guy, was looking over me with a terrified look over his face. I knew I was in deep trouble by his expression.

I remember thinking while the corpsman was working on me how lucky I was that I wasn't in Vietnam. Being that we were in the 21st century, if I could get to a hospital quickly, there was a good chance I would survive.

Laying there, strange thoughts crept into my head but were true nevertheless.

"Well thank God this isn't Vietnam. Well maybe the guy in Vietnam when he was injured thought, 'thank God this isn't World War II,' while the World War II guy said 'damn, at least this isn't World War I.'"

What a strange time to have these thoughts in your head, as I grinned thinking that at least my arm wouldn't be amputated like in World War I, when any injury was essentially a death sentence.

Drinkwater radioed in the following message to headquarters, "We have a casualty, urgent critical." When that call comes through the radio, all priority to the helicopters, air support, or whatever is needed is put on high alert and the pilots from wherever their base is, start running to the chopper to get in the air without a moment to waste.

With my shirt off and wrist bandaged from a piece of curtain that was cut off by my team leader, the QRF showed up. In came the captain of our company while the rest of the other platoon started fighting in the street. I walked shirtless into the awaiting Humvee accompanied by the driver and Doc Grimes.

I wish in all my heart I could say I had a Rambo moment and told the driver in the Humvee that I didn't need him. I would have taken the pain and just not cared about the hole in my chest and trouble breathing from lack of oxygen and stood up. I would've grabbed my rifle in my left hand and a machine gun in the right. One of the men in my team would take another piece of curtain that was used to bandage my wrist and they would fasten a headband for me. Shirt off, muscles out with blood dripping down my torso as I run into the street and lead the charge with my team behind me mowing down everyone in the street as we hunted down the man who shot me.

We always had fantasies like that. Being injured and not letting the pain affect you and having your hero moment. We definitely had enough Marines in the area where I wouldn't be in a situation where it was just me. I just couldn't believe how helpless I really was. It makes all the stories you hear so incredible about Marines who have been injured horribly yet they are able to continue fighting and earn these incredible medals for valor. Medals aside, even if the other men see you fighting so injured and every second closer to death, you will inspire the other Marines to charge and defeat the enemy. This is not a dream but has happened throughout the history of warfare time and time again. I am not sure how these men did it. I wanted to stand up and fight, but at that moment with all my injuries, I just wasn't able to.

The Possessed Spirit

Talking to Sergeant America years after my injury, he told me about an interesting tale involving the Big Guy. The thing about the Big Guy is that he isn't a real emotional person and isn't the kind of guy to just open up and speak about certain things. The strangest thing was that I was living with the Big Guy and still had no idea about it until recently.

After seeing me, one of his best friends with a huge hole in his chest probably going to die, a huge rage overtook him. The fire in his eyes was enough for our captain to stop whatever he was doing and stare into the eyes of not a man in that moment, but a spirit possessed by vengeance.

I could only imagine what everyone in that house thought when the Big Guy picked up the SAW and grabbed more ammo than any mortal man could possibly carry. I wish there was a video as this oak tree of a man weighed down by countless drums of ammunition, slowly made his way up the stairs. One by one he climbed, plotting his destruction on the city below him.

As Sergeant America personally told me, "The look on his face was not that of a man but of a possessed spirit. The only thing I could do was watch, get out of his way, and not say a word because I was afraid of him. He didn't have the look of a man who believed in an: *Eye for an eye justice,* but rather: *If you take my eye, I will take your whole body and soul with me."*

Sergeant America was still stunned as the machine gun laid waste from the roof above him with the sound of hundreds upon hundreds of rounds raining destruction on the city below. That area of the city looked like a small nuclear bomb went off from the destruction the Big Guy rained down upon Ramadi. The bodies also piled up and littered the streets with jihadists who met the anger of the possessed spirit that took over the Big Guy's body. *Revenge is a dish best served cold*, is not a saying that I agree with but rather: *Revenge is a dish best served from the bullets being fired by a big 6'3" two hundred fifty pound angry possessed Texan named the Big Guy bent on destruction.*

The Big Guy has no recollection of any of these events.

"Am I going to need surgery?" I asked the corpsman.

"Yes definitely, you have a sucking chest wound."

I couldn't stop talking with the two men in the Humvee whether excited or nervous with adrenaline I'm not sure.

"Doc, I'm starting to lose my vision."

"Hey Rosman, it is just because you are talking and you are struggling to breathe."

I then started to relax as we approached the Combat Outpost. Once inside, we drove to the large covered garage area where the medical room was located and I left the vehicle. This was the room where I saw the soldier go into without his arm a few months earlier. Now it was my turn. Walking into the room all the doctors and corpsmen were waiting for me.

I was laid down on the table and an oxygen mask was placed over my nose and mouth to assist with my breathing. One of the doctors then sliced open a large incision below my armpit going all the way to the edge of my pectoral muscle. It didn't hurt much, just a flinch or two. I was going in and out of consciousness getting closer and closer to death. All of the sudden, one of the corpsman slapped me in the face waking me up and making me angry. The anger caused me to stay awake and keep fighting while the medical staff was doing their very best to save my life.

Because of the critical situation I was in, the helicopter would be forced to land at the Combat Outpost to MEDEVAC me. Never having been in a chopper in the military before, I wished it could have been in better circumstances for my first ride. Laying on a gurney in the chopper, the flight medical nurse told me to focus my eyes on him. Trying to gather my thoughts, it all seemed to happen so fast. If I could make it to wherever they were flying me to conscious, I would probably make it. My lung was the only thing I needed to worry about because my hand had nothing to do with my immediate survival.

My thoughts drifted to my family so far away. I could only imagine in horror what the reaction of my parents would be once they received the call saying that I was critically injured in combat so far from home. I never felt so helpless in my life. A huge case of sadness and helplessness overwhelmed me. I could do nothing about my parents once they found out the news. All I could do was fight and live.

Once landing at a larger base in Iraq with proper facilities, I was transported to a large tent area where they had what looked like a full field hospital. I walked off and while they were getting ready to tend to me, I got really angry and started shadow boxing against the wall cursing at the heavens. I'm not sure why I did that, but in my situation, being angry was a good thing. Having the will to survive in any situation is what you need. I laid down on the table and I was asked how much I weighed. I remember thinking if I should be a jokester and lie about my weight while I cracked a little smile.

"I better not, I can joke around another time," I said to myself.

"How much do you weight?"

"One hundred forty pounds," I struggled to get the words out. I felt an excruciating amount of pain in my penis. "I'm peeing myself, I'm peeing myself," I yelled.

Being that I had shit myself only a few months prior, I was very sensitive to any bodily function not being disposed of in a proper fashion.

"It's ok, we put a catheter in your penis, it's completely normal."

I breathed a sigh of relief.

"Countdown from ten."

I thought, "This won't work on me, I bet I'll make it to zero."

I counted down in my head, ten, nine, eight, and I never made it to zero. At seven, the anesthesia kicked in and beat me at my imaginary game. I passed out not knowing when or where I would wake up. One thing was for certain, no matter where or when I would wake up or in what condition, I would survive and fight no matter what obstacles would lay in front of me.

I woke up with a nurse pulling a breathing tube out of my throat and I had no idea where I was or how long I was asleep for. All these years later, I still do not know how many days I was under anesthesia for. I would guess I was asleep for two days because I needed to be stabilized enough to be put on an airplane to be flown to Landstuhl, Germany, for an even higher echelon of treatment.

At the exact moment the breathing tube was pulled out of me, I was given the phone.

"Jason, it's your dad, are you ok?"

"I think so dad, where am I?"

I couldn't speak much, I had a very sore and raspy throat from the breathing tube and it was a struggle to communicate.

"Son, you are in Landstuhl, Germany, in the hospital."

"Thanks, it's really hard to talk right now, it hurts to talk."

"Jason, go to sleep you need to rest."

"Love you, I'll talk to you later."

That was the conversation I had with my father essentially word for word. It didn't even last fifteen seconds. I was in no condition to speak. I was also afraid, just having woken up with no idea who these people around me were or where I was.

Even though I was shot in the chest and hand, the first thing I did was check to see that my penis was still there. This is actually very common among Marines. As stated before, Marines only think about sex, sleeping, and eating. If you can't eat but are having lots of sex, life is good. If you can't sleep but are having lots of sex, life is great. If you can eat and have sex at the same time, life is epic. I have never had this happen to me yet. For example, eating a steak sandwich with honey mustard sauce while having sex, I have never done. So naturally the first thing I did was check to see that my only important organ was still alive and kicking.

I stayed in the intensive care unit for three days. I had three different chest tubes inserted into the side of my torso which explains the three smaller scars I have. The days went by slow but I spent the majority of the time sleeping. I got baby wiped by the nurse every day because it was the only way they could clean me. My hand was bandaged but no surgery had been done to it. I couldn't use my thumb on my dominant right hand making holding things a real struggle.

After the three days, I was moved out of intensive care to a regular hospital room where I shared it with another person. My voice was coming back and I was happy that I would survive my injuries. I got an endless amount of phone calls from my parents, grandparents, sisters, aunts, and cousins. I could hardly relax and it was all so worth it.

My only complaint, and it's far from a complaint actually, was that one of the nurses, who was a great guy and an Army medic, kept giving me dirty magazines. Well they weren't dirty like Playboy or Hustler but more like Maxim magazine stuff. When you haven't seen a woman in four months, women in lingerie may have well been porn mags for me.

Here was the problem. I hadn't seen a woman in four months and had a catheter inside my penis. Every time I would see a photo of one of the girls, I would get an erection and terrible pain would follow because of the catheter. I remember telling myself after waking up one night in agonizing pain with a huge erection,

"Jason, think boring non-sexual thoughts. Think about Tiger Woods hitting a long boring drive down the fairway, think about Alex Rodriguez playing the boring game of baseball and it lasting five hours. Anything but sex right now please." The pain slowly subsided but would return every time I would think about a woman.

Because my chest cavity was opened from my bullet wounds, this meant that the seal to my body was opened allowing all these foreign particles to enter. Because of this, I had to get the crap out of my body by coughing. I couldn't control the coughing and would non-stop hack up a lung. The chest tubes would collect all the gunk that would leave my body.

We'll Always have Landstuhl

Of the many memories I have from the hospital in Germany, one stands out the most. It involved me, another guy who I had never met, and in my own opinion one of the greatest movies I have ever seen. The movie was *Casablanca*, starring Humphrey Bogart and Ingrid Bergman.

It was around 9pm, when I was asked by the nurse if I wanted to see a movie and of course said yes. I was wheelchaired to the lounge with a small television where they played movies. I was on the left side of the room in my wheelchair with all my luggage, referring to the boxes that held my chest tubes and catheter. The other guy was more in the center and had something strange going on with his eye. It was all red like something I had never seen before. I remember him vaguely saying that he was passing a tumor or something through it.

We were just two men sitting in a room as if we were alone deep in our own thoughts. Where we came from, who our parents were, or what we were going through all didn't matter. There was no need to speak that night because there was nothing worth speaking about. The sound of our silence was the only noise that mattered that night and it was a too perfect miserable night to break it with senseless conversation.

There we were, one guy in a wheelchair with three boxes holding his chest tubes and coughing non-stop while the other guy in the room had this bloodshot eye trying to pass a tumor. All this was going on while we were watching a black and white movie made in the 1940s. Normally two men in their teens wouldn't watch a movie from this time period, but these were far from normal times.

I sat there going in and out of deep thought almost to the point that I was out of my own body. Somehow that movie got into my consciousness and in the lowest point of my life feeling so alone, so far from home, the movie crept into my soul. It was something about that night, that instant in time, that somehow that movie made a lasting impression on me. Every time I see a poster of this movie, I take a photo and momentarily remember that scared eighteen-year old kid in the hospital in Germany. I still get emotional whenever the movie is playing on television. It's like a time warp for me. *Casablanca* isn't just a great movie, but for that brief moment in time, it saved my soul.

Here's looking at you, kid

The Day I Almost Lost my Beloved Penis

Yes, the title is correct. If I was asleep I would have lost my penis. Sitting in the hospital room in Germany, I had many visitors. I wasn't really sure who they were or why they were there, but any visitor I was happy to receive. I was given a pair of sweatpants which meant I could finally get out of my hospital gown and wear normal clothes. I still had that annoying catheter in my penis and all the chest tubes inside of me. I could at least walk around now and not have my hospital gown open up showing the world my ass.

I had orders that in a few days I would be getting flown to a hospital in Washington D.C. to continue my treatment and recovery. As I saw the pastor walking around most days, I decided to talk to him a bit. I figured that since a pastor is a very respected person in the military, why not ask him if he could change my orders to the hospital in San Diego.

My whole family lived close to San Diego and would make everything much easier for them. Having to fly to our nation's capital would be a logistical nightmare for everyone. The pastor told me he would see what he could do and went on his way.

After a day or so of waiting, I received word that my orders were changed and I would be going to Balboa Hospital, in San Diego. I would be leaving in three days and would begin the long journey home. This would be a typical military journey where I would be going everywhere but my destination before arriving at my destination.

I would first fly to Washington D.C. and spend one night. From there, I would fly to Chicago for a quick stopover before landing in Northern California to spend one more night. The next day I would arrive in San Diego.

Being pushed outside on my gurney, I finally saw the German sky and got my first breath of fresh air in a long time. Waiting to get loaded into the ambulance it started to rain on me. Most people would probably think that they had shitty luck. Not only did they get shot and have tubes all over their body, it now started raining on them of all things. Not me though, I wasn't mad or anything because rain happens regardless if you are shot or you aren't.

"Do you want us to put the sheet over your head so you don't get wet?" one of the medics asked.

"I'm good, I'm not dead yet," I sarcastically responded in true Jason fashion.

I finally get loaded into the ambulance and we made our way to the airplane. I don't remember where the airport was but I imagine it was a military base airport because we drove up to the airplane. Upon being lowered from the ambulance I looked at the airplane and thought, "Fuck that isn't a jet, that's a fucking propeller plane. What in the name of fuck sakes does the world's most powerful military still use propellers for?"

A team of four carried my stretcher into the back of the plane which I again want to clarify wasn't a fucking jet. If I didn't have a giant tube in my dick or chest tubes inside me, I would've run to Berlin. It was too late now. I was strapped in and laying down on the stretcher ready to go. I looked around and realized this was a hospital airplane. I had never seen anything like it before. There were rows and rows of stretchers just like mine. We were stacked four high and I was the third in the stack. The guy on the bottom had the worst spot because he was on floor level which must have sucked for him. 3rd was a good position. Looking around at this huge airplane the whole fuselage was just like us, rows and rows of four stacks from front to back. The mobile casualties who could walk were in seats surrounding the interior of the plane. It was full and there must have been a hundred people easily in the airplane.

While the flight was midair, I realized that I would be laying down the whole time. The flight from Germany to D.C. would take twelve hours. That was a lot longer than a commercial jet no doubt because of the fact I was inside a propeller airplane. I made conversation with a major who also happened to be in the Marines and was stationed in Ramadi. I figured because he was in Marines, he got injured in a similar fashion as me. What a surprise I was in for.

It turned out that he had no idea about the Battle of Ramadi, and all the combat I was talking about. It seemed strange to me that even if you didn't have a combat position, you would at least know what was going on in the city. Wouldn't he at least have heard something?

It turned out a few days before getting on this flight, he tore his Achilles tendon playing basketball. After he revealed he had no idea about the Battle of Ramadi, which he was in the city for, he wasn't infantry, and how he got injured, it was hard for me to carry on a conversation with him. It was mainly because I had lost all respect for him and didn't care about his rank. I think he could tell once he saw the disgust on my face.

There was another character on the flight who had some serious mental problems. There were no physical ones but this guy was absolutely crazy. He had an escort with him to make sure he didn't do anything to hurt himself or anybody else. This crazed madman was running around the airplane yelling at people and going nuts. I thought it was great entertainment while everybody on the airplane was scared shitless of him. This whack job even took out a lighter and lit it, gaining instant attention from the flight crew.

"When you join the Army you go crazy like me, when you join the Marines you get shot up like yourself," as he spoke to me.

"I guess you're right," was the only thing I could say back to this crazed lunatic.

Landing in the middle of the night, I needed to be transported from the airport to the famous D.C. area hospital, Walter Reed. I was given a ride still laying down in my gurney in a kind of hospital bus. There were many people inside and I was the only one that looked injured on it for some reason. Looking out the window I could see the city lights and imagined all the fun I could've been having only a few short minutes away.

Getting to the hospital, I was left in the lobby and was told someone would be there in a minute to take me to my room. Minutes felt like hours as I waited all alone in the hospital. I felt alone and scared. I didn't know anyone, had little strength, and had tubes all over my body. My body was stiff from lying down for so long and I felt like I had rigor mortis.

A nurse finally came down and started pushing me to my room. I was excited to get some privacy and rest. Even though I rested mostly on the plane, I was still exhausted. Flying in the middle of a big loud plane with fucking propellers is not comforting to sleep in. I was also afraid of rolling over and falling five feet onto the ground. When I was finally put into my bed, I was so stiff from the flight I bounced. My muscles were extremely sore and the first thing I had to do was to start stretching as best as I could.

After a poor night's sleep, it was off to another propeller plane to continue my voyage. Again, being put in the airplane laying down, I was the second highest in order of the beds. There were two people underneath me and one person above. I still had all my equipment inside of me.

Slowly after takeoff, I dozed off into a deep sleep listening to the sound of the roaring propellers as we set forth towards Chicago. My long journey home was almost over, I just had to be patient for a little more. Landing in Chicago, I felt the thud of the landing gear hitting the runway and I was jolted awake by the sound of the brakes.

Taxiing towards the airplanes gate, I slowly drifted back off into sleep, only to be awoken by the back of the plane being opened. The back of this airplane was kind of like a garage door. The planes can be fitted for maximum storage capacity or in this case, a hospital plane. Once the door completely opens, the entrance is big enough for forklifts to enter.

Still groggy, I saw four airmen enter the back of the plane and approach the area where I was laying. They approached and verified by the paper tag on our beds that the man above me was supposed to get off. I was happy for him even though I never spoke to him, but I figured if he was getting off the plane, he was getting closer to home.

"One, two, three, lift," each airman grabbed a corner of the bed above me and started walking towards the exit of the plane. Slowly, I opened my eyes and thankfully I did. As the airmen were walking towards the back of the plane with the stretcher, the cord of my catheter attached inside my penis started stretching and stretching.

"What the fuck," I thought to myself.

I screamed, "Stoppp," the men stopped and looked at me.

"The cord, look it's stretching." I was lucky I said something. One more step forward, the catheter would have been ripped out of my penis.

The airmen were extremely embarrassed and wanted to get out of the situation as fast as possible. When I was loaded onto the plane earlier that day, the person put my catheter with the bag where the urine went and hooked it to the bed above me. The airmen of course had no idea and were just getting the bed above me off the plane.

"One, two, three, down," said one of the airman as the four men laid the gurney onto the ground.

"Look! Look!" I screamed as I pointed to the bag while the airman walked towards me.

He looked at the problem and removed the bag from the gurney and hooked it back to my bed. Extremely embarrassed at what almost happened, he quickly turned around and went back to the gurney on the ground.

"Up," he nervously spoke to the other airmen lifting the gurney with no count of any kind. The airmen quickly lifted the gurney and they hurriedly exited the back of the plane.

Shaking my head at the dramatic events that unfolded, I couldn't help but laugh as the sweat poured down my face. How much more could possibly go wrong?

"I should have gone to college," I thought to myself laughing as I laid back down. I have good news to report.

My penis was not harmed during these events.

After taking off from Chicago and landing at the base in Northern California without incident, I was brought to the hospital for the night where I was looked over by the doctor. My uncle who lived close to the base came to visit me and brought me glorious McDonald's. Chicken Nuggets, fries, and a Coke never tasted so good. After visiting me for two hours, he left and I could finally get some rest for the last leg of my journey home.

I was nervous going to see my family for the first time. I was ashamed for being injured and saddened to have left my squad and friends behind. I wished dearly that I could've been back there with them suffering every day. I was physically weak and frail. Not ten days before, I was a physical specimen full of endurance, being able to perform at a level that few humans could. The amount of physical labor we did on a daily basis would make most people vomit. I was young, motivated, and in shape for any obstacle. Looking at myself in the mirror, I couldn't even recognize myself. Skinny from losing weight and with hospital equipment attached to my body, ten days ago felt like a lifetime.

Landing at the airport in the always beautiful San Diego, my long journey home was over. I was taken out the back of the plane to my awaiting family. They were jubilated to finally see me after all the suffering they were put through. Not sure how I would react, I was very happy to see them but at the same time very sad. I saw my family while my squad would not be so lucky. I turned away from them as they hugged me on the gurney. Shame is the word I would use to describe how I felt.

Now inside my room at Balboa Hospital, I finally had some privacy and my penis would be safe from crazy Air Force people who almost ripped the catheter out two days earlier. I had a nurse come in and ask me if I would like a man or woman to take it out.

"You right now please take it out." I didn't care if it was a man or woman, just the first qualified person. The nurse deflated the catheter and pulled it out of my penis. There was a little pain but nothing compared to when it was put in. The catheter was out and I was free.

Thoughts of me dancing in the clouds free from the burden inside me filled my head. The catheter and the bag of urine connected to it were disgusting to look at. I was glad I would never see them again.

My parents were asked to leave the room while a military psychologist went in to speak to me. All that I remember from our conversation is that I told him I was happy I was shot. Not literally being shot but the fact that I would rather be injured than anyone else in my team. I knew I would be able to handle the pain and would never want anyone I cared about to go through it. If it had to be someone, better me than them. Why would I think that?

Unlike the civilian world where there is a culture of individualism, the military is the opposite. The team comes before the self. You care more about them and they care more about you. It's called sacrifice, but I would prefer to call it love. I loved the guys in my squad, every one of them including my asshole of a team leader Corporal Shepherd, and was prepared to sacrifice my life for every one of them in an instant.

I spent seven days at the hospital where my dad never left my side. He slept on the sofa the entire time. I was tired of being in the hospital and wanted to leave and go home. I had a drip of morphine that would automatically go into my system but I wish I could have controlled it myself. I understand why the drip is controlled and you don't have access to it whenever you want. Morphine is one awesome drug and unfortunately, it's not sold over the counter. It works and you sleep great.

One of my doctors came in and told me that they were going to pull the chest tubes out of me. I looked down at the big tubes and at the three small incisions not sure exactly how they were going to remove them. The tubes looked too big to be pulled out, but I was wrong.

"Ready?" The doctor asked.

"I'm not looking, just do it."

I felt the tube being pulled out of me and I lost my breath from the pain. It wasn't like typical pain but more like something inside of you that wasn't meant to be there being pulled out of you. Imagine a hose inside of you being pulled out. I felt relief as the first one was pulled out. The second and third ones were pulled out and the feeling was the same. I was relieved it was over and would now have no more luggage to carry around with me. My chest tubes and catheter were things of the past and I was a free man.

The next day I was able to drive home but before, I would have to stop at Camp Pendleton to my unit to have my orders for convalescent leave signed. Convalescent leave is just leave for medical reasons and I was given thirty days. Going back to the familiar base for the first time felt really good. Inside the headquarters for the remain behind element, I saw a bunch of the guys who were injured earlier including Cantu. One of the sergeants who I didn't know and didn't deploy, didn't yell at me in the conventional Marine Corps way because my dad was there but kind of whispered yelled and said, "You need to get a haircut."

I literally an hour earlier got out of the hospital with a cast still on my arm and bullet holes not yet healed. This asshole who didn't even deploy was getting on me about some stupid haircut. It is stupid shit like this why people hate the Marine Corps. We all love being Marines but hate the Marine Corps. If you don't believe me, just look at the reenlistment rates, they are very low and hover around 25%. Wouldn't this guy have common sense to just let it go and think that this guy didn't have time to get a haircut because he was fucking shot. I sometimes truly believe that the Marine Corps doesn't want thinkers because if they did, how did this guy make it to the rank of sergeant? I don't know who this sergeant was, but if you are reading this sergeant,

You can go fuck yourself you non-deploying piece of shit.

After getting my orders, my dad and I could finally drive home. Showing up at the house was a great relief and the journey seemed so long. I am not sure for how long I was asleep in Iraq, but I stayed one week in the German hospital, three days of flying to arrive in the hospital in California, and one week at the hospital there. It was a long time coming home and laying in my own bed felt so great.

It was during this time that I started slowly growing apart from my friends from high school. I was in a unique position because I grew up so close to where I was stationed. The other guys could only go home during long breaks. The jokes my friends from high school said were no longer funny to me. I could no longer relate to anything that they spoke about. They were in college doing college things and I was doing things that they couldn't even imagine. I was much more serious now and what they spoke about didn't seem that important and quite honestly childish.

Being back at home wasn't easy because I still couldn't use my hand and surgery was set for ten days into my convalescent period. Every day a nurse would come to the house and bandage my injuries. The hole in my chest would be cleaned with sterilized water and packed with gauze and bandaged. The hole was so deep, you could put half your index finger inside. It would heal from the inside out and it is amazing how the body heals itself while I watched the hole slowly being pushed flush into my chest cavity. My sides were also bandaged. Every day the nurse would tear the tape off my body and it would be excruciating. My skin became very sensitive to the constant tape being put on and taken off, so we would have to switch tapes because the skin became irritated.

The tendon in my right thumb was severed and I couldn't lift it up or down. Moving it left to right was still possible. (I can't write this all at once because thinking about it causes extreme pain to my hand and body). The doctor told me my options. They could stretch the tendon and reconnect the severed part. This would cause my thumb to permanently lock out. The second, would be to take the palmaris longus tendon from my forearm and graft it in place of my severed tendon. This tendon serves no function in the body except to be used for spare parts. It's incredible I know. We chose to do the graft with the palmaris longus tendon.

I was put to sleep and with the wonders of anesthesia, I woke up it seemed immediately after with the surgery completed. Being pushed into the recovery room still semi asleep, I remember telling the nurse that I wanted to go back to Iraq. This was not a conscious thought but came from my deep subconscious with no control of me saying it. It must have been true I guess.

After a brief stay in the recovery room, I was allowed to go home and rest. I began to have severe side effects from the anesthesia and had difficulty moving. Imagine the worst workout you ever had where your muscles were so sore you couldn't move. Multiply that feeling by ten and that is how I felt. I couldn't even get off the couch for dinner I was so sore. I just couldn't move. It took all my effort to even lift my leg off the couch and needed help standing up to get to the dinner table. I'm not sure why I had these side effects, but it was a terrible two days.

The Feeling of Uselessness

Being back at the empty base with all the wounded guys was a strange feeling. Nobody wanted to be there and everyone was depressed and angry. A few months before, every one of these men were at the pinnacle of their mental and physical powers. We were now weak and angry that our friends were still fighting in Iraq suffering while we were back home doing nothing. Injuries are not always the worst part. Being away from your brothers is far more painful than any hole in your chest or hand you can't use.

There was no doubt as to how badly I was hurt and to think I wasn't even close to the worst one. Once I have clothes on, you can't tell I was injured. Besides the scars, I pretty much made a recovery if there is such a thing. I was lucky that when you're young being the now nineteen-year old, I recovered quickly.

My roommate in the recovery platoon was part of Echo Company and was injured during the Battle of Ramadi. He had a gruesome injury that I don't think he could ever recover from. He got shot a few times in the leg and when he showed me, it took everything in me not to vomit.

All that was left was a bone with a thin layer of skin surrounding it. It looked like it was a twig. There was no fat or muscle, just a bone with some skin where you could still see the outline of his bone. I don't think you can recover from an injury like that.

To make matters worse, we were treated horribly by our command back home, known as the remain behind element. Instead of bolstering what little self-esteem we had left, they would make us do tedious work that was just depressing. Since all of us were injured, we had no issues going to our many doctor appointments but it was the type of work they made us do at the command post which was the most frustrating.

Instead of letting us get some college credits or speak to elementary schools, we were forced to do humiliating work. They made us paint the command post, move rocks, and rearrange furniture. The work wasn't hard but it was just humiliating. Why are guys who are injured forced to do this kind of work?

I still had a hand that I couldn't use and was lifting a sofa with the help of a guy who lost an eye and had shrapnel in his brain and shoulder. What kind of an organization can claim they care about their people when they force them to do shit like this? If you don't get angry reading this, I guess nothing will. Even after all this, I was still very proud of being a Marine and it hadn't seriously crossed my mind to get out.

The Return

In October, three months after my injury, Golf Company made their triumphant return home. The tension grew as hundreds of family and friends waited in the cool Camp Pendleton night. In the military, everything is hurry up and wait and today was no different. The wait was agonizing and the stress could be seen on the family's faces. Word then came that they were five minutes away from the base. They would first have to go to the armory and turn in all their weapons and I knew from experience that this would take a long time.

After another hour and a half wait, I heard the screams of excitement as the company started the long walk from the armory to the parade deck. The cadence grew louder and louder as the four platoons marched towards their loving family and friends. It was a long three month wait to see my friends again and I was never so nervous in my life. All the platoons stopped in formation and made a left face. The company commander led the formation and with a quick command,

"Golf Company, dismissed."

There was a huge scream of excitement as friends and family started running frantically looking for their Marines. All of us in uniform look alike and with one hundred fifty Marines plus family and friends, there was nothing but pandemonium. Wives crying reunited with their husbands, husbands seeing their newborn babies for the first time. There is no event, no sight so beautiful as the happiness seen from the end of a deployment.

Then I saw him, in uniform like everyone else, a little bigger and taller than the rest but there he was. We ran into each other's arms and started hugging and crying. It may have been the greatest moment of my life being embraced by the Big Guy again. Two men who couldn't be any more different who had been through so much hell, just holding each other crying and crying.

Just like that the deployment was over. Our battalion was devastated by injuries and at that time and maybe still today, we had the highest casualty rate of the whole Iraq War. Not all injuries require being sent home, but in total during our deployment, thirty-four Marines from our battalion were killed in action while we suffered an almost 30% casualty rate. We essentially single handedly saved the capital of the Al Anbar province from falling into the jihadists hands and started the process at least at the time of swaying that hostile cesspool of a city into our favor.

The Big Guy, not wanting to wait, got a tattoo on the first day back. I hope he gave it some good thought beforehand because I wasn't sure if he realized that tattoos were permanent. That weekend, with all the fun it went by too fast and before we knew it, we had to report back to the base. Because this was the Marine Corps, we had to have a fresh haircut and a uniform inspection the morning of our return. For the 1% of glamor being a Marine provides, it is about 99% unglamorous. For those incredible dress blue uniforms that the Marines are famous for that you see in parades, that Marine probably spent over five hours preparing it. People who hadn't seen their family for seven months, had to find a place to get a haircut and also prepare their uniform for an inspection. Getting a haircut is easy and doesn't take long, but my God, is it that important that these men would need to take time away from their family just for a haircut? Plus, preparing uniforms takes a long time. Like I said earlier, the Marine Corps doesn't care about you or your family.

The Day that Caused me to Hate the Marine Corps

After our uniform inspection, I started walking towards the battalion headquarters and when I saw it, I became full of rage. Despite all the shit I had been through, I still loved being a Marine and woke up every day proud to have a real purpose in life. People counted on me for their survival and mine theirs. That was a lot of responsibility for a now nineteen-year old. I still had a long time left in my contract. Upon our unit's return from Iraq, I was only in the military for fifteen months and I still had thirty-three more of them to go.

Seeing the battalion headquarters, from that second on, I hated the Marine Corps. I had thirty-three months of hell to deal with and wouldn't ever consider reenlisting. The battalion headquarters was tarped over and professionals were hired to paint and fix up the same building that me and the other injured Marines just worked on. My heart sank as tears swelled into my eyes as my veins started coursing with anger.

"Why the fuck did we do all this manual labor if they went and hired professionals to do it? This is fucking bullshit," I yelled out.

That's how they treated us Marines. Here you guys go, you are injured let's humiliate you even more by hiring professionals to do the job you were made to do because they had nothing better for you. One thought went into my head as I turned around and walked away.

I should have gone to college.

The Case of the Missing Claymore Mines

Rehabbing took me a long time because I was still having weakness in my surgically repaired hand and would need further therapy to help get my strength back. The other guys who were hurt worse than me and would be getting discharged from the Marines were still with our battalion in the wounded warrior platoon.

The now returned battalion was slowly starting to ramp up training and had some of the future team and squad leaders out training in the back of the 62 Area. When that night's training was completed, the wounded warrior platoon was assigned to guard three 7-tons with tarps over the back.

As to be expected because the Marine Corps isn't the smartest of organizations in the world, the command decided that it would be the wounded warrior platoon that would be assigned a three-day guard shift after training was done for the night.

We were simply told that the 7-tons needed to be guarded and were never told what was inside of them. Being winter, it would be cold and we weren't what you would describe as the "best of the best" anymore because the majority of us were on large amounts of pain and psychotic medications. We made for an interesting guard shift.

I don't think I am an overly sensitive person, but I think I can find it inside of me to have compassion for a man who lost his eye, had shrapnel in his head and shoulder, and that maybe he shouldn't be standing guard.

I also think I can find the compassion in me to say that a man who took shrapnel in the knee probably shouldn't be standing guard either.

But what the hell did I know. Maybe if I had gone to college, I could have figured out some of the reasons why these men who were in no condition to stand guard, were in fact standing guard.

On my first guard shift at midnight it sure was lonely. I was within viewing distance of the barracks but still far enough away that I felt incredibly alone. Wow, was it dark and cold. I could barely see my hand in front of me and just had my thoughts keeping me company.

My thoughts were pretty standard for a nineteen-year old who was standing guard at midnight all alone in the cold darkness.

"Wow, I can't believe how hungry, horny, and tired I am."

There were the three 7-tons and a bench where I could sit, but sitting down only made the time go slower and I needed to walk around to stay warm.

I actually had no idea what I was even guarding and honestly didn't care that much. I wasn't in any kind of mood at that time of night to jump on some huge vehicle and look around. I didn't even have a flashlight, so doing something as crazy as exploring the back of a 7-ton didn't even cross my mind.

All of the sudden in the darkness, I heard a noise like something was approaching me. I couldn't see anything and I hoped it was a small animal because I wasn't in the mood to talk to anyone. Getting closer to me, I could finally make out that it was someone approaching me.

I quickly remembered my boot camp training and what we were taught when speaking to someone approaching you while on guard duty. I still wasn't sure if what I learned in boot camp was still applicable in the real Marine Corps because what I had learned for this particular situation didn't fit the narrative.

Word for word just like I had been taught in boot camp I yelled out into the cold dark night,

"Halt, who goes there? Place your ID card on the deck and take seven steps back."

Why the hell would I tell him to put his ID on the ground? It was pitch black outside, this guy doing that would help me in no way. I guess I paid attention in boot camp too much even though this was completely useless.

The man approached me and I noticed he was an officer which meant I had to show respect even though at this hour in this cold I really didn't have any. The officer starting talking to me about absolutely nothing important and asked me no questions of any value. He didn't even look in the direction of the 7-tons which was the reason I assumed he was there. He then left and vanished in the direction he came.

"Strange," I thought to myself as I shrugged my shoulders. At least this changed the monotony of the night.

On my second guard shift the next night, I was paired with another Marine so I would at least have someone to talk to. This Marine was the guy who got injured taking a poop in the port-o-john in Ramadi and had a hand injury bad enough that he would eventually be getting medically discharged.

Because it was cold and he didn't give a shit, he actually drove his car to where we were supposed to be standing guard as we both sat in his car watching the 7-tons. It was another cold night and the 7-tons were in good hands under our watch. Standing up or sitting down, I preferred sitting down in a warm car than freezing for four hours.

Now that my guard shifts were over and it was the weekend, I went home to my parents' house. I was eating dinner when I received a phone call.

"Rosman, you need to get to the base immediately."

"Sergeant, what the hell happened?"

"Just get to the base and you will be briefed." The sergeant didn't seem in the mood to answer any questions. I told my parents that I needed to get back to the base immediately and left with my food still on the table.

In my head, I had visions that we were going to war with North Korea or Iran. I wasn't yet fit for duty but if we were going to war with those countries, I would've lied to the doctor to give me the all clear medically.

I left the house and jumped into my truck and made the forty-minute drive to base, with my mind thinking what could have gone so wrong that I was recalled to base.

I received a text saying to go to the battalion headquarters, so I quickly parked and made my way up to the building. Inside, I saw everyone sitting around a large table with no one saying a word. I grabbed an empty chair and just sat there silently. I knew I didn't do anything wrong, so I was more interested than worried about what was going on.

The executive officer (XO) of our battalion came into the room and told us the situation.

"There are six Claymore mines missing from the 7-tons you were assigned to guard. The whole base is being put on lockdown."

A Claymore mine, is a mine that you always see in war movies where on the front of it says, "face towards enemy." It would be horrible if you faced it the wrong direction and detonated it. These mines are used primarily for initiating an ambush and is a horrible invention of war. To set it off, there is cord connected to a trigger where you press on it three times. When it explodes, it sends hundreds of ball bearings through the air. It must be devastating when it goes off and hits people.

In training, the instructors set one off once. We were all huddled together hundreds of yards away and knew it would be coming from the countdown. The explosion was so massive and even though we were far away from the blast radius, I almost pissed myself from the loud bang. Pieces of debris hit my helmet from the force of the explosion.

Getting our orders, we would be sent to our rooms and not permitted to speak to anyone. The military police would be coming with their police dogs to smell for the mines in our rooms and cars. I wasn't worried because I did my job and watched the 7-tons so I knew nothing got stolen during my shift.

The police dogs came and they searched my truck and room and of course found nothing. The rest of the Marines in the whole battalion were put on line and were forced to walk every inch of the camp looking for the lost mines while the wounded warrior platoon would be hanging out in our rooms.

In the morning, we would need to report to another camp a ten-minute drive down the road and be questioned by the Naval Criminal Investigative Service (NCIS). I was excited because I had never been questioned about any criminal activity in my life and because I didn't do anything wrong. I had nothing to worry about. Being questioned by NCIS was definitely out of the ordinary and would make a normal mundane Sunday, not so mundane.

Waking up Sunday, I was in no rush because the area on the base I would need to report to was very close. I left thirty minutes early which meant I would arrive fifteen minutes earlier than the time we were supposed to arrive. In the military, you always show up fifteen minutes early and still wait an hour. This is called "hurry up and wait" and the military is famous for it.

I left the 62 Area and headed towards Camp Horno where my interview with NCIS would take place. Driving towards the area, I was forced to turn around because all roads going in that direction were closed due to a bicycle race being held on the base. I would now need to leave the base entirely to get on the freeway and drive south for thirty minutes and enter the base at a different gate and backtrack another twenty minutes to arrive at Camp Horno.

Now late, I was yelled at by the first sergeant for failing to plan ahead. In my head, I was thinking that maybe the first sergeant being a first sergeant should have known about the bicycle race and told us about it so we could have planned better.

Getting called into the back room to get interviewed, I was both nervous and excited at the same time. How many people can say they've been interviewed by the equivalent of the FBI before?

Upon entering the room, I noticed how beautiful the NCIS agent was. She was sexy and blond and had my complete attention. I ignored her male partner.

After a brief introduction, the agents started rambling about something that I probably should have been paying attention to. After about thirty seconds, I was no longer excited and was now bored getting interviewed. My mind drifted and thought about how hungry I was since I didn't have breakfast yet.

With my mind drifting away thinking about how beautiful the agent was and how I could sleep with her, I thought I heard the NCIS agents mention something about the President of the United States. After twenty more seconds of them speaking and me thinking if I had heard them right about the president, I interrupted them.

"Did you say the president was briefed about what happened?"

Both agents looked at me stunned and looked at each other with a kind of worry like something was wrong with me. They had mentioned the president like five minutes before and I suddenly out of the blue just blurted it out.

"Yes, he was briefed in the morning about what is going on."

"That's incredible," I excitedly responded.

I now know they were lying to me but my still gullible nineteen-year old self was excited and I wanted to help the agents find out what had happened.

"I'm here to help guys, whatever I can do, I don't want to let the president down."

I told them everything, well almost everything. I left out the part about me sitting in a car during my second guard shift being that I didn't want to get in any potential trouble. I am quite certain that in boot camp I was never taught that sitting in a car during guard was ever permitted.

I mentioned the officer with a name I didn't remember who came and talked to me for absolutely no reason and that was the only strange occurrence that happened during my shifts. I also learned that government agents have no sense of humor which was not good for me because I have a huge sense of humor.

The sexy female agent asked me if there was any possibility that somebody could have gotten into the vehicles without me knowing.

I told her that unless they had superhuman abilities like Superman or Spiderman there was absolutely no way possible for this to happen. Being that government agents have no sense of humor, they wanted me to clarify what I had meant by superhuman abilities as they looked at each other confused.

"Well," I responded,

"The three 7-tons were never out of my sight at any time. When I took a piss, which didn't last for more than eight seconds because it was so cold, I was still looking at the vehicles. So, if someone could somehow get in the vehicles making no noise while I was watching the vehicles, they would need superhuman powers like Superman or Spiderman."

The government agents still with no sense of humor nodded their heads. They gave me a business card and sheet of paper they wanted me to fill out and turn back into them when I was finished.

This sheet of paper was even more useless than the interview. The paper had the most ridiculous questions that I needed to answer and I was amazed at the absolute stupidity of the questions. Some of the questions were as follows.

How do you think the Claymore mines were stolen?

List the steps you would take to prevent this from happening.

If you stole the mines how much would you sell them for?

These questions were stupid because I wasn't getting paid to solve the case for them. In fact, I had no idea of any real solutions because it wasn't my job.

Some of the answers I gave to prevent the theft from happening were simple logical things, like not having guys missing eyeballs with shrapnel in their brains standing guard duty. Another good idea would be to tell the men what they were guarding. The Marines make no distinction in guarding things with more vigor depending on what you are guarding. Let us be honest, I wouldn't want to fight to the death guarding pencils if that was indeed in the back of the 7-tons. If there were nuclear weapons, I would definitely guard with more vigor. It does in fact make a difference what you are guarding.

The last question about how much I would sell the Claymores for, well I was just being honest. I was making $1500 a month and had no idea of their value on the black market. 50 x 6 = $300. That was a lot of money. I wrote $50 each and turned in the paper and left.

This response gathered interest because a truly innocent person wouldn't be tricked and would have said something like $0 because they didn't do it.

Sorry, but if you don't like my answer, don't ask me the question.

Four days later I was summoned back into the same office and was forced to answer the exact same questions as before. I wrote the same answers except the last question I smartly wrote $0 and went on my way. I never heard from NCIS again.

The Claymore mines were never found.

Returning to the Platoon

It wasn't just my body that had to recover but also my mind. I was psychologically weak and had to get back to what I once was. Being nineteen, I was still so young that my injuries didn't really hurt that bad. I never even took pain pills once I left the hospital. Being a Marine takes a certain mental attitude and just being in superb shape is not enough. Waking up day after day going on patrol is less about the body, but more about your mind not letting yourself quit. We didn't get vacation during our time in Iraq and to go seven months in a crazy deployment like that takes all the mental toughness you have.

I was tired now of the process and felt I accomplished everything I wanted to do. I had seen combat and that's all I really wanted to do in my career. After being so close to death, I realized how precious life was and wanted to get out. There is no shame getting out of the military with a medical discharge. You receive all the same benefits and nobody in your unit would hold it against you. Lance Corporal Cantu and the guy who shot himself in the ankle were both discharged medically. In my case, a medical discharge was not possible because I guess I healed enough that I was brought back into full duty.

I hope women like scars because I see people's faces whenever I take my shirt off. Their expressions are always the same and say, "What the fuck happened to that guy?"

I was definitely far from what 100% was supposed to look like, but here I was standing in front of our first sergeant and the platoon sergeant from 3rd platoon. For some reason, this platoon sergeant liked me and always had a good thing to say about me. I was a bit scared of him because he was an ex drill instructor and enjoyed killing, but I guess not everyone in the world could hate me.

Standing in front of the two men, the first sergeant asked, "What platoon do you want to go back to?"

I told him, "I want to go back to my old platoon 2nd."

The platoon sergeant chimed in, "2nd platoon sucks, are you sure you don't want to go to 3rd?"

"No staff sergeant, I'm loyal to 2nd and if they suck, I want to go back and help them."

The first sergeant nodded his head. I was going back to my beloved 2nd platoon.

Courage with a Question

While the insurgents were free to use whatever methods that worked without their own political structure, we have a structure that causes delays in getting new technologies to the troops to counter new insurgent attacks. This is not a critique of the American government, but just the realities of every government in the world. It is impossible to evolve faster than the insurgents. Funding must be approved through various committees, then the money will be allocated. The factories must then develop and produce the product before being delivered to the troops. For example, you can't just add armor to all the vehicles at a snap of your finger.

With American forces taking heavy losses in the volatile and confusing civil war in Iraq, the American people were angered by the stunning amount of our soldiers being sent home in caskets. The war wasn't going as promised and the Iraqis weren't taking to "democracy" very well. The majority of our soldiers were getting killed and injured because of IED attacks. The American people wanted answers. After a speech by the Secretary of Defense Donald Rumsfeld, he answered some questions from the audience. One of the questions came from a soldier.

"Why do we need to dumpster dive to find armor for our vehicles?"

The secretary of defense's response may have been right or maybe wrong, but the one thing for sure is that a skilled politician should never say anything that could open him up to scrutiny and criticism involving our military.

"You go to war with the Army you have, not the Army you want."

What a blunder from a career politician. He came off as an arrogant asshole, which was his reputation and for someone who wasn't looking out for the troops. The criticism against him came faster than the winds of a class five hurricane. The great people of the United States, who love our military and hold them in such high esteem, were now angry because they felt the military were being let down by the people put in charge of them. Nobody can get away with taking advantage of our military, especially when their lives are in danger.

The criticism against him only grew and I'm not sure why he didn't resign after the company who was responsible for making armor for all the vehicles came out almost the next day and said they were only working at 40%-50% capacity. They had the will, desire, and the manpower to increase production, and they were just waiting to be told to produce more. That order never came until after the secretary of defense made his blunder.

I know the military quite well and four years is enough time to get a true understanding of what it is all about. I most certainly was no general, but I know a thing or two. That young soldier who questioned the secretary of defense probably got in trouble. The military doesn't want thinkers, they want people who without question follow orders. Once you start thinking and asking questions you will be labeled a shit bird or told you have an attitude which means your career is essentially over. How is it possible that in the movie, *Forrest Gump,* he wasn't what you would call a smart man yet during boot camp he was an absolute genius? Of course it was only a movie, but there was still a little truth and you can laugh in the way they parodied the military.

The fact that a reporter asked the soldier to say the question doesn't matter. The question being asked packed a harder punch coming from a soldier in uniform than if the civilian reporter asked for himself. It took a lot of courage for the soldier to stand up in uniform and ask his boss a very critical question. In the military, you are taught to never question anybody higher than you in command and make them look bad. The secretary of defense is very high up on the list. Since the soldier made his superiors look bad and so up the rank structure, this soldier who unknowingly helped saved lives, probably received a lot of scrutiny from his fellow servicemen. I on the other hand, would thank him. His actions helped speed up the process to get more armor to vehicles, yet other members of the military would criticize him instead of thanking him. I don't get it and I hope you don't either.

I would like to thank that young soldier and the American people for forcing our government to fulfill their duties to our servicemen fighting overseas.

The Final Tale of Greg Rund

With my battalion now home, Greg Rund deployed to Iraq with 3rd Battalion, 5th Marines. His unit would end up being part of the Second Battle of Fallujah. In November and December of 2004, the eyes of the world were on the Marines as they cleared building to building and faced quite possibly the most intense combat since Hue City in Vietnam.

To avoid civilian casualties, the residents were given advanced warning of the impending attack for months, allowing them to make it out of the city before the fighting started. The people remaining in the city were all hard-core jihadist prepared to fight to the death knowing they would all eventually die in the city.

With time to prepare for the battle, the jihadist barricaded all the doors and blackened all the windows. Every house was a potential ambush but the Marines would have no choice. They had to clear the whole city of insurgents and if that entailed entering every house, then that was what they would do.

Rund who was a team leader, tried entering a house through the front but it was barricaded, so his team entered through the backdoor and slowly made their way into the house. The ambush came from upstairs pinning Rund and another Marine in the kitchen behind a refrigerator. Trying to get out of the house, they were trapped because fire from another house was preventing their escape. The other Marines outside weren't able to enter the house and help rescue the trapped men because they were trying to return fire and find out where the secondary shooters were coming from.

Outnumbered and under heavy attack, Rund and the other Marine decided to fire and move out of the house. As the team leader, Rund would go last letting the other man escape first. The other Marine ran first under a hail of gunfire when there was a massive explosion behind him, sending shrapnel into his lower back while he screamed out to Rund.

There was chaos outside because everybody was under fire and there was a trapped Marine inside. They couldn't call in an airstrike or a tank to destroy the house until all the trapped Marines which now was just Rund, were safely outside.

I knew that receiving a letter is the greatest morale booster you can have. Even though Rund and I were only acquaintances, I knew that when you are in that hostile situation, any kind of support is so uplifting. I wrote letters to all my friends in that unit because while I was back home injured I became very close to them.

Life is full of regrets and the only thing you can do is learn lessons from your mistakes and never repeat them. I still beat myself up all these years later for how lazy I was and I am still ashamed of myself. One thing I have done because of this and all my friends can attest to is that I am always the first to call and to keep in touch. No matter how far away I may be, distance is never too far for me to just simply say hello and ask how are you?

What caused this to happen to me?

The letter I wrote to Rund never got sent to him. Every day I would wake up and see his letter on my table ready to be sent. Then the letter went inside my drawer, still visible every time I opened it. All that letter needed was one little stamp and for me to walk downstairs and drop it off. That letter to give hope to someone so far away knowing that he wasn't forgotten about and that he was in my thoughts. My letter was never sent because of my utter laziness.

I was back home at my parent's house for the weekend when I felt the vibrations from my cell phone ringing.

"Hey Ben, what's up?"

The voice on the other end wasn't the cheerful voice that I always expected whenever we spoke.

"Hey man, it's Rund, he was killed in action, shot in the head."

I got a huge knot in my throat as the tears welled up in my eyes. My parents who were on the couch knew something was wrong. I walked outside holding the tears back just enough until I couldn't hold them anymore. The guilt was too much as I remembered that every day for months I told myself I would mail that letter off to him. I never did, and now he was dead.

A month later, I would meet his family at a restaurant near the base with my letter in hand. Not sure why I still had it or wanted to give it to his family, but with my head buried in shame I gave my letter to his younger brother and explained what happened. This is the reason that I am the best at keeping in communication with people, better than they ever will be with me. They don't have the memories, heartache, sadness, or the regret that I have.

I am sorry Rund.

He fought to his very last breath with courage I could only imagine. After the intense battle, his fellow Marines entered the house and saw him surrounded by dead insurgents. He fought to the very end using hand to hand combat.

Greg Rund was killed December 11, 2004, at the age of twenty-one. He was awarded the Bronze Star for his actions.

The Circle of Life

The vast majority of Marines leave after the completion of their first four-year contract. The few who do reenlist get sent to another unit or can become instructors. The higher-ranking Marines who have already reenlisted before, usually keep reenlisting until they retire. They almost always get sent somewhere else too.

We received a new captain, first sergeant, new platoon sergeants, and a battalion lieutenant colonel. Fox Company's first sergeant was promoted to sergeant major and stayed with us as the new sergeant major of 2/4. Fortunately, our beloved Gunny stayed with our company.

Sergeant America was the only one who reenlisted in our squad and stayed in Iraq, never coming home with Golf Company. Unfortunately, my mentor Lance Corporal Cantu couldn't complete his dream of spending his whole career as a Marine. Around 40% of our company moved on in one form or another.

Since all of our senior Marines from our Iraq deployment were now gone, the Marines that went in at the same time as me would now be put in leadership positions. There were also the new Marines who came to us straight from infantry school who would be the new boots. We also had a strange group of Marines who came to our unit and some even had more rank than us.

These Marines were infantry Marines who came from the security forces. They weren't embassy guards but were infantry Marines sent to guard nuclear reactors all over the country. The ones that were sent to us came from just outside of Seattle, Washington. I had never heard of security Marines before and had no idea how these men were sent there, instead of the normal infantry like I was.

There was now a struggle for power. We had a certain swagger and confidence about us finishing off a combat deployment with all of our new ribbons. We thought we were untouchable being part of the

Marines that were made famous from the Battle of Ramadi. The sad part was that we were still mostly lance corporals and these security Marines were mostly corporals and outranked us. Since they had the rank, they would be given the positions of squad and team leader. If there were any available positions, we with the rank of lance corporal with the combat experience would fill in what was left.

I would never be given a team during this upcoming deployment because I missed almost all of the training rehabbing from my injuries. We would be deploying to Okinawa, Japan, as part of the 31st Marine Expeditionary Unit (MEU).

A new adventure filled with prostitutes, jungle patrols, and a monkey would be awaiting us.

Okinawa

The island of Okinawa was where we would do all of our jungle training. Even though it was a deployment for us, it was similar to being back in Camp Pendleton; except once we left the front gate we were in Japan. We lived in two-man rooms and the base was no different than any other. Unless we went on the Navy ships to do some training, it was just like being back home with some small exceptions.

During the long flight, I was excitedly writing down all the things I wanted to do while I was over there. Definitely trying new food and snorkeling would be my first priorities.

Even though we were told that porn magazines were not allowed in the country and that we would be inspected upon arrival, of course we brought loads of magazines with us anyways. Upon landing at the airport, we were put in formation and even before being welcomed into the country, we were ordered to dump our sea bags so the authorities could check for porn mags. We all looked at each other and soon almost everyone must have picked up ten pounds of magazines. The earth shuddered as they were collected and piled in the center.

After all this, it came down that we could have porn mags in the country but with no penetration. All of us looked at each other thinking, "Who would have a porn without penetration?"

The whole pile stayed put being that pictures of tits and ass were not sufficient for us animals.

The reason we were there strategically was for the protection of Japan. Since the end of WWII, the Japanese are not permitted to have an offensive army and it must only be used in self-defense. Not only does the United States provide security for Japan, but it gives our country a massive amount of military personnel to protect our interests against the Chinese and North Koreans.

It wasn't just in Okinawa that had all the military bases but in a bunch of other islands and countries as well, including a massive troop presence in South Korea. Even though we were deployed to Okinawa, there were many units that called Okinawa their home base. It was the same as me being stationed in California, but for them in another country. They could drive and live in base housing and even bring their families with them.

The rules would be strict for us. After fifty straight years of having drunk servicemen every weekend get smashed and destroy the city, the local Okinawans were sick and tired of us. The lowest point in the relationship between the Marines and the people of this island was no doubt in 1995, when three U.S. servicemen including two Marines, raped a small girl. Unfortunately, whenever you wear a uniform, it makes us all look bad and ten years later, we were still paying the consequences for the actions of those low life scum. If college kids do something stupid like that, they go to jail and that's the end of it. Nobody goes around thinking or acting like all college kids are to blame for the actions of a few. Every day, there were protests in front of the base demanding that all U.S. military leave Okinawa.

The rules in place for our liberty were as follows: Whenever leaving base, we needed to have a buddy with us. We had a midnight curfew which didn't just mean being back at the base, but also being checked into our unit by midnight. Even though Japan was a country where you could drink below the age of twenty-one, the Marines had a rule that the law of the United States was the law anywhere we went in regard to drinking. Whenever we wore civilian clothes, we would need to wear a collar shirt and have a belt if our shorts or pants had belt loops. We would also not be allowed to wear sandals unless they were the ones that wrapped around your feet like for hiking.

Since we lived on an island near the beach, we always wanted to go snorkeling or just hang out by the water. It was a real pain in the ass having to bring your beach clothes and change once leaving the base. Coming back was an even a bigger annoyance because you would be all sandy and before entering the base again, you would be forced to change into your collar shirt and shoes. The Marine Corps never made our lives easy and always complicated things with stupid unnecessary rules.

A guy in my platoon who was a first-generation Muslim American whose family was from Somalia, before joining the Marines never had sex, drank, or smoked in his life. Hell, he probably never even cursed before. In Okinawa, his first deployment with us, this all went away. He started drinking, he started smoking, and he started having sex. It wasn't only like one or two times with a prostitute but once he got the taste of that honey, it was every weekend. He told me that some weekends he slept with four prostitutes and this was a normal occurrence for him. He told me that all the brothels on the island knew him. This poor innocent man who never did anything wrong in his life, had now been completely corrupted by us animals.

Maybe he should have gone to college.

Training

Training in Japan was great at its best but horrible at its worst. The jungle I learned was a combination of being part Marine and part gymnast. Walking through the jungle, one slip and you could roll down a hill and break your arm. With your rifle and gear on your back, you would need to grab onto branches and hope they wouldn't break. One second you were patrolling and the next you are grabbing a branch praying that it could support your weight while you pulled yourself up. The jungle was always wet and uncompromising. The humidity was like steroids for the bugs and made them seem twice the size. There was so much life in the jungle even though these training areas had been used by American forces since the end of World War II that I could only imagine how much thicker and more wildlife would be around if there wasn't a steady influx of people training in it all year round.

I guess it's a good thing that we have been fighting in more desert open terrain than we used to. Just training in the jungle gave me even more respect than I had before for the men who fought in the jungles of Vietnam. Our advanced technology is rendered almost useless in the jungle. Our big impressive tanks can't drive through the jungle and our advanced aircraft won't really bomb a target they can't see. It's impossible to look from above into thick triple canopy jungle like that.

In jungle fighting, the fighting is close and personal. GPS doesn't work so your skills at reading a map need to be excellent. Reading a map in the thick canopy jungle is very difficult because other common map reading techniques are ineffective. City navigation is easy because you can use the tall buildings to know where you are at all times and use them as markers. Land navigation in big open areas is also easy because you can use big terrain features in front of you and see it clearly on the map. In the jungle, you have none of that. All the trees look the same and everything looks flat even when it isn't. My squad leader was a genius at land NAV and didn't even need a map to do it in the jungle.

I was the point man for much of this training. This was a different type of feeling than being the last man. There were also different types of pressures involved. In the front, you would control the pace of the patrols and had nobody in front to keep up with. In the front, you needed to be hyper vigilant because there was a good chance that you would able to see the enemy patrols and you could set up an ambush.

In Japan, the enemy were the other platoons that you would be fighting against. Since open space in the jungle is limited, you couldn't spread out like in open terrain. Most of our patrol formations were in what is called, "Ranger file." This means that the patrol is done in a straight line because it is easy to get lost in the jungle, especially at night. I was given a machete to cut and clear all the brush in front of me.

Not knowing that we were on hill, I approached the top and looked down at the valley below. The hair stood on the back of my neck as I turned around and looked at my squad leader. He motioned me to continue the patrol as I again looked down below. What was staring back at me looked like one huge giant spider web. The whole valley below which I would be the first to walk through was so thick with spiders that if I didn't have a fear of spiders then, I sure do now.

Walking through the valley trying to chop away at every web was an impossible task. There were too many. The webs got on my neck, face, and all my exposed skin. Walking through all the spider webs, a familiar thought went into my head and forced a small smile.

I should have gone to college.

The Interesting Tale of the Drunk Irishman

Daniel McGuigan, where do I start with this crazy bastard? He always called himself Irish, even though he never went to Ireland before, nor did he speak a word of Gaelic. He didn't even have an Irish passport, so the Irish government didn't even know of his existence. He was just proud of his Irish ancestry I guess. Some nationalities seem to be more prideful at least when talking about it. If someone is from an Irish background even if their family immigrated in the 1800s, you never seem to hear the end of how Irish they are.

He came to our unit during the first deployment in Iraq as a combat replacement along with another guy named Richard Quill. They were both with us only about a week before I was injured. He was junior to me by about five months in the Marines but was about three years older than me. He joined the Marines a little later than the traditional age and I never knew why. During the Iraq deployment, he was grazed by a bullet in the helmet that knocked him out unconscious. He awoke and suffered no ill effects from what could have been a catastrophic injury. He showed me the impact of the bullet on his helmet he was allowed to keep and I remember thinking that this guy used up all of his luck for the rest of his life.

Danny Boy, was a great guy and a real drunkard which made him even funnier. Wow, could this guy drink and the next morning act like it never happened. In Okinawa, where almost everyone develops a drinking problem, Danny was an absolute mess. In formation when our squad would have to run, I would always be behind him. The stench of alcohol was so horrendous blowing back in my face, I would either have to make my own row in formation to get away from the blowback from the stench, or I would have to vomit. Every morning we exercised and I had to suffer through this. If I were in his position being that I hardly drink and not "Irish", I wouldn't be able to move in the morning. Danny Boy not only could drink like it was his last day on Earth, but wake up and run three miles like it was nothing. He was a real piece of work and I really loved that drunk bastard even though he made my life miserable.

In Okinawa, with the endless amounts of jungle training, we also sat around afterwards in fighting positions hoping our poncho over the tree branches protected us from the rain. We would patrol for hours on end then just go back and sit in the hole we dug for hours. Laying down trying to sleep was horrible with hundreds of ants, mosquitos, and every other bug attacking you from all directions.

These insects crept into Danny's subconscious while he was sleeping and he would have terrifying nightmares.

"Ahh, oh shit," he would scream as he woke himself up, "Bugs, bugs they're getting me."

All night he would scare the shit out of us while we would be trying to sleep only to awoken in the dark jungle by hurling screams. On a night patrol, we were ready to step off when we heard Danny yell, "Oh shit, there's something inside my uniform." He then proceeded to completely strip down, panic, and start running around in his underwear slamming his uniform on the ground trying to kill whatever bug that may or may not have been inside his uniform. Everybody in the squad couldn't contain their laughter as this guy was almost buck naked in the middle of the jungle at 0200 running around seconds before our patrol started.

Danny Boy was an incredible talker and charmer. He could get any woman to like him. I'm not exactly sure how he did this or I would have done the same thing. We needed to get haircuts every weekend, and near our area in San Clemente, California, there were only a few choices for us. I'm sure the women who work at these places get hit on by hundreds of Marines all weekend and they are used to it and don't even think twice about it. Danny, not only charmed one of the women into going on a date with him but later also gave birth to his kid. Of all the Marines who must have tried to impress that woman every weekend, it was somehow Danny who made it happen.

He was the only person I knew that actually slept with a woman while on the Navy ship. I had no idea how he even did it or where he even did it. I guess since the woman was a sailor, she knew the ship really well and knew all best hiding places where you could do the deed without getting caught. The ship is a small place so anything that you want to keep secret would last about five minutes. It also didn't help that a woman would call our phone in the berthing area and ask for Danny. After telling the voice over the phone that he wasn't available at the moment, she would hang up without even saying goodbye.

I really wished I knew how he convinced her to sleep with him and where they met. Of the whole ship, there were only a few dozen women on board. On ship, fat or skinny, ugly or pretty, it doesn't matter. A woman on ship is like water in the desert. They are all precious and after not seeing women for months on end, they all end up looking like Brazilian supermodels to you.

Danny was just one of the many colorful people that I have met in my life. He is a good person and I will always remember him for his rowdy drunken behavior, the hours of sleep he caused me to lose almost nightly, his contagious smile, and his stench from the booze he drank every night. I am happy to call Danny McGuigan a friend.

Our Beloved Gunny

In Camp Pendleton before being let off for the weekend, we would always have safety briefs that would take forever. The Gunny would speak for ten minutes, followed by the first sergeant, then our captain. They would always just repeat what the other guy said before and waste forty minutes of our lives.

The message was always the same. Don't drink and drive. Even though it is illegal to drink before twenty-one in the United States, the command would never say it to our faces but would turn a blind eye to us drinking underage. As long as we didn't do anything stupid and followed the golden rule we would be fine. *Do unto others as you would have them do unto you* wasn't the golden rule in this case: *Don't drink and drive* was. If you got in trouble for just being drunk and stupid, your punishment by the command would be far less than if you got behind the wheel drunk.

We were lucky that our Gunny continued on with our company to Okinawa. He could have easily been given orders somewhere else, especially if he would have been promoted. As colorful as ever when we were training in the Philippines, being that he was Filipino, for some reason he decided to tell us about his loyalties even though no one would dare question his.

"You guys are probably thinking because I'm from the Philippines what would I do if we ever went to war against them?"

Everybody stopped what they were doing and stared at each other because that thought never crossed any of our minds.

"I would slit their fucking throats."

There must have been a lot of pressure on him because of the intense rules that governed us during our time Okinawa. The rules were really strict and it was easy to get in trouble for even the smallest offenses. We could actually get in trouble for underage drinking even out in town in sovereign Japanese territory. If there was a random asshole gunny or first sergeant who saw you at a bar drinking and wanted to show his power, he could find out what unit you were in and report you. Instead of being able to sweep this under the rug, the command would be forced to act.

Non-Judicial-Punishment or (NJP) is the way your command punishes you without the use of the court system. When facing an NJP, the Marine has the right to refuse and take his case to a court martial. The court martial is going to a real court with your own lawyer and there is a judge and jury. The problem with going to a court martial is that if found guilty, the punishments can be anything from getting a dishonorable discharge or even going to jail. For something as simple as getting in trouble for underage drinking, it was just better to take whatever punishment your command gave you.

The main reason for so many people getting in trouble was the Marines' continued policy of needing to be twenty-one to drink and the majority of us were still less than that. With the Navy's policy, they could drink at whatever age the law of land was. In Okinawa at times, it felt like a prison so many people turned to hard drinking.

After so many cases of underage drinking and problems because of it, our Gunny had enough. Instead of having their NJPs take place in the company commander's office, he held a company formation and marched all the accused in front of us. There were about twenty Marines from our company standing in front of us getting read their punishments. Our Gunny wanted to show the rest of us that there would be zero tolerance for stupidity and the command was being serious.

Their punishments were mostly the same. They consisted of sixty days base restriction and forfeiture of half pay for two months. Overall, we had more people than that get in trouble, but those twenty got in trouble around the same time. I was happy that I hardly ever drank because being forced to stay on the base sounded like torture.

Because of the Gunny's horrible creaking knees, he couldn't stay with our company anymore. He fortunately would stay with 2/4 but would move to the battalion headquarters. His replacement would be a familiar face from our time in Iraq.

Not all familiar faces were good though.

Shit Bird Training

Our platoon was unlucky in some ways but lucky in others. The Marine Corps made no sense to me most times, but it always seemed to work out one way or another. In the Marines, once you reenlist and want to make a career in the service, you need to do something called a "B" billet. A "B" billet is a secondary duty that has nothing to do with your regular job. This must be done in order to continue your military career. The three choices are drill instructor, recruiter, and embassy duty.

Everybody has experience with both the drill instructor and recruiter. The recruiter sells you the idea of the Marine Corps and does all your paperwork to send you to boot camp. Recruiters have to be nice guys because they need to sell the idea of the military to not only the typical high school kid, but also his parents. If the recruiter acted like a psychopath, he probably wouldn't get anybody to sign up.

The recruiter has many challenges because his work is done far from any base and lacks the support network of being around other Marines. Since I grew up close to Camp Pendleton, my recruiter wasn't far from where he lived and would return every night to his house on the base. He was in the far minority as the rest of recruiters weren't so lucky and could be sent all over the nation to big and small cities where they would need to order supplies from catalogues for new ribbons for example. They spend most of their time at the high schools in their region and other locations where young people gather. The job of the recruiter is very difficult and from what I've read, the Marines actually send the best to do this duty.

The drill instructor is the heart and soul of the Marine Corps. They are with the recruits every minute of the day during their training cycle. They are loud, they are intimidating, and they are intense. The three or four drill instructors you had will haunt your nightmares for the rest of your life. They mold young men into Marines after thirteen weeks of intense training. The drill instructors have immense challenges that I can only begin to describe here. They need to mold eighty young men who act as individuals and turn them into a team. They need to teach the recruits how to walk, talk, and act like Marines. We were infants and their job was to teach us everything about how to survive in our new lives. The relationship built between the recruit and drill instructor is based on fear whereas the relationship you have with your recruiter is based on friendship.

I only met one person that ever served in an embassy. The only time you have experience with embassy Marines is if you were one yourself. I have no idea of the challenges and difficulties of this particular "B" billet. A recruit would never see one of these Marines either in boot camp or the recruiting process. They do not have the same notoriety as the other two, because the other two jobs leave a lasting impact on every Marine who ever served.

I can proudly say I was probably the only person in the history of the Marines to have stayed not only in the same platoon, but also the same squad. From the time I entered my unit, to the day I checked out of the military, I was always in Golf Company, 2nd platoon, 2nd squad. In your first contract, it is rare to change companies but if you did, you would at least be in the same battalion. I never heard of somebody actually changing their battalion during their first contract in the infantry. Everybody changes squads or even platoons within your own company. It is as easy as being moved around because you are now a team leader and move to 3rd squad from 2nd squad.

Most likely this happens after a deployment when Marines get out of the Corps and new infantry Marines arrive to your company. It is chaotic because at first the new guys don't have a platoon and bounce around from one team leader to another until everything gets sorted out about two weeks later. New squad and team leaders are chosen and new teams are formed.

Why is this important? I think I have a good perspective how people judge other people or groups based on information that is not true or inconsequential. During my first time in Iraq, our platoon was known to completely destroy the area in any firefight. As soon as there was enemy contact, our platoon would crush the enemy with overwhelming fire and no mercy. We destroyed the city block from wherever the fire came from and true or not, we were known for this in our company. At first, I thought this was cool because who wouldn't want to be known as the platoon who completely destroyed the enemy and their soul after each battle?

Marines are very competitive with each other. In boot camp, we are bred to compete and always win. Since there was no real enemy, the other platoons were viewed as the enemy that needed to be defeated in any competition. In every facet of training, we would look at the other platoons like scum and do everything to beat them in everything we did. Your mind and body were trained with the mentality that if it was just you against five hundred enemy soldiers, every one of us would expect ourselves to fight to the death and die gloriously killing all of them single handedly. This frame of mind, this will to succeed and never quit, gave us our edge in combat.

Even in Iraq where there is real enemy, you still are competitive against the other platoons. Even though we were all friends, every platoon wanted to be the best. Nobody wanted to be known as the shit bird platoon. The shit bird platoon always got treated like shit and was never given any respect. In Okinawa, 2nd platoon was considered the shit bird platoon.

Here is the reality of the situation. We all went to the same boot camp and had the same training. Our team and squad leaders all went to the same leadership courses and were equally qualified. Our platoon sergeants all were just as qualified as the other one. Unfortunately for us, our platoon sergeant was the only one who wasn't a former drill instructor in the higher command and the other platoon sergeants treated him like shit. Everyone from platoon sergeant to first sergeant in our company came from the drill field except him.

Since drill instructors think they are better than recruiters, they would treat him with less respect because he didn't yell at anyone. Our platoon sergeant was just as qualified on his own merits without the need to be judged because he didn't yell like a psychopath.

If you hadn't noticed by now, I am a very logical thinker and don't let emotion cloud my judgment. I viewed every platoon as the same because we all had the same training. To say one platoon was way better than another simply because our platoon sergeant wasn't a former drill instructor and then magnify every mistake we made into something it wasn't just to fit into a pile so our shit bird name had more merit, seemed childish to me.

Being the shit bird platoon wasn't all that bad though. The better Marine you are or platoon you are deemed to be, the "better" training you get. The problem is the better training isn't any better, it's just more work. In every single training exercise, my platoon was given the security detail which is considered the most boring and unrewarding. The assault platoon, which we were never given in training, got to do the fun stuff. They would assault the objective and with blanks in their guns, hit the target and pretend to shoot at things that weren't really there. The training was always a letdown and many of my friends felt the same way

My "shit bird" platoon got the honor of sitting in the Amphibious Assault vehicles (AAV) until getting the order to run around and provide security. This would entail that I would get out of the vehicle walk about 50 meters away and take a knee. I would stare into the trees and look into absolutely nothing. Nobody even know where the assault element was or where the target was. There was never any shooting from the blank rounds that I heard. Every once in a while, I would stand up and stretch and go take a piss. We would then get the word to go back into the AAVs where we would all go back to sleep. That is how training went 99% of the time for 2nd platoon, the shit bird platoon.

How I learned Spanish

Excited and motivated that I helped save the lives of an Iraqi family by speaking Spanish to them, I wanted to improve my level to that of a fluent speaker. My level at the time was that of someone who took two years of Spanish in high school which is a shame being from Southern California. This is similar to almost everyone in the United States. The level of Spanish education is pretty poor and once leaving the classroom you forget everything you learned. Being how Spanish is such an important language, it is an absolute shame that the system isn't better so that everyone by the age of fifteen is already fluent. I know that Scandinavian countries speak incredible English and there is no reason with all of our resources, most importantly being that we have so many Spanish speakers, that as a nation we have so few speakers with Spanish as a second language.

In Okinawa, if we didn't have some kind of training going on, we would always get weekends off. The liberty restrictions being so tough didn't help, and at times it felt easier to stay on the base and not deal with all the hassle. Due to these restrictions, I saw very little reason to leave the base. It was during this time, I decided to fully dedicate myself to learning the Spanish language. Inside the base library, I checked out the book, *Dummies Guide to Learning Spanish.*

Almost every minute I was awake, I studied from that book. If bringing the book wasn't possible, I would bring dozens of flashcards and study vocabulary. Sitting in our fighting position after jungle patrols, I would study like a man possessed. There was nothing to do because the fake enemy would never come. Ten feet in front of my fighting hole, there was a fence which was real Japan, so no training enemy could come from there. Instead of smoking cigarettes and talking about tattoos all day, I was there studying my notes. While on patrol, since I knew we wouldn't be fighting the Chinese or North Koreans anytime soon, I was practicing vocabulary in my head.

All the Spanish speaking guys in my unit and we had a lot of them, must have hated me. I would ask question after question to them about Spanish grammar and vocabulary. When one would get tired of me, I would move on to another guy and ask him questions. This is the kind of dedication you need to become good at something. Learning a language is never easy and I learned in Japan from a book. I arrived in Japan speaking hardly any Spanish and I left Japan speaking at a very respectable level for the conditions that I had learned in. Everyone thought I was crazy for learning Spanish in Japan. Now those same people wish they spoke Spanish like me. I have no sympathy when people tell me they have trouble learning a foreign language. If I could learn in the middle of the jungle, I promise you, anyone can.

Whenever someone asks where I learned Spanish, I always smile when I tell them Japan, and I see the expression on their face.

Shit Bird Platoon Fun

During our Okinawa deployment, we would be spending some time on the Navy ships. I heard that the ships were due for repairs so we would be spending less time on ship than what was customary for this type of deployment. When we finally got on board, we would go for training in the Philippines. Well the other platoons trained, but because our platoon sergeant wasn't a former drill instructor and we were the shit bird platoon, it was no surprise to us when we were selected to be the platoon that would be segregated from the company and be punished by not being able to train.

As usual, not being able to train was actually a blessing in disguise because training sucks. While the other platoons got to train in the jungle with Filipino Marines and sweat their balls off, our shit bird platoon would be mainly sleeping with prostitutes. I didn't personally sleep with any and I'm not sure why, but I was in the minority.

Our platoon would be taking a school bus and going about four hours away from the company and we would provide security for a group of engineer Marines, who would rebuild a roof in a school that was damaged by a cyclone. This was very easy work and would involve us sitting in chairs at the entrances of the school and stay awake doing nothing. While the other platoons were probably hating their lives, we had people from the town do food runs for us as they came and talked to us. I never ate so much bread and pizza in my life. We would do guard duty for six hours and be done for the day. We used the school gym to sleep and that was mainly what we did. We even got to walk down the street into town and order food and do some shopping. Danny Boy, being the charmer he always was, even got a ladyboy to show us his tits.

This was a small town with no tourism that I could see. I am not sure where the prostitutes came from, but as soon as they heard the Americans had arrived, they all must have taken buses to the city. One of the Marines, even lost his virginity to a prostitute on the very same school bus we had taken to the city. He would later be in my team and I was very proud of him because nobody should potentially die for their country being a virgin.

Our platoon sergeant was one cool and funny guy. He told me this story that when he was a recruiter near his hometown in Chicago, he went to the police station to do a background check on a potential recruit. In a complete coincidence, his wife showed up at the same time to turn in her divorce papers. What bad luck.

He allowed us to do anything we wanted as long as we stood our watch. If we wanted to bang prostitutes, he would support us and even potentially join in. I forget who it was, but one of the guys even fucked a prostitute with his night vision goggles on in the school bus. Marines are far from normal people, I can promise you this. During all this craziness, one of the guys adopted a monkey named Junior

It is obvious that being the shit bird platoon was much better than being considered the best. The best got unrealistic training for any of the combat we would see in either Iraq or Afghanistan and get to suffer in horrible heat and conditions. The shit bird platoon, yeah so what if the other platoon sergeants didn't like our platoon or platoon sergeant, we got to be separated from them and have fun, and at least a couple of our guys lost their virginity.

I got the feeling training in the jungle that if we went to war in a place like this, it would be hard to win. It wouldn't be just the enemy I was worried about, but the elements. In Iraq, it was terribly hot no doubt, but it was mainly a dry heat. As bad as the heat was, it would have been nothing compared to fighting for real in the jungle.

"Sir, if we go to combat in the jungle, would we wear our flak jackets?" I asked my lieutenant.

"Absolutely," he responded, "We take them off only for safety during training."

Because of safety being paramount at all times in training, certain precautions had to be made to ensure we didn't overheat in the jungle. Going from the base to the training area, we would always wear our flak jackets with the ceramic inserts inside. As soon as we got off the vehicles, we would take our vests off and put it in our packs.

Have you ever thought you were good at something then you saw somebody who was actually good at it?

I had that feeling in a sense because I thought we were doing good training getting in great shape for whatever the jungle had in store for us. We would carry our packs for miles until we reached our staging positions, then from there we would do patrols. Dealing with the heat, humidity, sweat, and all the bugs, I honestly thought I was getting the hang of it. Once my lieutenant told me we had it easy, I got a huge reality check. I was exhausted with horrible prickly heat with bug bites all over me and I thought I accomplished something. The idea of doing everything we did in the jungle, but then adding a forty-pound flak jacket to your body, then throwing a real enemy in the mix, showed how far away we truly were from mastering the jungle.

In one memorable training, we went to the north of Okinawa to a place called the Northern Training Area. I'm not exactly sure what this training area meant or how it was different from any of the other trainings we went to, but it was at least a longer drive away. The jungle appeared denser, meaning to me that there had been less training throughout the years. The trails were hard to spot. Again, I shivered at the thought of us having to fight some enemy in terrain like this.

Some of the most fun I ever had in training was here on the north of the island, when on our last day we got to do an obstacle course where our platoon was split into two teams.. It was an intense course which involved climbing down ropes and crossing rivers. I remember having to jump and swim under mud with turtles looking at me.

During the last four hundred meters of the obstacle course, our team had to put the heaviest guy on a stretcher and carry him till the end. Of course, the heaviest guy happened to be the Big Guy. This wouldn't have been easy on a flat track, but there was nothing flat about these final four hundred meters. We had to climb rocks, go down and back uphill. The poor Big Guy was even submerged underwater while we had to cross a small river. We all finally crossed the finish line completely exhausted, but had a great time nonetheless.

Completely covered head to toe in mud and missing a toenail, I now had to rinse off. Waiting for us at the finish line was the now promoted Gunnery Sergeant Psychopath. He was the new gunny of Golf Company. What fucking luck! He told us to cover our balls with our hands as he took a fire hose and sprayed all the disgusting mud off us.

Returning Home

The journey home was anticlimactic as we flew home the same way we came to Japan. Some of the Marines went home a week earlier than us in order to get our barracks ready for the arrival of the main group. Gunnery Sergeant Psychopath fortunately was one of those guys. I couldn't imagine being on a plane with him for sixteen hours.

Since we weren't coming home from a combat zone, the welcome back didn't have the same feel as when the battalion came back from Iraq. Regardless, it was good to be home because it had been long seven months away.

After reuniting with our families, I walked with my dad towards the barracks where we would be getting our rooms. From at least four hundred yards away, I could hear the yelling. Who could possibly be crazy enough to yell when they knew there were families around?

We arrived at the barracks and of course it had to be the same guy as always. He was on the second story screaming about not letting any of us go home to our families. My dad looked at me and asked,

"Who is that guy screaming like a psychopath?"

"Well dad, that's Gunny Psychopath, and that's what psychopaths do."

He looked at me and shook his head, "Are there a lot of those here?"

"Yes, there's a lot, but this guy is the biggest one."

My dad shook his head again and asked, "And how many more months of this crap do you have left?"

I stopped for a second to calculate, "I have a year and seven months left."

"That sucks for you," my dad chuckled, "let's go home."

My Okinawa deployment was officially over.

The Circle of Life Again

Not everyone in the Marine Corps is this perfect workhorse. I would say in my defense that I was far from the only person like this. The Marines want you to be as close to a machine as possible and I was far from that. The Marine Corps deems who they think are the smartest and sends only certain people to all the special schools that are offered. Only a few Marines in the company have all this knowledge and get all the experience. These schools are very challenging and always emphasize little food and sleep. They would never send me to these "elite schools" because they knew I would just give no effort and fail out on the first day. I wasn't worth wasting a hard to come by slot on and I didn't blame them.

When you come home from deployment a new cycle begins. Typically, the first thing that happens is that everyone goes on leave for thirty days. The company headquarters and barracks are essentially deserted. When everyone comes back from vacation, there is a lot of downtime. A good portion of the returning company is processing out of the military and the company has very thin ranks. They need to wait for a new batch of young Marines from the infantry school. Since we were the most senior Marines left in the company, all the Marines that came in with me were now team and squad leaders.

In order to get more experience for our new responsibilities, the vast majority of us were sent to division schools where all the specialty schools are located. There are very few open spots at division schools because it isn't just members from your unit that are trying to go, but all the different companies on the whole base where they feel going to a specialty school can help their unit.

In the Marine Corps, they think that by not sending you to a special school is some sort of punishment. Being sleep and food deprived sounded like punishment to me. Spending time at the gym and getting off work early seemed like paradise to me. I was in paradise while a lot of the guys were getting shit on in the forest. I couldn't escape going to a division school forever though and I was finally sent to one. I can only imagine the discussion they had at the company headquarters about me.

What school should we send Rosman to?

We need to send him somewhere because he has never been to one before.

Well looking at this list, I think we should send him to the easiest one because it's a waste of time.

OK here is an interesting one, let's send him here.

Done.

I would be going to a division school. Knowing how the Marine Corps worked, they thought they would punish me by not sending me to corporal or squad leaders course. I on the other hand, thanked my lucky stars. While some of the guys in my company would go through hell and back, I would be punished by going to a course where I would literally just shoot my gun all day. That's right, I would stand almost in one spot and shoot three-hundred rounds a day. It was the coolest and easiest Marine Corps course that I think existed. I would learn to engage targets from fifty yards and closer and learn to shoot on the move. There was no sleep or food deprivation. It was simply shoot my gun all day and learn cool things about my M-16 that I didn't know before. I felt like I was six feet tall, not because of how great I felt, but because there was so much ammunition on the ground that I was probably six feet tall standing on top of all the spent shell cases.

On the last day of class, we took a shooting test and I passed. I think the class was called, Close Quarters Shooting Package or something to that cffcct. That was thc only class I was ever sent to and it lasted five days. Every night I went to my room and slept. It was like an 8-5 job except we finished at around 1400. I absolutely loved every second of it. Instead of a normal field exercise with my company, where we would have to wait eight hours for transportation but told to be ready at any moment, things were a little different with division schools. Here, you didn't wait on transportation but the buses waited for you. Since everyone in this course was in the infantry, we were all shocked and looked around at each other not sure what the buses were doing waiting for us. None of us had ever experienced anything like this before.

But since I have always been 100% truthful, I think that I must be honest about something else too. I have been very critical about myself when I could have easily lied. I must now defend myself a little and make something very clear so there are no misconceptions.

When the bullets started flying or we were in any chaotic situation, my performance was beyond exemplary. When it mattered most, when my men needed me and lives were on the line, I was just as good as any Marine I served with. Making your bed perfect every day has nothing to do with you kicking ass in combat. No matter how much the Marine Corps tries to brainwash you into thinking that things that have nothing to do with anything make you better in combat, it's not true. For example, having nice rolled sleeves shows that you are disciplined and makes you more effective in combat. They forget to mention that in combat you have your sleeves rolled down, so how great you are at sleeve rolling has no impact at all. Another great one is that having a fresh haircut somehow makes you more of an effective fighting unit. I had a nice new haircut every week and my shooting or hiking ability never seemed to improve. Strange, isn't it?

I was always there and never missed any patrols or standing any guard shift. No matter the pain I was in, I never talked about it. When the stress of combat was hard on people, I was always smiling and joking. My personality changed very little while others changed dramatically. I was there for everything and I was very dependable and that fact is indisputable.

By the time everyone starts finishing their individual specialty school, the new batch of Marines start arriving from the School of Infantry. From there, you start your pre-deployment training and then you finally deploy. I was in the military during a time of war, so the turnaround was very fast. Seven months deployed then seven months at home. That cycle stayed the same for my whole contract.

The seven months I refer to is the time finishing your last deployment to starting the next. In a perfect scenario, we would get our new Marines five months before the deployment started. In an imperfect scenario like for my first deployment, we arrived a little over a month before deploying to combat.

Types of Deployments

From my experiences, there are two types of deployments in the Marines. First of all, being stationed and deployed are two different things. Being stationed somewhere means that place is your home. Being deployed means leaving your duty station and going somewhere else for a set period of time before returning home. I was always stationed in Camp Pendleton, California, but have been deployed to Okinawa and Iraq.

During my first deployment to Iraq, we flew on a chartered civilian jet to Kuwait. From there, after a week we took a convoy to Iraq. We had a base we would go to and a unit we would replace. Although not known the exact date of our return, you could calculate around seven months because that was the length of time for typical Marine infantry deployments. This deployment was pretty regimented and everything was essentially known beforehand.

My second deployment to Japan we were part of the 31st Marine Expeditionary Unit (MEU). The actual ships were located in Okinawa, Japan, yet we would spend most of our time on land. What is a MEU then?

An MEU is truly what makes the Marine Corps different from the Army. The MEU is a group of ships with lots of Marines inside. From all these ships, the Marines can sustain themselves in combat. There are different MEUs all over the world constantly patrolling. The 31st MEU patrols the waters in Asia.

There are no permanent personnel inside an MEU. The units are all chosen and then go and join together, forming the individual parts needed for the mission. We were chosen as the infantry battalion and therefore formed the infantry part of the MEU. Every type of job you could think of was filled in the MEU. We needed helicopter and jet pilots so there was a unit for that. Engineer and tank Marines were called in along with nuclear, biological, and chemical weapons (NBC) specialist. These are just a few of the hundreds of examples that compose an MEU.

The MEU makes the Marines a very agile fighting force. It would take forever for the big Army to get all their equipment shipped and ready for a fight. If the president has a situation that needs to be resolved quickly using the military, he has at his disposal MEUs all around the world with Marines ready to fight in less than forty-eight hours. No force in the world is that mobile and can provide such a global presence.

Because of this rapid ability to respond in case of a natural disaster, the MEU can provide disaster relief. It is very common to see Navy ships helping out immediately after a terrible tragedy around the world. There is a good chance Marines are on those ships too.

In addition to following orders to go to combat, the MEU has a few specific things it does as well. If an embassy is under attack and a rescue is deemed necessary, it is the nearest MEU that gets the call. If a fighter pilot is shot down, the MEU would probably get the call. These multiple roles require unique training for all the different possibilities that we could encounter.

In the real world, you will most likely never be called upon to do any of these kinds of missions. The odds of one of our sophisticated fighter jets being shot down by some guy in the Middle East with an AK-47 isn't happening. The last time our embassy was attacked and destroyed in Benghazi, the Marines weren't even called in to help. It would have been an incredible feeling sitting around the ships doing nothing, then all of the sudden somebody would burst through the door and say,

"Something has just happened, get your gear and wait for the brief."

It would be awesome to be on the landing team when the order, "Send in the Marines" is given, but that order never came.

After every deployment, the MEU empties itself of all the units inside it. All the tanks crews, infantry battalions, fighter squadrons, etc. finish their deployment and they go home. These units then will be replaced.

The Circle of Life One Last Time

We were told that we would be the infantry unit for the next deployment of the 15th MEU. This MEU is headquartered in San Diego, California, and patrols the water near the Middle East. Unlike the 31st MEU sailing close to home in Japan, once we left for the deployment, we wouldn't be able to go back to the barracks until the end. Before our deployment started, we still had a lot of training to do and had to train the new guys for all the unlimited scenarios we could be facing.

Our captain and first sergeant would continue with us through our next deployment. The platoon sergeant from 4th platoon got promoted to gunnery sergeant while we were in Okinawa and would become our company gunny. Our platoon sergeant fortunately would be staying with our platoon. The sergeant major would also continue with our battalion in the same position.

I would finally be given my own team and I couldn't have been given better men. Lance Corporal Raposa had already been to Okinawa and had some experience. He was the guy who lost his virginity to the prostitute on the bus in the Philippines. He was a very motivated Marine and sounded like he wanted to make a career out of it. He was strong and most importantly, he was highly intelligent.

The other guy in my team would be a newcomer by the name of Lance Corporal Bobby from Washington State. He was an incredible runner who could get close to a sixteen minute three-mile run. My best time was a little over twenty-one minutes, just to give an example at how fast he was. He had a great personality in the sense that he was always smiling and wouldn't let anything bother him. I was truly blessed to have them both as team members.

My job as a team leader would be to put my men in the best position possible to succeed. My men were so self-sufficient, I never even had to yell at them. In all actuality, they were better Marines than me but I had the one thing they both didn't have. I had actually been to war before and that experience isn't something you can learn from a book.

After being injured, I knew my own mortality but my men didn't know theirs. I told them time and time again that at the end of the day, the only thing that mattered to me was them coming home safely to their families. Everything else didn't matter to me. In whatever situation we would face, if we had to take twice as long to do the job safe, I would take it every time.

Training Starts

Once we started training, it seemed like a never-ending training operation. We would finish one then have a few days to prepare for the next one. I think that it is only fair to count the training as part of your deployment. Yes, we were in California, but we never seemed to be at home. The last three months is the most hectic time during the cycle because you need to get sea qualified for the MEU. The training includes going on the ships we would be using for the upcoming deployment to simulate anything we could encounter during real-world missions.

Our three infantry companies each had their specialty. This didn't mean that you would use your specialty in the deployment, but your training was geared more towards your specialty. During our first deployment in Iraq, Golf Company's specialty was never used. In fact, the other two companies never used theirs either.

Fox Company was the boat company of our battalion. They had those high-speed rafts that you see Navy Seals using in their secret missions. A good portion of their training focused on waterborne assaults even though in Iraq, they were just walking around the streets like the rest of us.

Echo Company had an awesome specialty being the helicopter assault company. They would train and do SPIE-rigging and other essentials for an infantry company being brought into the fight via air. Sharing the base with Echo at the Combat Outpost, I never saw anyone being brought into combat by HELO. They walked around just like we did.

Golf Company would specialize in using the Amphibious Assault Vehicle (AAV) for use in combat. These incredible vehicles (incredible until you actually have to use them) were so versatile and powerful, they could be used for many missions. These vehicles had tracks like tanks and could be used in the ocean and land.

Inside the vehicle hangar of a Navy ship, the Marines sit inside the AAV and close all the hatches. The hangar bay is filled with water, then the AAV drives off the ship and dunks into the water for a split second before coming back up. The AAV with machine guns, drives up to land and has similar but far from equal capabilities as a tank on land. With a crew of thirteen Marines in the back, when the order is given, the ramp drops and the Marines charge out the back and half turn left and the others right and charge forward towards the enemy. Sounds cool right? Anything that sounds cool in the military usually isn't.

Nicknamed tracks, they would always break down and you would train just in case they sank while out in the ocean. Inside was the most basic thing you can imagine with two benches bolted to the ground and space for the crew to hang their packs. Part of the roof could be opened once on land, having two Marines facing opposite directions standing up and looking outside.

Still being the shit bird platoon, we got the most boring training out of the other three. We still got the primary role of security like always. We would run outside the track and take a knee and hang out for a few hours. We would get the call to get back inside and off we would go to another objective. The next objective would be much of the same with our platoon sitting around most of the time. Since it was so dark inside the track, all of us would immediately fall asleep as soon as the ramp closed.

Our main training exercise would not be consisting of Navy ships or tracks, but would take part in the middle of the unforgiving desert base of 29 Palms. This base is the largest training base in the Marines with ranges that seem to go on forever. I could have easily been stationed at this base near Palm Springs but got lucky by being at Camp Pendleton.

This thirty-day training evolution we would be doing was known as Mojave Viper, formerly known as, Combined Arms Exercises (CAX). The training would be split into two parts. The first consisting of massive training ranges that would stretch for miles on end. The second part would involve us going to a simulated Iraqi village where we would do everything possible to simulate the real thing. They even hired real Arabic speakers to play the villagers. It would be the realest simulation that the Marine Corps could provide.

Doing all this running under the summer sun in the Mojave Desert was absolutely terrible. Every step I took running, I had to tell myself not to pass out. For safety purposes, we would do two practice runs before being given any live ammunition for the range. The first would be a walk through, then starting over again for the second one at almost full speed. A couple hours later, we would be given live ammunition for the final evolution.

The range would consist of a lot of fire and movement and never-ending running under the 115-degree heat. The sweat would sting as it went into your eyes. Being focused was crucial because you could easily shoot someone if you didn't realize they ran in front of you. Once the exercise ended, we would walk back to the tents where we would await transportation back to the sleeping area.

The second part of our training took place in a mock Iraqi town where we would occupy a small firm base in the center of it. Since this was a real-life simulation, the situations we would encounter would always be changing. If we responded to an attack with too much force and killed innocent villagers, the script would change and the villagers would become more hostile towards us.

We would suddenly have to respond to a riot outside our base and while trying to calm the situation down, a simulated bomb would explode. We would have to treat all the injured Marines and Iraqis while listening to hysterical women screaming at the top of their lungs. I'm sure the new guys found the training intense but it's impossible to simulate the real thing. All the guys like me who had been to combat before, thought the training was more humorous than realistic.

With the training now complete, we took the buses back towards Camp Pendleton. If everything went smoothly after arriving and turning in our weapons, there should have been a few hours for everyone to go to the bars considering it had been a month since we had any fun. We were completely finished with everything by midnight and we were told we couldn't leave the base because two packs were missing. Everybody was just standing around doing nothing because we all knew what was going on. The bars in the area all closed at 2am and we knew they were waiting for that. Sure enough, right at 0200, they found the missing packs. Since everything was closed and there was nothing to do, we all went to our rooms and went to bed.

The Final Deployment

This deployment would be starting at the end of September 2006, and my contract would finish on July 13, 2007. I was in the final long stretch of my contract, and it was a case of the countdown clock. I couldn't wait to get out and not worry about my legs getting blown off, yet I still had to remain focused on the mission at hand. Even though we didn't know exactly where we would be going, my mission was simple; to not get killed or injured and make sure that didn't happen to anyone in my team and squad.

At the port waiting to board our ships, we had a few hours to hang out with our friends and family. It's always an awkward silence making small talk to your family when you won't be seeing them for months on end. No jokes are funny and the mood is somber. We decided to go to the base Taco Bell, because that was the only place open.

Waiting for the food, I received a phone call from my mom in Seattle telling me that my grandma had just suffered a stroke and was in critical condition. There was nothing I could do. We were in less than an hour about to start a deployment and during a deployment only the death of immediate family grants permission to go home. Immediate family is mother, father, brother, and sister. If I was in Camp Pendleton and this happened during the seven months I was home, I would've been able to go to my grandmother no questions asked.

With my grandmother's health clouding my thoughts, it was time to board the ship. Our ship's name was the Comstock or better known because of the maturity level of us Marines, as the "Cumstock". I hugged my dad and stepmom goodbye and boarded the ship. Nobody can tell the future and that could've been the last time I ever saw my parents.

On the ship, our platoon sergeant took roll call and once we were given the all clear, we were free to go to bed. We would spend the night in port and when we woke up, we were already underway sailing towards Hawaii with a trajectory for probably the Middle East.

Ship Life

The Navy ships hadn't changed much from what I imagined they looked like in World War II. The technology and weapons were much more modern but the living facilities seemed as spartan now as any tour of a ship I went on when I was young. The Navy sailor takes pride in her ship and that ship is their home. Life on the ship was boring for us Marines with nothing much to do. In the berthing area, our whole platoon lived in tight quarters next to one another.

Each bed, or coffin rack as it was known, had a curtain for a little privacy but was not big enough to sit up in without hitting your head on the rack above. The rack would open in the middle and would have steel rods where you could lock your rack in place. The inside storage would be where you put all your clothes. You push in the metal rods to collapse the rack and it closes, then put your padlock on so nobody steals your stuff. Each rack had an electrical outlet so you could read or plug in your electronics. The rack itself was a hard-uncomfortable mattress that if I was the age I am today, I would've needed a chiropractor to walk in the mornings. When you are a young man in your late teens and early twenties, your body is indestructible.

By this deployment, porn magazines were a thing of the past. I had one of those portable little DVD players so I could watch movies on the ship. Most of the guys by this time all had laptops. I highly doubt they were spending time on their computers doing research for anything because we didn't have Wi-Fi. Most of the storage space was used for one thing and one thing only. This was porn and just porn. If you could've somehow transferred all the porn files into what the equivalent would be in magazines, the ship would have sunk.

We were so bored on ship, guys would watch porn in their beds. We were so bored, guys would even watch porn together. That was how animalistic we were being on ship with no release. Our routine was pretty straightforward. Wake up and everybody cleans the ship for an hour. Then, we wait in line for breakfast. Once breakfast was over, you go take a nap and probably watch porn. Then, you go outside and smoke a cigarette and return to your bed to finish watching whatever porn you fell asleep to. It would now be time to stand in another long line and wait for lunch to be served. After lunch, it was time for another nap then maybe a class or weapons cleaning. After turning in weapons, it was time to stand in that long line one more time for dinner. After dinner, we would await word on what to expect for the next day. This meant more of nothing. After word came down, we were off for the rest of the night. This was when we would shower, hygiene, and watch movies to pass the time.

The big screen TV in the berthing area was connected to the ship entertainment system where they would play three movies a night. The small sweatshop of a gym we had was segregated between Navy and Marine personnel during certain hours and also for officers. Because there was so little room on ship that was the only way to get any exercise.

Besides waiting in lines to eat, we just watched lots and lots of porn.

During this deployment, my father and I had a plan once getting home to visit Europe and see a few soccer games during my leave. Unfortunately, it was impossible to know so early during a deployment when you will come home. Although every day there was a new rumor of a date coming home, the truth was nobody knew. The rumors become so strong, you wished you could just block it all out because it really messed with your motivation. I am not really 100% sure how they start, but I have my theories. Regardless, they are not professional and just saps motivation and the focus of everyone when they need it most.

On the ship, we had access to an email server that would be very slow if it worked at all. It wasn't a traditional email account like Outlook or Google but some kind of government email server. It was strange to use and never had to use anything even similar since. It was through here that my father and I communicated.

I would try to predict when we could possibly come home and how long after coming home it usually takes to be given our post-deployment leave. Depending on the date, I would look at the season schedule in both Spain and England and my dad and I would fly and see a game in both countries. We wanted to fly to England to watch an Arsenal game then fly to Barcelona to see Barcelona play. It would be a week trip just to watch our favorite sport and as a celebration for surviving four hard years in the military. I really enjoyed planning theoretical trips in my head while waiting for the slow internet to download the schedules of the teams we wanted to see.

Most of the rumors we heard probably started from the wives and parents back home with nothing better to do than just talk to each other and form support groups. One person in the group must think they know something or want to feel important and they might say they heard that the unit is coming home on this certain date. Then, this rumor spreads like wildfire through the wives who then tell their husbands. The Marines who contrary to popular belief do not like to fight, be dirty, or suffer, take to the rumors like they are the gospel. If they enjoyed being dirty and fighting, why would they always talk about coming home when the deployment just started? Rumors spread through the platoon and everyone thought they knew more than the captain who would repeatedly tell us that he had no idea when we were coming home.

The young Marines who have only a high school education and have such a low rank know nothing of the big picture, talk as if they are scholars on the Middle East and they know exactly when, why, and how we are coming home. These guys had no idea what we would do the next day, yet they could theorize the most complicated issues. Let's not forget that most of them couldn't find Iraq on a map.

Pirates

Despite the fact we were on ships whose AO was the Middle East, we still weren't told officially where we would be going. I don't know if our captain knew and was under orders not to tell us, or he truly didn't know. He did tell us a couple possibilities which I found to be quite comical to be honest.

One of the possible missions we were told was that we could be fighting pirates. They were causing havoc near the Somali coast by kidnapping and holding ransom big shipping vessels from around the world. These Somali pirates were made even more famous when they kidnapped the captain from the Maersk Alabama. This kidnapping was brought to the big screen by the Tom Hanks movie, *Captain Phillips*. The main reason for the pirates doing this kidnapping behavior was because they viewed these big companies as threats to their fishing and way of life.

The big companies would overfish causing the locals to lose out on the little food they needed to actually feed their families and live. Of course, we are never told this and just assumed that these poor men were the evil people in this situation. Somehow, these big global conglomerates were the good guys and we, who got paid $1500 a month, were indirectly responsible for protecting these companies worth billions. You don't really think about this stuff when you are so young and dumb and just blindly nod your head. When you view that everything you do is the right thing, you never stop and think that for every action there is a reaction and consequences. You simply cannot affect someone's way of life and not expect them to strike back.

Once our captain left the deck where he would relay all the information to the company, his words of us potentially fighting pirates starting creeping into our subconscious. As we started filing into our berthing area, his words took full effect.

"We're going to fight pirates, fuck yeah!" somebody screamed when they entered the berthing.

Our whole platoon let out a simultaneous cheer. Somebody put on the movie, *Pirates of the Caribbean* from their laptop and connected it to the big screen in our room, as all thirty of us squished in together trying to watch. Our excitement grew and grew until it exploded. About thirty minutes into the movie, everyone in the berthing started having simulated sword fights and speaking like a pirate. We held mock executions and I'm happy that nobody got seriously hurt. We always had the tendency to go past the limits of what was considered safe. Were we Marines or school children? From the looks of it, we were more like children, but our actions proved one thing that I knew all along. Deep down all Marines want to be pirates.

Yo ho, yo ho a pirate's life for me.

I knew we were going to Iraq because a few months earlier President Bush, desperate to save face and public support after Iraq had turned into a disaster, ordered the surge. It couldn't have been a coincidence that we were sailing to the Middle East at the same time as the "surge" could it? Since I wasn't an easily brain washable person anymore, I wouldn't be fooled. Many of the people that I entered the Marines with were still gullible and thought that we were still fighting a war for the freedom of the American people. It always seemed strange to me that we were fighting for freedom for our own people who were already free ten thousand miles from home. I would say I am a really logical thinking person and that I make decisions based on logic. It is very frustrating when another Marine who had seen and been through everything that I had been through was still a bit brainwashed.

"I'm here because I want to be here," he told me.

I found that very interesting because I didn't necessarily want to be "here" and I could have thought of a million other things I would rather be doing. Sitting on a nice sandy beach next to two beautiful Brazilian women drinking colorful alcoholic drinks, would be much more preferable than being on a ship sailing to Iraq again.

The truth was that this Marine had no choice, just like I had no choice. He was under contract and if you didn't show up to work, you broke the law and could and would be sent to military jail. His wanting to be here or me not wanting to be here really didn't matter. We both had no choice.

It also surprised me that most of the Marines still didn't understand why the Iraqi people didn't like us. It was very simple. We were not wanted in their country. As the saying goes: *After three days guests start smelling like fish.* We overstayed our welcome, made promises we couldn't keep or probably didn't even attempt to, and we wondered why they hated us.

Seasickness

Since Marines are soldiers of the sea we should be used to the open ocean. Unfortunately, this couldn't be further from the truth, Marines actually spend very little time on ships in comparison to our Navy brethren. While we are not on a sea deployment, the Marines stay on land in the barracks, usually in a shared room with another Marine. The Navy at least in the lower ranks, stay on the ships. Even when the ship is in port, the ship is where they work and sleep. There is no privacy and they also share the berthing with thirty other sailors. It must be a horrible life living so long on the ship.

Marines with our lack of time on the open ocean, suffer from seasickness while the sailors don't. The seas become rocky, the Marines start puking. Seasickness is horrible and anyone who has suffered from it knows exactly what I am talking about.

On the long sail towards what would eventually be Kuwait leaving from San Diego, seasickness hit our platoon hard. Because there is nothing for Marines to do on ship besides sleeping, working out, and watching porn, our lieutenant would have classes to keep our minds prepared for any missions we could soon be going on. I can't remember what this particular class was about, but it didn't last too long.

Trying to pay attention to the lieutenant while sitting down on the floor was very uncomfortable and the classes were very boring because they were repetitive. All of the sudden, one guy left and ran out of the room. Everyone looked at each other and kind of shrugged saying,

"Ok, that's weird."

Everyone turned back towards the lieutenant and the class continued. A minute later, two more Marines stood up and sprinted out of the room. Again, everyone looked at each other and shrugged their shoulders. Then, three more Marines sprinted out of the room, then five more, then eight.

"Class is cancelled," the lieutenant announced as the rest of the Marines including myself, sprinted out of the room. Seasickness had hit our platoon and now there were thirty Marines running through the ship looking for any available toilet. Our berthing only had two toilets and the Marines holding onto their vomit as long as possible charged into other berthing areas with complete strangers and ran right into their bathroom to the awaiting toilet. The sailors knew the signs of seasickness and were pointing and laughing at us while we ran through the halls with looks of terror on our faces.

After throwing up a few times and cleaning up, there was only one thing left to do. All of us got into our beds and tried to sleep the sickness away. It sounded like thunder with all the Marines moaning and groaning as it felt like there was ship inside us rocking back and forth. It was a tough night to say the least. I laughed thinking how although we were on a big ship, this couldn't be further from a cruise ship.

Marines although soldiers of the sea, hate the ocean. The vomit all over the ship proved it.

Fear of Failing the Team

The gunfire is in the distance. It's not far away but not too close to worry. I'm laying down in a deep sleep when somebody probably my squad leader kicks me in the leg to wake up. We get the word that we need to get our gear on because we are going to investigate the gunfire. I am groggy and want to stay asleep but I awake like I do every time. My gear seems heavier this time as the weight of my flak jacket weighs me down and that uncomfortable trapped feeling overwhelms my body.

I am a little slow getting ready and my team is in the distance. I try and walk towards them but they seem to get further and further away. Every time I get closer, I feel like I forget something and need to stop. A rush of uncertainty overtakes my body as I realize I forgot to refill on water. I run back as fast as I can and refill my canteens and camelbak. I now need to run to make up the time and start sprinting towards my squad at the front gate. I can see them and they are yelling at me to hurry up. I finally reach them and look down and realize I forgot my rifle.

I wake up in a cold sweat unsure exactly where I'm at. I look around and realize I'm not in Iraq anymore, in fact, I'm not even in the military anymore but living on an island in the south of Brazil. It has been ten years and the nightmares continue and are always similar. I always forget something and let my team down. The dreams are very rarely about me getting shot by a machine gun because my team is more important than I am. It's 3am, too late to do anything, but I know I won't be able to fall asleep again tonight.

The nightmares will always continue.

Tales from Liberty

Sailing to Kuwait, we were lucky to stop in Singapore as a liberty port. We had been sailing on the open water since Hawaii and hadn't touched land for what seemed like months. I loved the idea of boats, but in real life, being on a boat for so long is not appealing at all. You are always sweating, bored, and always waiting in long lines to eat. I don't know why Singapore was chosen, but all I knew about the place was that it was modern and very strict. The stories I heard about them caning people who chewed gum were famous worldwide. Stupid little things like that are always on your mind because the simple thought of chewing gum being illegal is so unexpected.

Not having seen land for a long time and knowing we wouldn't be seeing women after Singapore, it must have played a role in how crazy things were about to get. Five hundred Marines and even more sailors hitting a city with only two missions in mind, get drunk and get laid but not necessarily in that order. Zero hour for the destruction of the city was set to begin and everybody in the berthing area was nervously waiting, pacing back and forth in anticipation of the few days we would have off before setting sail again.

Permission was given and the process of offloading all the troops began. Each of us was given condoms in line before leaving and had to be inspected that we were wearing the appropriate civilian attire. It took us another two hours to disembark and once getting off the ship, all hell broke loose. We attacked the bars like there was enemy on the other side. People ordering five shots of tequila just for themselves. It was absolutely amazing how so many people could get drunk so fast. Even more amazing was how easily the prostitutes would approach us and how the Marines would never say no. The prostitutes wouldn't even have to give their pitch, it was like, hello, how are you?

Marines would be like, "Hello, how much? Let's go right now."

Since I do not drink much, it is very easy for me to get drunk. One drink turns into a few and the next thing I know I have no idea what the hell is going on. I am constantly in amazement how other people I know can drink alcohol like it's water. Beer after beer, it never stops. I find it difficult to drink water let alone beer when I'm not thirsty anymore. Yet many people I know can drink a twelve pack like it's nothing. At least I make for a cheap drinking partner. When their tab costs $80 and mine is $12 and I am drunk too, they usually have no problem paying for me.

Imagine if they had to pay for them and someone else who could compete drinking with them, their bill would be outrageous.

In Singapore somehow, well, not somehow, of course Danny Boy met a Navy chick who was stationed there and she took a liking to him. With little effort, he went to a popular hangout spot for military personnel and as usual his fucking charms worked. I don't remember what she looked like but I remember she was very pretty and I was happy for him. Well that's a lie, I was extremely jealous and probably angry at him.

Since the guys in my platoon had never really seen me drink before, I guess they wanted to see me get wasted drunk. We were staying in the house where Danny Boy's girl lived in and we started partying and making drinks. It seemed like every other shot was for me. I turned around and noticed that it actually was. I really didn't care that much, I knew that it was OK for me to have fun and relax and live a little and not always worry about all the consequences.

Drink after drink I took and kept up with everyone and more. They weren't traditional shots but mixed shots so you wouldn't taste all the alcohol. After a few and then a few more, I couldn't taste the alcohol anymore, which made it even easier to drink. I remember I kept thinking,

"I must be a better drinker than I thought because after all these shots, I still don't feel the effects of the alcohol."

I sat down on the chair then holy shit it hit me like a tidal wave. I went from completely sober to the most drunk I had ever been in one second. I was pulled into the chair and out of breath from the alcohol and my thoughts went crazy. How could I lose control so fast? My vision was hazy and I became instantly hot. The night just started and I wanted it so badly to end already.

Now the group was leaving the house as we were walking towards the area with all the bars in the city. The more time passed by, the more drunk I became, unable to control anything I said screaming at the top of my lungs. As we entered a bar for military personal, I could barely open my eyes and almost fell into the pool. I offered to buy strangers at a table a round of drinks which is definitely something I would never normally do. I begged the strangers with tears in my eyes to let me use someone's cellphone so I could call my dad at home.

Drunk and stupid I called my dad and made a complete idiot of myself crying to him on the phone saying absolute nonsense. (Note to self, never call your family when drunk to the point you can't even form coherent sentences).

Looking around, the group I was with left me. I guess they thought it would be funny. I got scared because I was alone in a foreign country not exactly sure how to get back to the ship and surrounded by people I didn't know. Being so drunk, not being able to think clearly didn't help much either. Then appearing out of nowhere like a knight in shining armor, Tommy suddenly appeared. I don't know how he got there or who he was with, but I didn't go out with him that night. He saved me from myself when he saw how drunk I was and I really couldn't be alone in my current state.

Tommy led me to an area where we could take buses back to the port where all the ships were docked. They were provided by the military because everyone on board was military personnel. Still disgustingly drunk, I proceeded to scream, cry, and sing during the twenty-five-minute drive back to the ships. Everybody on the bus started getting sick of my screams and turned around and told me to shut the fuck up. Tommy decided to put me in a choke hold so I would pass out and fall asleep. I pretended that his choke worked and closed my eyes just to open them again. I got under control for a few seconds then started screaming again.

I got off the bus and Tommy needed to help me walk up the ramp onto the ship and report. The request if I remember correctly after all these years goes something like,

"Corporal Rosman requests permission to come aboard."

The duty commander would then grant you permission and you enter the ship. Reporting properly this particular evening would be difficult while being carried over Tommy's shoulder. Our company first sergeant was waiting at the entrance of the ship asking for our IDs. Now shirtless, I mustered all the strength I could and threw my military ID at him. Somewhere deep in the back of my mind, I kept asking myself what the hell was wrong with me. I just couldn't control myself.

Tommy dropped me off at my berthing area and he went off to his platoon. Entering the berthing, it was absolute clown show pandemonium. Thirty drunk Marines screaming, crying, and fighting with each other. People running around naked through the aisles, others vomiting but missing the toilet. I was in the right place. I fit in perfectly with everyone else, drunk as could be and joined the screaming party. I jumped into my bed frothing at the mouth and started talking shit to one of the junior Marines.

"I can take you anytime anyplace in football. Right here right now."

"Really, you really think so?" he snapped back at me.

"Right fucking now."

"Get in your three-point stance then and we will do it."

"Not that kind of football, I meant NCAA football on the PlayStation," I yelled back.

I had never played real football before, but we had a PlayStation in the berthing and I was really good at the game. We were two drunk people arguing over football, him thinking I meant real football rather than the video game type. Marines getting a chance to drink after being deprived for a period of time causes extreme amounts of retardation.

The next morning, we held a quick company formation. I tried my hardest not to vomit and I think everyone was feeling similar to me.

"Dismissed."

I sprinted away from formation running at full speed. I climbed down the flights of stairs and into my berthing making it just in time to the bathroom as the vomit came out of me.

Marines are only motivated by sex, alcohol, and fighting.

It quickly became apparent once docking in Kuwait, we wouldn't be fighting pirates or going anywhere else besides the Middle East. The base we were at was used as an intermediary base between troops coming and going from Iraq. The base was massive and you would need to walk for at least a mile to the nearest chow hall. For our purposes, we would acclimate to the desert climate and do a lot of running. Being stuck on ship for so long, your level of endurance disappears quickly.

In Kuwait, a good portion of the Marines still didn't believe we were going to Iraq and they would listen to even more rumors back home. I'm nearly 100% certain that these people back home who didn't know anything, wanted to feel important and just made things up out of thin air. How could family members know before us? I was there and had no idea of any plans, but some wife or girlfriend in the middle of nowhere Kentucky knew more than me about our current situation. If we weren't going to Iraq, why would we be in Kuwait?

We still didn't know our mission, but we would be flying in big C-130 transport planes to Iraq. It was a short forty-five-minute flight and before we knew it, I was back in the country that had given me and all of my friends so much pain and grief only a few years earlier.

Hitting the Ground in Iraq for the Second Time

We landed at Al Asad Airbase and it was absolutely incredible. This was an "Awesome fucking base". We had hot showers every day and even fast food, if we wanted to buy it. I couldn't believe that people could actually be sent to Iraq and never leave this base. Even though we were infantry and do the majority of the fighting, that didn't mean we were paid any different from anyone else. The American military pays you by your rank and that's it. A person who stayed in the luxury of Al Asad and did paperwork as long as he was a corporal like me, received the same salary. Because Iraq as a whole was a combat zone, just someone being there meant they received combat pay too. The base was so large, it was impossible to even know where the entrance to the base was.

A few days into our stay at the base, we finally received our mission orders. We would go into one city and move in line and clear every single house of weapons before moving to another city. The three cities we would clear would be in an area known as the Haditha Triangle. I'm not much for geometry, but this didn't sound good. These missions would be very intense with very little rest while clearing the cities and we would have no base to sleep at afterward. It would be just us with no support and we were expecting heavy enemy contact.

During our first deployment to Ramadi, we were told that we only had to bring our weapons with us because they were the rules. We were to expect no combat and be loved by the Iraqi people and viewed as heroes. I think it is fair to say they were wrong. Never under any circumstance trust intelligence. Everybody in the infantry hates and doesn't trust intel because they come off as almost arrogant. Who the hell are these people who probably never leave the base, yet they think they know what's going on in the streets or what will happen.

This time we were told to expect the absolute worst. Every house would have house to house fighting and every alleyway would have IEDs waiting for us. Even the palm groves would have IEDs hanging from above. The intelligence reports meant one thing to me, death was certain for many of us and we would take many casualties.

Upon receiving the intelligence reports and knowing from my first Iraq deployment that I was not indestructible, I wrote a letter home. This letter would not be sent unless I was killed in action and would be held by the Big Guy in his flak jacket. I would do the same for him. It is perhaps the hardest thing in the world sitting down on your bed in the sleeping area in Iraq, surrounded by your platoon imagining your death. If during my first deployment someone came and told me that everyone in your company will die except one person, who do you think that would be? I would without hesitation say myself. It is impossible to imagine your own mortality and process yourself actually dying.

The letter I wrote, I couldn't go more than five seconds without crying. Saying goodbye to all the people you care about in your life is an unimaginable burden and I got unbelievably sad, hiding my tears in my hands hoping nobody saw me. Saying goodbye to your parents, sisters, grandparents, and one of my friends, was enough to make me almost vomit. The only specifics I will mention of the letter that I wrote, is the part where I told my father that I wanted him to evenly split the insurance money he would receive upon my death to my sisters. The one friend I mentioned in my letter is no longer my friend. This is the first time I have ever mentioned this letter and the Big Guy and I are the only ones who know I wrote it.

Writing this brings back many bad memories that I haven't thought about for ten years.

We had our mission and we were soon told the plan. Each platoon would be given one Humvee and the total seven vehicles would leave a day earlier than the rest of the company. The three extra vehicles that weren't assigned to a platoon would be used by the headquarters element of our company. I was assigned as the vehicle commander for our platoon and would now have a lot of responsibility put on my shoulders. The rest of the company would be taking helicopters to the objective and we would be meeting them there at the exact same time if possible.

I figured the soldier asking Donald Rumsfeld the question about armor only a few years earlier really did work because by this time, all Humvees and 7-tons were fully armored. This was a big difference from two years earlier when even the smallest IED could have been deadly. At least now with the strong armor on each vehicle, we had a fighting chance against the enemy's most formidable weapon.

The Memories

It's all just memories now. A flicker of the past, of battles fought long ago that every day seems further and further away. Besides the scars on my body that I see every day, this could've happened to somebody else. These memories could've been from a movie that I saw long ago because I still can't believe that it was me who lived it.

The night patrols, the day patrols, the long guard shifts, the marketplace, the battles, and the tombstones of friends lost, are just memories of who they once were. They are all just moments in time long ago captured in a brief second, like a photograph.

A photograph from my mind is of my squad leaving the Combat Outpost at night with me as always in the back of the patrol. A big truck drives by and the smoke and dirt is lifted in the air surrounding the squad. From the back, with the dirt, smoke, and the lights from the city, I was the only one who could see it. We looked like we were walking on a cloud and I remember thinking that I would never forget this moment. The beauty of it, I freeze framed in my mind as we looked almost at peace. We were thirteen men, still kids to some, from every background imaginable and for that split moment, it felt like we were the only people left on Earth.

The IED

The IED was the most feared weapon in the enemy's arsenal. Marines fear these silent killers because we fear what we cannot see. IEDs can be hidden anywhere and can be made of almost anything. Our enemy like any good adversary changed and adapted their tactics throughout the years. In a game of cat and mouse, the biggest question was, who was the cat and who was the mouse?

This devastating weapon was responsible for more casualties than actual gun fighting during the war. They have a demoralizing mental effect because they lie in wait and you never know if they are there or not. When you question every step you take, while at the same time every step can be your last, this is where the psychological effect of these powerful yet simple weapons pack their strongest punch.

How fast the enemy adapted was the most impressive. As a unit, we underestimated the capabilities of the enemy in Ramadi. I most certainly didn't but I could tell by the way people in my unit talked about the insurgents, the general belief was that they didn't know how to fight.

Standard operating procedures (SOP) are commonplace in any industry, as well as the military. An SOP is basically if this happens, we do this. An example of an SOP, was on the flak jacket where we would all put our medical kit in the exact same place so that nobody would waste time looking for it in the event it was needed.

On our first deployment to counter the IED threat, we were told that if we drove faster than forty MPH, we would be safe. When the person responsible for setting off the IED pulled the trigger and set off the explosion, if we were driving more than this speed, we would have driven past the bomb by the time it exploded.

The most powerful military in the world yet that's how we were told to counter the IED threat. Something so simple, yet I have no idea if that even worked or not. The invasion of Iraq started and ended very fast and the real war slowly began afterward while the pace vigorously increased. We were now dead center in the heart of what could be described as the Iraqi Civil War, and somehow driving more than forty MPH apparently could save our lives.

Since the two years had passed since the last time we were in Iraq, the situation had taken a turn for the even worse. Every day, there was a new death being reported on the news. They were usually caused by IEDs. They had grown more powerful since our first time in Iraq and were much more sophisticated. Going over the possibilities from the adaptations the enemy made of how they could kill me caused me to get wheezy in the stomach. Every possible countermeasure we were taught in one sentence was in the next sentence thrown out because the enemy knew what we would do and they would counter it themselves.

One example would be while driving on the road, if we saw a pothole to never drive over it. We knew the insurgents would usually plant the IEDs in potholes and so as an SOP, we would never drive over them. The insurgents after watching us for years knew this and they would plant the IED next to the pothole knowing we would swerve around it. Just to make it even harder to detect, they would bury the IED and pave over it. How is it possible to win? You drive over the pothole you're dead, if you swerve to avoid it, you're probably dead too.

During our stay at Al Asad a few days before departing friendly lines, I was sent to a course to learn about how to identify IEDs before they blew us up. Since I would be the vehicle commander, I had better learn quickly how to identify them or risked being sent home in a body bag.

The things that this course taught me were quite amazing and nerve racking. We were shown a type of copper wire that the insurgents used to attach to the explosives. They had reports of the copper wire going up to five miles away from its source. A spotter would just radio the trigger man a few miles away and just like that the explosion would take out a vehicle or a patrol. That whole forty MPH thing we were taught the first time in Iraq was now a laughable suggestion that would get everyone killed every time.

The insurgents would now set multiple IEDs so that after the first vehicle for instance was blown up, they knew that the other men in the patrol would come and help try to save the injured men. The secondary IED would lie in wait and boom! The responding troops would also be killed. Every single thing you could think of, the insurgents would adapt and anticipate.

We were told of a story of a group of very intelligent soldiers who came up with a brilliant idea. They designed a contraption that stuck out about six feet in front of their vehicle and dragged onto the ground. Their thinking was that if there was a bomb, it would blow up their design and give them a six-foot barrier between them and the explosion. The men left the base in their vehicle with their new design attached. Sure enough, they hit an IED and their design worked. It was completely destroyed but their Humvee and everyone inside were safe.

They turned around returning to the base excited about their design and thinking they solved the IED threat. A quick turnaround later, they had put another one in front of their vehicle and left the base once more. Within an hour, the insurgents had put another IED in the exact same spot and buried it. This time, the insurgents placed a two second delay on the IED. The vehicle drove directly over it and the bomb went off dead center under the vehicle. It was a catastrophic hit.

There was some good news in the fight against IEDs. We took the fight against IEDs hi-tech and it really worked well for a period. On the back of our Humvees, these small satellite looking things were attached to them. When activated which was anytime the vehicle was on, it provided an invisible shield around our vehicle against the insurgents most effective IED attack.

This attack was a remote control activated IED. The remote could be a cell phone or even a landline. The insurgents would punch the code into the phone and instantly the IED would explode. This satellite looking thing attached to our Humvees prevented their cell phone from sending a signal to activate the bomb until we were a safe distance away. What was most exciting, was that this new device caused the drop of these types of remote detonated attacks by 95%.

We went hi-tech and the insurgents went back to low-tech. The copper wire which I mentioned earlier, was now the insurgents weapon of choice. Holding it in my hand a few inches from my face, I could barely even see the wire. This wire would be impossible to spot outside in the real world. I had no idea how we would spot the IEDs before they blew us up. Needless to say, leaving that course made me even more uneasy than before.

Every step I took could be my last.

The insurgents had also evolved in other ways than just IEDs. According to the intelligence reports we were given, they were paying snipers from the Chechnya region of Russia to kill Marines. These snipers were highly trained and would gladly accept the bounty put on the head of Marines.

During our first deployment, our personal safety gear was the traditional helmet with the flak jacket. The flak jacket with the ceramic plates inside worked great when hit by bullets. The flak jackets left the side of your torso exposed only. These contracted snipers were so good, they would now aim in the exposed area of the flak jacket and shoot Marines through their side leading to a fatality. Because of this new threat, we were given an addition to our flak jackets. They were little inserts that had a small ceramic plate that we attached protecting our sides. Again, the game of cat and mouse was being played.

Before these additional inserts were given to us, it was extremely difficult to move. With the ceramic plates plus all the ammunition and water we carried, I wouldn't hesitate to say I carried forty pounds on me at all times. These new inserts didn't weigh much, but took away from whatever little maneuverability we had to begin with. Now it was impossible to be agile on my feet and if I needed to turn around, I actually had to physically turn around instead of just looking over my shoulder. That is how much weight and how uncomfortable everything was. The worst part of all this was that I never got used to the feeling. Every time I would put on my flak jacket, I would say the same thing,

"This fucking sucks."

This new sniper threat not only caused a modification to our gear but also to our actions. What we used to do during the first deployment was now considered a sure way to get killed. When coming to a stop during a patrol, it was normal to go to the corner of the street and have a wall protect part of our body. We would look towards one part of the street while the next Marine would do the same thing looking somewhere else. Because of this, everybody was looking somewhere else protecting everyone in the squad. This security halt could be anything from waiting for the squad leader to decide where to go next or simply stopping to rest.

Our new procedures changed completely. We would now never take a knee and instead always be moving. If we were on a halt in the patrol, we would now never stand still. You could walk back and forth, go left and right, but never stand or sit still. This also was true for actual patrolling. Instead of just walking straight, we were told to be random. If you felt like randomly running around in circles, then do it. If you felt like throwing a smoke grenade to conceal your movement just because you wanted to be unpredictable, then just do it. The idea was to assume the enemy sniper was always aiming in on you about to shoot. It was comical when two of us would speak together during the patrol. Instead of standing and exchanging information, we would both be a few feet from each other randomly moving talking to each other. It looked like one weird salsa dance with heavily armed men doing strange random movements back and forth to each other.

The enemy sniper chooses their target the same way our trained snipers do. They look for people reading a map, the group leader, the radioman, and people who look older, therefore being more important and having more rank. The sniper always aims center mass which means dead center into the chest. Why not the head? The head is a smaller target than the center of your chest. Even if they miss dead center they will still hit somewhere in the chest cavity. They aim in, breath, and at the end of their breath when there is a pause between inhale and exhale, they slowly pull the trigger back and fire, delivering a perfect shot center mass. The idea was that if you were always moving, when the sniper aimed in and fired, he would miss our vital organs and maybe hit our shoulder.

The most powerful and well-trained military the world has ever known, started dancing to avoid being killed by a sniper.

On this deployment, we were sworn to secrecy and would not be able to tell our families what city we were going to. I am not sure what technology the insurgents had where they could find out if we told our families or not, but I wasn't about to be the guy who broke the vow of secrecy and be responsible for the people I cared about being needlessly killed.

Since the vehicle convoy would leave one day before the rest of the company, we were able to use the satellite phones and call home. Having the last phone call you may ever have with your dad makes for a difficult conversation. For security reasons, I couldn't tell him where I was going or when I was going but he was smart enough to know that this was it. The last time I talked to him, I told him our next phone call would probably be my last one.

I do not remember word for word our conversation but it went something like this.

"Where are you going?"

"Dad, I can't talk about it for security reasons, but I wish I could tell you. Just know this will be the last time I will be able to call for a long time."

"Are you going back to Ramadi?"

"Dad, I cannot even tell you where I am not going. For all I know my own superiors are listening to our conversation."

After a few minutes talking about other stuff, my dad asked me in Spanish another question that I thought I could finally answer.

"¿Vas al mismo lugar donde fuiste la primera vez?" (Are you going to the same place as the first time?)

"No."

We said our last goodbyes and my father reminded me to always be vigilant and never let my guard or focus down. He finished by saying,

"Get through this deployment and be done with this shit once and for all." The goodbyes were over.

My last deployment would truly begin.

Here We Go Again

Getting in the vehicles preparing to leave, I was truly nervous. The IED threat was so grave how couldn't I be? The only thing I could do was stay vigilant and have the courage to say something if I saw anything suspicious. Stopping a moving convoy and it turns out to be nothing but just a big waste of time was a fear everyone had. I truly didn't care because I wanted to come back with all my arms and legs.

Our small convoy arrived at our halfway point without incident. From the intel reports, I am honestly not sure how this happened. The halfway point was another random nameless base to me scattered throughout the country. Our stay entailed us parking all our vehicles in a straight line and getting food. After all this, we decided to sleep in the vehicles instead of going to the makeshift sleeping area they found for us. It would save time just being in the vehicles so we wouldn't have to rush the following morning.

The following morning after a horrible night sleeping, we would continue our drive towards the rally point with the continued goal of meeting the helicopters at the same time they arrived in the city of Barwanah. We were again blessed with no IEDs blowing up any of our vehicles.

Finally approaching the city, I looked out the window to my left and saw the rest of our company flying in on helicopters. I had not been in a helicopter since I was injured and seeing my friends getting a ride in a HELO was one of the coolest things I had ever seen. In my mind, the movie, *Apocalypse Now* played where all the helicopters were flying overhead playing the symphonic music on the way to shoot missiles into the city.

The helicopters landed and the Marines poured out from behind. They acted like they were under fire which they weren't and immediately hit the ground doing buddy rushes with their assault packs until they arrived at a wall. I found my platoon soon after in the rush of all the Marines and was told once we found them to separate from the convoy and follow them.

My squad leader wanted to put all the packs in the back of the Humvee but I didn't want to. I was worried because we were expecting so many casualties that if we put packs in our vehicle, there wouldn't be any room for the wounded. I was quickly told to "shut the fuck up" and the packs from my squad were put into the back of my vehicle.

The first twenty minutes after the company landed, it was chaotic. After that, things began to slow down a bit because we weren't under any fire like we expected to be. I was fortunate to be in a vehicle so my job was much easier than the rest of my platoon. The platoon would split up and start clearing houses on both sides of the street while my vehicle was in the middle of the road. Lance Corporal Raposa was the turret gunner and his weapon was the M-240 machine gun. This gun was similar to the SAW but bigger with 7.62 ammunition instead of 5.56.

Since I believed the intelligence with danger lurking on every inch of ground, I wanted to stay with the vehicle at all times instead of helping clear houses. To a lot of people, it looked like I was being lazy but the truth was different. They were just jealous that I was sitting in the vehicle while they were working their asses off. It wasn't me who chose to be in charge of the vehicle, that was picked by someone else.

The problem with a lot of people is they just see what's immediately in front of them and fail to look at the bigger picture. One extra guy helping to lift mattresses wouldn't have helped make our day go by any faster. If for example, I was upstairs in a house searching and we came under attack, I would have been far away from my vehicle. The vehicle would have two inexperienced Marines under fire and I would be nowhere to be found. I thought this through logically and decided it was best to stay with the vehicle as often as possible.

Once sunset came, the searches ended and our lieutenant and squad leaders had to find a house suitable for our whole platoon to sleep in, plus a Humvee to park. This was not an easy task finding a home that met our security requirements. They were basically a good size wall surrounding the house and a way for us to get onto the roof. Once we found a house, thirty exhausted Marines would have to wait to rest because the family inside would argue with us about not wanting to leave.

The family was given ten minutes to leave with the promise that we would neither break or steal anything. I think our lieutenant gave them a piece of paper with an address, where they could take it and get paid for us using their home. I cannot confirm this 100%, but I believe I either saw this happen or I overheard someone mention it. Either way, I felt terrible for the families we did this to almost every night. We treated their homes with respect and never stole or broke anything. War is a cruel business and unfortunately people always get hurt.

The first night was absolutely miserable because we still weren't used to the conditions. We still were expecting action at any time and dressed accordingly. Inside the home, we slept in full uniform with our Kevlar vests with our boots unlaced. We even used our helmets as pillows. The house that night was too small for a full platoon and we literally slept on top of one another.

The reason why we didn't have a base to stay at night was the fact that this wasn't a typical Iraq deployment. My first deployment, we lived at a "Pretty Shitty Base". We came and replaced the soldiers who were there before us. This time around because of the abundance of extra troops due to the surge, we arrived with nobody to replace. We were just extra troops given a mission and had to figure out the rest, seemingly ourselves.

As expected, the days become repetitive with the long grueling hours of nonstop work. Monday, Tuesday, Saturday, it all didn't matter. Days of the week lose their meaning as you go from one patrol to a guard shift then to sleep before starting all over. Shift to shift is how the days and weeks would go.

After a few days clearing Barwanah, we found a house that was more suitable for the size of our platoon. This house was structurally completed with four bedrooms, but the inside was not touched. Each squad would occupy a bedroom and do as best as we could to stay warm. The floors were still dirt and there was no electricity. Unlike the majority of the world, Iraq didn't have a culture of getting bank loans. By this I mean, to build a house and you could only afford a brick, you have that brick. When you can afford ten, you add those ten bricks to your home. The house we would occupy for the next three days, the guy probably ran out of money and was saving to install flooring and electricity.

Food was a major issue as well. Since we were always on the move, we had no time to eat even if there was any. The cold weather which made patrolling easier would also dehydrate you because we would be shivering at night. We would boil eggs that we took from a market to cook in the mornings from a field stove we had in my vehicle. Cooking in our room kept us warm as we tried not to starve.

I lost weight no doubt during these operations. I love eating more than anything else and I was doing everything but that. I lost a good ten pounds I could tell when I finally took off my undershirt. During the patrols, other Marines would take shotguns and blow off locks to store fronts so we could all get candy and cookies. Since I don't like sweets, I refrained from taking or eating any of the food from the stores. In a black and white world, what we did was no doubt wrong. In the grey world, where nothing is black or white, what we did was perfectly fine. We were hungry and looking for food while clearing out enemy insurgents so the locals could live a peaceful life.

Sitting on a roof with a younger Marine, we did the worst thing imaginable and talked about food while being hungry. He told me about a magical place in Texas, where you could eat unlimited pizza for $5.99.

"It must taste like shit being that cheap?" I asked him.

"Actually, for the money, it tastes really good. You can even order the pizza and they will make slices for you. Anything you want, even pizza with macaroni and cheese on top you can order."

My mouth was watering with the thought of unlimited pizza with every taste I could desire. I promised that one day, I would visit this magical place called Cici's Pizza as soon as I saw one. After being hungry for so long, I made a promise that I have always kept. I vowed that if I could survive this deployment, I would never take food to go. I would sit down and enjoy my meal instead of being in a rush to eat all the time. We should always enjoy our meal and never need to rush. If necessary, I will leave twenty minutes early to eat comfortably inside instead of taking it to go. Ten years later,

I still haven't broken this promise to myself.

Since we rarely stayed in the same house twice, the command didn't know exactly where we were. They knew the general area and if somebody from command wanted to come to our house, we would need to meet them down at the main road to guide them to our house.

As the vehicle commander, I was told to never be the only vehicle driving around. We would always need to have another vehicle with us at all time. Sitting in my vehicle in the late afternoon relaxing after our platoon's long day, we finally could get some rest and bed down for the night. We suddenly got a call saying that command wanted to come into our house and they wanted us to meet them halfway on the main road to guide them.

Lance Corporal Raposa wasted no time and jumped in the vehicle excited to go out. He started yelling in his excitement, "We got to go, we got to go out, they will be waiting for us." He actually got mad at me because I told him we couldn't leave until the other vehicle was ready. We couldn't drive by ourselves and had to wait for the other vehicle to load up and we would drive together to the rally point.

Facing towards the road sitting in my Humvee, the engineers who had the other vehicle next to mine were finishing eating. I saw the company command vehicles below and knew we would have to rush to meet them in time. The other vehicle was finally ready as we turned on the engine.

Boom!

An IED detonated under one of the command vehicles two hundred yards in front of us. I saw the whole thing in front of me happen. If I had listened to Lance Corporal Raposa and left as soon as we received the word to meet, we would have met the lead vehicle and been blown up at the exact same time. The sound was so loud it felt like we had been hit even though the IED was far away. My breath was knocked out of me as my heart started pounding against my chest. I double checked to see that my balls, arms, and legs were not harmed just in case as we started driving towards the site of the explosion.

Thirty seconds later we arrived and I dismounted from my vehicle and started running. I couldn't see, I couldn't hear, and I could barely breathe. The fog of war set in as I tried to figure out what I could do. The Humvee that was hit was blown up and rolled over down the road. I remembered my IED training class that I took ten days before as I gathered my thoughts.

I told Bobby that after five minutes, I wanted him to drive the vehicle forward fifteen feet. Often there would be secondary IEDs in the area and we would have to do a security sweep. We could have stopped on top of another IED and not even noticed. That was the reason why you move positions every so often to better check your surroundings.

Our executive officer (XO) or second in command of the company was injured. Another guy named Big Thompson, (no relation to my friend Chris "Tommy" Thompson) was also injured. Big Thompson was one unlucky bastard. His original contract had expired but extended his contract so he could deploy with us. He didn't want to go four years in the Marines without seeing combat so he extended. He lasted three days in combat before being injured. Another guy that was injured got in the

Marines roughly the same time as me. When the vehicle was blown up, he got thrown out of the turret and sustained a serious concussion and would need to be MEDEVACED.

We now had to gather the injured and drive to the MEDEVAC point. The injured got dispersed throughout the remaining vehicles as we all drove providing security. After a ten-minute drive we stopped at the side of the road where next to us there was a big open field large enough for helicopters to land.

Our XO who played college football, was a heavy man. He was in a stretcher and it took the full strength of four men to lift him up. They took him towards the awaiting helicopter while I helped the Marine with the concussion walk to the same HELO. The dust and noise were horrible caused by the helicopter's propellers. I couldn't see or hear and had to put on my big ski goggles in order to guide the injured Marine to the helicopter. Right before putting him in, I gave him a hug and told him that I hoped to see him soon.

The helicopter lifted off and I stood there gazing at the beauty of such an incredible machine as it quickly disappeared from our sight. Now I had to remember how to get back to our platoon's house. I knew this would be tough because I was bad with directions and with the chaos of what just happened, I forgot where the hell we drove from.

I started following the engineers hoping that they had some idea as to where the hell we came from. After a few wrong turns, we found the main street and turned towards our house. My lieutenant was waiting for me and asked how the XO was doing. They were both friends being they were both junior officers.

"Sir, I think he will be fine, he had his arms and legs but looked like he broke his nose because there was blood all over his face. I couldn't tell if anything else was broken because his uniform covered everything up."

The scary thing about this IED was how it was hidden. This wasn't planted and hidden during our first three days there but must have been waiting for a long time. There were hundreds of us who drove and walked over the IED every day since our arrival. Anytime during those first few days, I could've been blown up and killed. It was impossible for an insurgent to place such a large IED, dig a hole, place the IED inside, and then repave the road without anyone noticing. This IED was large enough to cause a catastrophic kill to the Humvee and with enough force to destroy the road it was hiding under.

After a few more days, Barwanah was finally cleared. Besides the one IED, we found no significant weapon stockpiles and didn't have any enemy to fight like the intelligence told us. This city took about ten days to clear and we would leave the city and go to the Haditha Dam.

The Haditha Dam was used to provide a majority of the country with electricity. The dam was used as a base and was guarded by soldiers from the country of Georgia. I have no idea what our government promised them in return for them sending their soldiers to Iraq, but I promise it was far from free. I was just happy that we didn't have to guard the base and could get some rest. Here we would do laundry, shower, and eat real food. We could take off our gear and walk freely around the dam during our few days of rest before the next mission.

After resting for three days, our next mission would take us to the city of Habbaniya. The mission would be the exact same as before. For ten days, we would again search every single house in the city. We encountered absolutely nothing again. There were no IEDs, no enemy contact, and no weapons. It was a complete waste of time. I had no idea where the bad guys went or if they were ever there. Again, intelligence wasn't that intelligent and they were completely wrong.

The Miserable Story of Checkpoint 12

After Habbaniya, most of our platoon wasn't going back to the Haditha Dam right away. We would be going to Checkpoint 11 and 12. We had no idea what that was or what it would entail. We just finished clearing the city and I don't remember exactly how we all got there, but we had two of the three squads in our platoon who would be going to the checkpoints. 3rd squad which had the lieutenant would go to

Checkpoint 11, while my squad with our platoon sergeant would be at checkpoint 12.

Checkpoint 12 or hell as I remember it, was more like a hut. On one side was an enclosed wooden structure with a couple of cots inside. On the other side, there was an open area with cots with camouflage netting above it. There was another small tent somewhere else for the bathroom. There was no food or water from what I remember. There wasn't any type of built in security like concertina wire, berms, or even those dirt filled twelve-foot high barriers.

This was literally a basic lookout position on top of a hill in the middle of nowhere with no protection. We were told to make sure nobody put any IEDs on road below us. We weren't told how long we would be up there or any friendly units in the area, absolutely nothing. It was simply being dropped off and told to watch that road, goodbye. The road we were supposed to watch was a small stretch as well. It was a good distance away too, maybe two hundred fifty meters or so. Because of the hills in the surrounding area, it was possible to only see a small portion of the road anyways.

It was miserably cold on this windswept lookout point. I didn't have a thermometer but at night, it must have gotten down to 20-degrees or less. I was sleeping outside on a cot and I didn't have a sleeping bag. My bones shivered to their core as another gust of wind overtook the hill.

I woke up in the middle of the night and because we were trying to be tactical, I didn't want to use a flashlight but had to use the bathroom really bad. The only problem was that I had no idea what it looked like from the inside. Waking up I didn't have time to wait, I had to take a shit right then and there. I ran outside and went in the tent that I had never been in before. There was no modern toilet to speak of. In fact, I'm not even sure if that was the bathroom. I just saw some kind of hole in the ground and hoped that was it. The diarrhea shit I had to take wasn't going to stop as I pondered if I had found the toilet or not.

"A hole is better than my pants," I thought to myself remembering the time I shit myself in Ramadi.

It wasn't that going to the bathroom felt so good but more the satisfaction that my pants were safe. It was late, really dark, and extremely cold. Squatting over the hole hoping that no shit hit the back of my boots, I couldn't believe the situation I was in. This really sucked and this was only the first night.

During the next day, there was really nothing to do because no cars drove on the road we were looking over. We didn't see military vehicles or normal cars. It was still cold even during the daytime and I was getting sick. I tried to get some rest and warmth in the Humvee but that didn't help much. I was too restless as I tried laying on the cot, but since that was outside and we had no blankets that was even worse.

I went to the other area that was enclosed which was where our staff sergeant and squad leader were sleeping. Even though their structure was made of wood and a little warmer, it wasn't exactly comfortable either. There were loads of Maxim magazines that whoever we replaced left, and my squad leader and platoon sergeant started taping all the semi-nude photos on the wall. They also started taking bits and pieces of the wood from the structure to start a fire inside to keep them warm.

By that night, I felt so sick I wasn't sure if I had pneumonia or not. If I didn't, it was as close as possible. Laying there in my cot late at night, I remember thinking that I had never been this miserable in my life. This was worse than being shot. I felt so miserable that if I was given the option to die warm at that very moment or continue to live this miserably, I would have chosen a warm death. This and the next night were the two worst nights of my life. Getting critically wounded a few years earlier was nothing compared to this.

After the third day, we were picked up by vehicles and driven back to Haditha Dam. The wood structure was now barren except for the minimum necessary to hold up the walls with the women's pictures taped to it. The rest was used for firewood. I imagine, I was far from the only person who had to use the bathroom as badly as I did, and if that hole I used was indeed the toilet, then they would need to build something else.

In the vehicle, I couldn't lift my head up and was hoping the dam would appear and I could go as fast as possible to the showers. At the base, I couldn't even lift my head up as I was walking to find the medical unit. Some Marine from another unit, looked at me and told me to lift my head up and "Walk like a Marine." I was so sick and weak I didn't even have the strength to tell him to, "Shut the fuck up."

The worst part of my life was over. I got pills for whatever sickness I had, but it wasn't pneumonia. I took a long hot shower and remembered that the clock doesn't stop. My end of service date July 13, 2007, would come and no matter what happened the clock never stops and that day would eventually come.

Looking back in life, sometimes things weren't as bad as they seemed when you were actually there. Just to confirm how bad it really was and it wasn't my imagination, I recently asked a friend who was there with me. He told me that the checkpoint was one of the worst experiences of his life and that it made him into the man he is today. No matter how stressful life gets, he always looks back onto his time at the checkpoint and remembers that it can never get worse than Checkpoint 12.

The most miserable point of my life was over. After a few days of rest at the dam, there would be another city to clear.

War Sucks

Since we are a generation brought up by movies, it seems normal that I always look back in movies for great memories. Movies can inspire and teach you. Every moment in your life seems to have a connection to some movie. The movie, *Saving Private Ryan*, I believe is the greatest war film ever made not because of its depiction of the violence which was very realistic, but rather for one particular scene of non-violence where the men were just sitting around exhausted talking in the church.

The medic of the team said his mother would work the night shift and he would usually be sleeping when she came into his room. He would sometimes try to stay awake, but the harder he tried the faster he fell asleep. Sometimes his mom would come home early and he would pretend to be asleep. She would stand in the doorway and look at him while he kept his eyes shut. All she wanted to do was say hello and see how his day was.

His biggest regret was that he never just said hi to his mom and he wasn't sure why he didn't do it. Now so far away in horrible combat where he could be killed at any second, he may never have the opportunity to see her again. He would die later in the movie. For all its great combat scenes, this small anticlimactic scene showed war for everything that it truly is.

War is nasty and I'm not proud to have gone to it. There is nothing noble about having to fight and kill other human beings. It is actually a shame that men are put in a situation where this becomes necessary. One of the things that angers me the most is when people just callously say things like, "We should go bomb them" or "Let's just send the military in." They say these things like it's just entertainment for them and don't understand that there are real consequences, because they won't be affected by them. Even if we just send our airplanes to drop bombs from the sky, that doesn't mean pilots don't suffer either. Our smart bombs aren't as smart as we think they are. They still miss often and even if they do hit their target, a five hundred-pound bomb hitting its target will kill innocent people too. That's a big explosion for only the bad guys to get magically hurt.

Before people just think fighting is the way to solve every problem and sending our troops into harm's way is the only choice or easiest, I want you to really think about the consequences. The people who are sent to war never come home the same. Every single person I know that went to combat with me has some sort of problem. There are no exceptions to this.

Do you want to know what war is like? War is pain and suffering. War is waking up every day and not knowing if you will be alive the next. War is calling home any chance you get even if it's 3am because you aren't sure if you will ever hear your parents' voice again. War is scary and war is brutal. War is you or me and I choose me. War is not politics but war is affected by it. War, there's no patriotic music playing in the background when you are fighting. War is when your friend dies, it hurts and the pain never goes away. War is life and war is death. Are you sure you still want to know about war?

Al Bundy & PTSD

Many people I know from the Marines suffer from what I call, Al Bundy Syndrome. Al Bundy, is the character from the TV series, *Married with Children*. He was a shoe salesman in an empty mall who hated his life. The only thing he ever did and was proud about was score four touchdowns as a high school quarterback playing for Polk High School. That was the high point in his life and everything went downhill afterwards. Many of the people I know suffer from Al Bundy Syndrome, thinking their greatest moment happened during a firefight in 2004. That's all they think about, that is all they have ever done, and it's all they will ever do. It is time to move on and have new goals. The past can never be changed and the future hasn't been written yet.

I know the biggest strongest men who have problems. I know the smallest most average looking people that have problems. One thing for sure is that everyone I know has some sort of problem. There are no exceptions to this. Everybody's symptoms are different but they all fit into the broad range of possibilities for Post-Traumatic Stress Disorder. Most men abuse alcohol which acts as a lighter fluid for their issues. Some men abuse prescription pills given to them by the Veterans Administration.

The VA which is backlogged by the hundreds of thousands, over-prescribe medication for veterans to try and speed up the backlog. This is not just a problem in the VA, but a larger nationwide problem where doctors just prescribe pills and create overdependence on drugs. Prescription pill abuse is just as dangerous as the common street drugs that have more fame. Unfortunately for our veterans, they are caught up in both ends of the problem. The country itself has a huge problem and the VA who is supposed to help these veterans, sometimes hurts them.

Every single person that I served with including myself has some sort of issue. Some are major and some are much more minor, yet everyone I know has mental scars. The biggest strongest guy I know gets anxiety for reasons I will never understand. He will be in a restaurant and all of the sudden he starts acting paranoid and strange. There may be four people sitting inside minding their own business but you cannot speak to my friend because he is hyper alert and on edge. He always needs to sit facing the window or entrance to the restaurant or he will start getting anxious and get extremely restless with his hands. When he enters into a room everybody stops and must think, "Wow, that guy is big." PTSD doesn't care about how big or strong you are. It affects everyone.

Many people have problems sleeping and suffer from nightmares. When you don't have a good night sleep, the rest of your life is affected. Many members from my battalion have attempted suicide and a few of them have killed themselves. Someone I saw not too long ago needs a comfort dog for their daily lives. His experiences were so traumatic that he needs a dog to help him get through his daily life.

I don't know anyone from my military service who is still married to the same woman as when they were in. I may be wrong, but it must be close to a 100% divorce rate. Of course, their divorces could have been due to many factors but no doubt their military experiences didn't help.

People always wonder why I can never sit or stand still for too long. People think that I am hyperactive but that is the furthest from the truth. I can sit at home and watch movies all day but outside in public is a different story. If I'm waiting for a store to open because I arrived early, there is no way I can just sit in my car and pass the time. I need to get out and walk around until it opens.

At my sister's dress rehearsal for her wedding, everyone thought it was funny while we were all practicing for the big day with everybody standing in their assigned positions except me. I was the only one walking around, angering bridezilla and the wedding coordinator. When people asked me why I always walked around and never sat still, I always joked around and said, "So the sniper doesn't get me."

I get anxious in public when I sit or stand in one place too long and get bored. Maybe it is because I was always the last man on patrol and looking behind me constantly, I would never see any friendly faces and I would either see potential threats in Iraqis or vast nothingness. It could also be that during our last deployment in Iraq we never sat still during the deployment. Because of the anti-sniper techniques, we were taught to make ourselves a hard target, I never stopped moving the whole deployment. I don't get anxious in crowds in the same fashion as the Big Guy, where you can see that something is bothering him. It just looks to everyone else that I am hyper.

I have trouble enjoying myself. When I go out to a bar and should be having fun, the truth is I am really not. It gets annoying being around a lot of people. The sensation I feel is that I am in a glass bottle where I can see everyone having fun and I am happy for them, yet for me it feels like I am watching the events on a television even though I am there with them. This is a real condition caused by the nature of military work and the attitude you are forced to have to survive. If your best friend dies you have no time to grieve. All you have is your next patrol or next guard shift. After time, this hardens you and you lose the emotion that you need to have to become the person you want to be. Why shouldn't I enjoy myself when I go out? I am no different than anyone else. This condition is called the Flattening Effect.

I suffer from the Flattening Effect and it makes my life less enjoyable.

To me, the long term is thinking in three-month increments. This is by far not what experts consider long term, but it is for me. Long term is usually five to ten years. The reason I think three months is long term, well I really don't think that but that's the way my mind acts is because I know how precious life is. Thinking longer than three months in the future seems crazy to me when nobody knows if they will be alive tomorrow, let alone in five years.

Trust me, I know this is stupid. There is retirement planning that you need to start saving for young. One day I will wake up really old and nobody wants to hire an old guy starting at the bottom of a company. You need to spend years at a company and get promotions to make more money. It doesn't look good on a resume when an employer sees that you quit all the time. I know all this yet there is something in my mind that prevents me from doing the smart and logical thing. I can't explain it, but that is the way it is and probably will always be.

The Clearing Continues

The third city we would clear was Haditha. This city was made infamous about a year earlier when Marines in response to an IED attack went crazy and started killing innocent civilians. I think a few Marines went on trial and were convicted. We were told to be very vigilant because the residents of this city would hate us because of the previous attacks. This raised the anxiety amongst us as we again cleared house to house expecting to find insurgents around every corner and IEDs on every street.

We again found absolutely nothing. No insurgents, no weapon stockpiles, nothing. The only thing that remained a constant besides the horrible intelligence was how hard the work was to clear house after house. Your shoulders are the first to go lifting all the mattresses over, then your back, and finally your legs.

Christmas was celebrated in the city and just to have some fun, I decided to take my team on a special patrol. I decided that we needed to get out of the same rut we seemed to be in day after day. I told the guys that we were going to knock on random houses and sing Christmas carols to them.

Knock knock. An Iraqi man answered a few seconds later.

The three of us started to sing, "We wish you a Merry Christmas, we wish you a Merry Christmas, and a happy new year."

The Iraqi man smiled at us. I know he didn't understand a word we said to him, but smiled at the strange sight of three heavily armed men singing to him during the middle of the day. That was one of the best times I had during the deployment and makes me smile whenever I think about it.

Our three-city sweep was finally over. In total, nobody shot their weapons and no significant arrests were made. It was a big waste of time. We would go back to the dam for a few days and celebrate the New Year.

I got to call home and was able to speak to my dad.

"Hey dad, its Jason."

"Hold on, your sister is on the line, let me try and make this a three-way call."

"Hello, can we all hear each other?"

"Yes, yes we can, awesome."

"Dad, how is my grandma doing?"

My sister chimed in, "she passeee."

"Allyson be quiet," as my dad cut her off.

Right then and there I knew my grandmother had passed away. A few minutes later, I called my mom in Seattle to confirm the news. I told her that even though my father hadn't told me exactly, I knew him well enough and knew he didn't want to tell me. He acted the same way when my dog died. He didn't want me to lose focus during patrols and I guess would rather have told me after returning home.

I went back to my bed and laid down. I wanted to cry but couldn't. I was angry at myself for not crying and I wanted to so badly. I was a machine now, incapable of showing much emotion. That's what the military wants from their troops and that's what they got. I tried to sleep but had another restless night thinking about her. There wasn't anything I could do, she was gone and I was a million miles from home. We would be celebrating New Years at the dam and all I could do was stay focused for the next patrol. The next morning, we would be briefed on our next mission. The missions never stopped coming and the pain I felt from her passing would need to wait.

Another brick was put in my wall.

Our new mission wouldn't have us going to a new city but back to a familiar one. We would be going back to Barwanah to continue providing security and to prevent the insurgents from regaining a foothold in the city. I wasn't exactly sure what foothold they were talking about because we never encountered any insurgents when we were there three weeks earlier.

With our return to Barwanah, we wouldn't be needing my Humvee anymore and it was given back to headquarters. Somehow our chain of command also got us a massive house to stay in and we wouldn't need to sleep in a different house every night.

I know what everyone's thinking. After all the crap Jason and his friends went through, finally they got something nice. Just because I said the house was big, that didn't mean it was nice. The house could easily fit the two platoons staying there, plus much more if need be.

The house nicknamed, the Playboy Mansion, due to its size, had no electricity or running water. The house was on the banks of the Euphrates river and almost seemed peaceful. The floors were dirt and you had to be careful and pick up your feet when you walked or you would kick up dust everywhere. This FOB, made the Combat Outpost two years earlier look like the Waldorf Astoria Hotel. The Playboy Mansion was the very definition of a "I Should Have Gone to College Kind of Base."

To use the bathroom, there were three wooden structures to give us some privacy. In the inside, there was a bench with a toilet seat in the middle. Underneath was a massive bucket that would be collected once a day by a junior Marine and he would be forced to burn the shit. If he was smart, he would wear a gas mask; if he was dumb, he wouldn't. Once the shit turned into essentially black dust, it would be buried on the side of our compound.

The Playboy Mansion would house only my platoon and 4th. 1st and 3rd platoon would be together along with the company command in another house on the other side of this small city. Our routine would be pretty straightforward and nowhere near the absolute crazed schedule we maintained when we cleared the three cities in a month. One day my platoon would be on patrols and 4th would have security, then the next day we would switch. On our patrol days, there was no QRF or any of the constant readiness levels we had while in Ramadi two years earlier.

Once we settled into the Playboy Mansion, we had a regular food delivery. The food came from the other house where 1st and 3rd platoon lived. Every morning, they would make the food and it would be driven to us by the gunny. The food was basically tray rations designed for big groups. They had about the same taste as an MRE, which was little to none.

The majority of our meals consisted of spaghetti with some vegetables. Easy to prepare and simple, yet tasty enough not to get too many complaints. Although food was no longer a problem because we were in a fixed location and could get care packages sent from home, there was still no way anybody was gaining weight. Most care packages consisted of socks and blankets with cookies being the primary food that we received.

Since we had opposite schedules as 4th platoon, we would usually see them when we all gathered for dinner. Because of the schedules, it was funny how little we saw of them even though they were in the rooms next to ours. It was also comical seeing our platoon sergeant and theirs always bickering with each other. Since our platoon sergeant of course came from being a recruiter and theirs was a drill instructor, it was fair to say they never got along. It is also fair to say that their platoon sergeant was an asshole.

After getting a feel for this small city, I wasn't sure why we were here. There was nothing to do and our AO was so small we could walk it in thirty minutes. We were never told of a specific threat and it felt like they had nothing better for us to do, so we were just sent to this small town of seven thousand people. There was no comparing

Barwanah to Ramadi. The biggest building here was just two stories and there was no main market place. It was basically just a farming village where we would see the same people almost every day.

Besides the repetitive nature of patrols and standing guard, thus far in the deployment, there was no stress. We never executed any raids at night and I unfortunately never had to break any street lights to feel like an elite Special Forces soldier. When we went inside a house at night, it was mainly to stay warm while a few guys were outside. Most of the houses here were one story and didn't have a roof to climb up. If the homeowner had a TV, we would sometimes just hang out with him for a few hours and watch a movie to pass the time.

With the one generator we had at the mansion, it was always a race to charge our iPods and portable DVD players. Since I had one of the few DVD players, I usually had preferential privilege to charge my stuff first. We would all huddle around my little six-inch screen and watch whatever new set of movies my dad sent to me in a care package.

In one package, he sent me an absolute gold mine. They were, *Casino Royale*, *Borat, Rocky Balboa,* and various pornos with titles I prefer not to mention here. Since the screen on my DVD player was so small, it was impossible for everyone to watch all at once. I wasn't about to let people use it without me there, so I sat there and watched *Casino Royale* four times until everyone that wanted to watch it could.

Even though there wasn't much going on in our small city, there was still work to be done at the Playboy Mansion. When we arrived, the house was just a house with no protection from incoming fire. We never did any remodeling on the inside because we had no materials to cover the ground floor with wood for example. Since this was the military, what we did have was an abundance of sandbags. Many hours of each day during the daylight was spent filling sandbags to fortify the outside of the mansion. Before the sandbags were placed during the day, the light would come through the windows like any normal house. By the time we were finished sandbagging, it was almost always dark inside.

The Playboy Mansion from ground to the roof was now covered completely by sandbags making it the ugliest mansion in the world. As for now, there was still never incoming fire but if there was, we would be protected. Remembering how during our first Iraq deployment, one of the guys got injured taking a shit or jerking off in the port-o-john, our three makeshift toilets were sandbagged as well.

In the last few days of January, we would have the Playboy Mansion to ourselves and would need to do both the patrols and security. 4th platoon was sent on a special mission where they would again be going house to house looking for weapons.

The month of January ended without incident, but February's history hadn't been written yet.

Richey Baby

My good friend Richard Quill III or as I called him, "Richey Baby" was a member of 4th platoon. In our first deployment, he was a combat replacement and was a member of my 2nd platoon. He was from Georgia and a huge Bulldog fan. He was tall, blond haired, good looking, and muscular. He also was a kind person with a good personality which made him in baseball terms, a 5-tool player. I imagine he was every woman's perfect guy. On the Navy ship, he was always in the weight room which was common for everyone because there was nothing else to do aboard. He was such a good guy which makes what happened to him even sadder. He was let down by leadership. The hardest part of recounting his tale is that there are still so many unknowns after all these years. Nobody knows exactly how or why it happened because nobody was given that information.

Murphy's Law

There are many sayings in the Marine Corps. Usually they involve some contortion of Murphy's Law. *If it can go wrong it will go wrong*, is probably the most famous of all the laws, especially in a military setting. Mr. Murphy affects us every day. Have you ever tried looking for an ATM with no success? Why is it that whenever you don't need one, there are a million, but when you are desperate for one, you have a better chance finding snow in Death Valley.

So how did this affect daily life for me in a combat zone. First of all, I would always assume that Murphy was just around the corner waiting for me to get complacent. This would mean that I would always have my canteens and camelbak full. With my luck, we would be called on a mission with one minute to prepare and leave. I would never want to go thirsty and run out of water in a firefight. I would also pack extra batteries in case I needed them for my NVGs.

After another patrol ended and we made our way back to the mansion, I noticed something that wasn't there before and after three years in the Marines, I knew this was a bad omen and didn't like what I saw. It was a row of Humvees meant for us. Normally Humvees would come once a day from the other base on the other side of the city to drop off our food, but this was different. They were just there empty ready for us to use.

Walking past the Humvees for the first time entering the front door of the Playboy Mansion, I took off my helmet and wiped the sweat off my forehead thinking to myself, "Fuck, if it can go wrong it will go wrong."

A few days later I was proven correct.

The Final Days of Richey Baby

4th platoon would be sent on a special mission away from the Playboy Mansion. I remember the night before eating dinner and joking to Richey about how skinny he was becoming. This would be the last time I would ever see my friend. I am not sure what caused his death and I don't think I will ever know because the information has either never been released or is just not known. I've talked to his father a few times through the years but never had the courage to ask him if he knew what happened to his incredible son nor thought it appropriate. Since I wasn't there by his side during his final days, I think it was only right that I asked his squad leader to help tell the rest of his story.

***

I couldn't tell you what caused Richey to get sick. It started getting concerning six weeks before he passed as he started losing weight. He would tell me he felt weak and disoriented. I stopped taking him on patrol with us two weeks prior. He seemed so depressed at that time. We couldn't get him to eat much and I even had Marines bring him food. He was assisted to and from his rack to go to the bathroom. I requested a MEDEVAC a week before we went to the "Pretty Shitty Base" where they housed the battalion level staff.

The commanding officer came down for a non-related reason and he told us that since we would be leaving soon, just to wait until we could get him to see the medical officer at the medical clinic. When we got there, he took a turn for the worse. We had to carry his gear, weapon, and even carried him. After we arrived to the base, I believe we stayed there for four days before we left. I asked everyone I could to get a bird to fly him out on day one. I got the usual run around about priority for air and he didn't meet the requirements for pulling assets away from the battalion.

I begged our platoon sergeant who had a rank of gunnery sergeant and the lieutenant to go take him to the command and medical officer. They did, but nothing came from it. In the meantime, Richey was getting worse and was still being brought food but now we had to feed him. In a period of less than three days from our arrival at the base, he went from horribly sick and weak to not even able to feed himself. I asked one of the other Marines from my platoon who was on guard if we could put him in his berthing because they had heat, because Richard was constantly shivering.

We put him in there and I had a watch posted on him 24/7. One of the guys on watch came over and told me that he had defecated on himself. I lost my shit and after asking a couple of the Marines to clean him up, I went to the Medical tent and yelled, begged, and pleaded for him to get immediate care. The answer was the same. Since we were due to leave the next day they would say the fastest way to get him out was on the already scheduled ride. The only thing was our mission kept getting pushed back. The military is always hurry up and wait, but this time this was actually preventing Richard from getting the help he needed. Since all my previous requests were denied to get him to a higher level of care, our scheduled ride was what he was waiting for. Who knows if he could have survived if the battalion did more to get him the help he deserved and needed.

The night before he passed, one of the Marines from the tent he was staying in came in to tell us that he was having trouble breathing. The platoon sergeant and I ran in to help. The platoon sergeant found a piece of an orange stuck in the back of his throat. By this point, Richard was out of it completely. He didn't recognize us anymore. He bit our platoon sergeant's finger when he was sweeping to clear his airway. He pissed himself in front of us and we carried him over to the medical tent again. It would be for the last time.

We were told later that Richey had gone into cardiac arrest and soon after that, he had passed away on his flight out. I miss him, he was a true friend, a great person, and I'm blessed to have had him in my life.

The only thing I was told was that he passed from "natural causes". Whatever the hell that means, for such a young man to go the way he did. At the time he died, he went into cardiac arrest and stopped breathing on his own. They attempted to start his heart multiple times. They found particles of food in his lungs that indicated that he was too weak, having trouble properly eating and breathing in his last days. Even though my opinion carries no medical weight, I think that a combination of depression from problems back home, the constant battle field stress, and fatigue just put him in a downward spiral. Like I said that's just my opinion I have nothing to back it up.

During the whole six-week ordeal from when Richey started to have problems to when he died, yes, our platoon sergeant called him names like pussy and bitch. At first, he definitely did but I think it was because it was so sudden and quick his sickness. One minute, Richard is this strong muscled guy and then seemingly overnight, he can't patrol anymore. Missing a patrol is a big deal because that means you are letting your team down. I'm not defending our platoon sergeant's actions, but to be honest it crossed my mind at first too. Not that he was a pussy but that maybe he wasn't telling the truth about how he felt. It wasn't until he came to me and asked for a break that I truly accepted it was true. Him asking this was totally out of character for him. He was a strong guy and was able to muster enough fortitude to finish doing his job even with everything going on with him. That will to continue and the heart to be there patrolling with us gave us the perception that he was fine.

Our platoon sergeant was an asshole but he was no more than any other person in a similar leadership position in the company at that time. He lost a lot of respect from the platoon by making his assumptions out loud to them. He was the type of guy that didn't have a filter. He constantly disrespected our lieutenant and would undermine anyone that challenged him, myself included. The one thing he did right was ask higher for help every time I asked him to. The lieutenant was a coward, too afraid to stand up to him. Our platoon sergeant made all the decisions for my platoon So yes, he did call him names but at the same time he was prior service with the Navy as a corpsman and he did what he could to help, but it was too late. He put up too many barriers with everyone out there.

A Dagger Straight in the Heart

With the Playboy Mansion feeling really empty because of 4th platoon being gone, we were summoned to one of the main empty big rooms of the house because the captain wanted to speak to us. Our platoon started getting antsy anticipating we would be extended again in our deployment. I was busy calculating how another extension would affect my European vacation I wanted to take with my dad.

Our platoon was waiting in the room as the captain walked in.

“Men,”

I was expecting the word extension to come immediately out of his mouth but what came out next was devastating unlike anything I had ever felt before. I wish we would have been extended instead of this.

“I don’t know why or how this happened but Quill has passed away.”

There was gasp of disbelief from us, as the men like me who knew him best were overcome with emotion. I couldn't stand up and had to sit down before collapsing. People had to run out of the room to cry in private. We were hardened warriors trained to show no emotion but the loss of Richey was too much not to cry, scream, and not be angry.

Richey was a great young man with his whole life ahead of him. There is not one day that goes by that I don't think about him. We were all losing weight and looking back he was losing more weight than anyone else. I wish he would have told me something, anything, so I could have helped him. I deeply cared for this man because of his caring good nature and big smile that would light up a room. Whenever I drink a beer, I always leave a little in the glass in memory of my friends who couldn't come home. I always leave a little for men like Richey Baby.

My friend Richard Quill III, from Georgia, died of mysterious conditions on February 1, 2007. The men who fought with and loved this man like I did, will never forget him and we will always fight and carry on. His memory is carried on in our pain and remembrance every day.

With the news of his death affecting me greatly, I had no chance to grieve. Fifteen minutes later, it was my squad's turn to go on patrol. I wanted to disappear, I wanted to go home, I just wanted to say goodbye one last time to my friend Richey Baby. All this wasn't to be as I put on my flak jacket once more and felt the weight not of the forty-pound vest like normal, but of my sadness.

Leaving for patrol with what seemed like the weight of the world on my shoulders with tears still in my eyes, I needed to remind myself.

Stay focused Jason, one step at a time, stay focused.

Suicide Bombing

Another day of patrols came as usual but this time it was different. Although the Humvees were there, we wouldn't be using them because there really wasn't anywhere to drive to. Walking our normal route through our boring and quiet farm town, we hit the end of our AO. The end of our AO was a checkpoint where the Iraqis could cross from one point to another. This checkpoint was manned by our 1st and 3rd platoons. Their house was located behind the checkpoint up the hill a little distance. Instead of turning around like normal, our squad leader who was the smartest Marine I've ever met, decided to enter the checkpoint.

I had never been inside the checkpoint so it was exciting to see something different. Our squad leader walked quickly through the checkpoint going up the hill towards what I assumed was where 1st and 3rd platoon lived.

"I'll be back in a bit," he told us.

With time to kill, I walked into the checkpoint to see what was going on and see my friends from the other platoons. The checkpoint was pretty typical, with the entrance with serpentine wire and reinforced walls, forcing the people to walk in specific directions. Walking past them, I saw how men and women at the entrance were separated so that women would go one way and the men another. It was against Iraqi customs and for the military for men to check women. At the checkpoint and this was a big deal because it had been a long time, I saw two women. "Women," I said to myself like I was some caveman seeing the other sex for the first time.

I've said many times before, Marines only think about eating, sex, and sleep. My imagination went into overdrive as I looked around thinking how and where I could have sex with one of them in or around the checkpoint.

"Slow down devil dog," I said to myself.

"You can't sleep with them unless you talk to them first, so stop being a pussy and say something."

Being the pussy I was, I walked by both of them without saying a word.

Inside the checkpoint, I saw Tommy for the first time it seemed in months. He was a squad leader and was working inside the checkpoint and finishing his shift in a few hours. It was great seeing my old friend.

"Tommy," I yelled, giving him a big hug.

Although he was a sergeant and I was a corporal, we were on a first or just last name basis if nobody else was around. If he was around his squad and I walked by, out of respect for him and for the authority over his squad, I would always refer to him by his rank as a courtesy.

"Tommy, I heard you were reenlisting, why?"

"Well, it's a lot of money and tax free if I enlist in a combat zone. Plus, once we get back, I can essentially choose my next duty station."

"Tommy, I love you buddy but you are a fucking idiot. I'm serious dude what the fuck is wrong with you? We have five months left in our contract. We've survived hell and back and you just want to say fuck it and do it all over again for some money?"

"Yeah man, it's like $35,000, that isn't just pocket change."

"Dude, please don't," I begged, "You're making a big mistake," as I walked away.

A few hours later, death would come calling. Fate wouldn't take Tommy on February 7, but fate wasn't so kind to others.

Walking back towards the entrance to the checkpoint and with the other platoon busy doing their job, I decided to walk over to the side of the checkpoint to a covered area where you are supposed to go if you aren't doing anything. It just keeps extra people from standing around doing nothing and had great protection from any sort of mortar or any other attack that could happen.

The two female Marines whose job it was to search the Iraqi women as they walked through the checkpoint were inside there with me cooling off because there was a lull in the foot traffic coming through. I finally had the chance to talk to both of them and shoot the shit.

I was interested how they got to the checkpoint every day and where they came back to. I really had no idea and they could've been in the house with 1st and 3rd platoon for all I knew. We were that isolated from the other platoons in our company that I truly had no idea what they did on a daily basis or what or where their area of operations even consisted of besides the checkpoint.

It turns out that the women were actually picked up and dropped off every day by our gunny. They lived in the "Pretty Shitty Base," where we went once a month to shower. I remember thinking how beautiful both women were. Not just water in the middle of the desert dying of thirst kind of beautiful or because I hadn't seen a woman in so long, but really truly beautiful. One of the female Marines could have been a model. Maybe it was her second job I don't know, but she was that beautiful.

After all these years, I do not remember what the three of us spoke about and I don't believe in making up or dramatizing stories. Most likely with my lack of game with women at the time, I probably said something stupid like,

"How do you guys like the weather?"

Two hours later one of the women would be dead and the other would be critically injured. I may have been the last person she ever spoke to.

Our squad leader returned from the other platoon's house and it was now time to get back in formation and walk home. After a quick thirty-minute walk back to the Playboy Mansion, we entered the compound and I saw something that I thought was both strange and interesting. Instead of just 3rd squad, which included the Big Guy preparing for their patrol, this time there were a lot more people. The sergeant major was there along with his security. The battalion commander was also there along with his personal security. In addition to him, there was a warrant officer along with his security. Instead of a patrol of thirteen people, this new patrol would have around forty people.

At first, I was curious as to what was going on. My curiosity quickly turned into fear as the sergeant major locked eyes with me.

"Rosman, I see you didn't shave your shitty little mustache."

What shitty luck. Why of all days did he have to come to our little base for the first time? Why couldn't I have just snuck by him without him seeing me and gone inside?

"Fuck," I muttered under my breath.

"So why didn't you shave that shit?" he repeated.

"It's hard to shave without electricity or running water sergeant major."

"I see," as he sarcastically nodded his head.

I hurriedly walked by him and took my gear off entering the front door of the Playboy Mansion.

The sergeant major would be dead in the next few hours.

Walking into the Playboy Mansion at noon we would have six hours off. These six hours would include our sleeping, eating, hygiene, and whatever else you wanted to do. Coming off a patrol and having to sleep at noon isn't the easiest thing in the world and by the time you actually fell asleep, the food truck would arrive. If you didn't wake up in time you wouldn't eat. These six hours weren't really six hours of sleep but more like two or three. That was the routine and yes, I still got paid around $1500 a month.

While half asleep in our squad room, I started hearing commotion in the main area of the house where the radio and big map were located to keep track of the squads while they were patrolling. When patrols are out of friendly lines and they reach a checkpoint, the radioman would call in and say something like,

Playboy Mansion, this is Joker 2/3 over.

Send your traffic 2/3.

2/3 is at Checkpoint Wizard out, copy?

Copy, over and out.

The location of the patrol is then plotted with tacks that move once a new location is radioed in. Since we were living in a town with no action going on, it was very boring. Hearing all this commotion was something new. I gingerly stood up and made my way to the radio.

There wasn't a lot of information that was readily available but what I could gather from asking people, was that there was a suicide bombing at the checkpoint where I was two hours earlier. We didn't have any word on any casualties or the current situation. It just sounded like a lot of commotion over the radio. Nobody on our end in the Playboy Mansion was doing anything except listening. It almost seemed like a radio broadcast where the reception was horrible.

Since we had vehicles, (I told you something bad was going to happen), the QRF which was 1st squad, was sitting in the vehicles waiting for the go ahead to drive to the checkpoint. My squad was too anxious to go back to sleep and we moved into the Ready 2-position. I don't know if it's called the Ready 2-position or if I just made that term up, but it sounds cool.

Since QRF was activated with 1st squad in the vehicles, my squad was put on alert as the next to go in case we were needed. 1st squad's shift quickly finished and they got out of the vehicles and my squad replaced them.

We got the order to proceed to the checkpoint. I had no idea what to expect but I was expecting the worst. I'd seen hell on earth before and was ready for it once more. The men in my team, young guys, had never seen thus far any kind of real intense action. I was still young too, but I was a grizzled combat vet with a shitty mustache who was the ripe old age of twenty-one.

Sitting in the vehicles, I looked at Raposa and Bobby and felt bad for what was about to happen. No matter how smart or tough you think you might be, nothing can ever prepare you for seeing dead bodies and mangled limbs. Their innocence would be lost in the next few minutes.

Looking at my men's faces, I shook my head and thought to myself,

"They will never be the same."

And they never were.

People lost limbs and their lives because of the stupidity of the people put in charge of us. The higher ranked people you don't get close to because you never see them. The relationship once you see or speak to them is a relationship of one-word answers.

The problem is when these people's dumb actions cause the deaths and injuries of people that you see and work with every day. The people you went to boot camp with, then to infantry school with, and finally after all that, they are in the same Marine Corps infantry company as you. The kind of people you would die for in an instant because they would do the same for you. The kind of people you can literally identify from the way they walk and even from just their earlobe. These were the people I truly cared about, not some guy I've seen a few times and never spoke to before. These people put my friends Tommy and the Big Guy in a position for them to get killed needlessly.

I write this part of the story for them, so that the truth comes out. I write this part of the story for the guy in my platoon who lost his legs and the other guy who lost fingers. I write this part for the guys who weren't physically hurt but the scars from what they saw will haunt them for the rest of their lives. I write this part of the story for the two men in my team that shouldn't have experienced what they saw that day. I write this for us!

After a short drive towards the final straight away leading into the checkpoint, we stopped and saw our approaching lieutenant and our third squad leader. We stopped and opened the door as he threw a helmet into the back seat. I got out of the vehicle and got into the backseat so he could get into the front. Still not sure what exactly happened and unsure if anyone was hurt or not, I asked the lieutenant if anyone was injured.

"Wait for the brief," he responded.

"Yes sir."

I knew this would be bad if he wouldn't tell me who was injured or killed. Knowing that there was no reason for him not to tell me, he quickly changed his mind a second later.

"The sergeant major was killed. Two men in our platoon sustained horrendous injuries and could die at any moment. One lost his legs and the other one took heavy shrapnel. One of the female Marines was killed and the other one was critically injured. Dozens of Iraqis were killed and injured by the suicide bomber."

I closed my eyes not wanting to believe what I was being told could possibly be true.

The sergeant major being killed was a big deal. The death of someone so high ranking would be a huge deal all around the Marine Corps because that there are so few sergeants major. In the Marines, after so many years in service where you have made thousands upon thousands of connections in your career, his death would reverberate around the Corps.

I was relieved that Tommy and the Big Guy were neither hurt nor killed. We continued to the checkpoint arriving a minute later. Leaving the vehicle, the fog of war went into immediate effect. I had immediate tunnel vision and was out of breath even though I was only walking. The adrenaline in my body was causing my heart to beat so rapidly that I could only hear my short-panicked breaths gasping for oxygen. The chaos of the situation was horrifying.

The Marines from the other platoons sealed off the checkpoint leaving frantic Iraqis stuck on one side or the other looking for their family to see if they were killed or wounded. Looking around, the other platoons did a great job and cleaned off a lot of the blood. Besides the chaos at the checkpoint, I was in awe of how fast and professional everyone acted.

Our lieutenant was frantically trying to help an Iraqi man find his son and he wasn't being helped by the sergeant from the other platoon. Feeling like I was watching all this take place like I wasn't there but rather watching the chaos through a television, our lieutenant took the Iraqi man by the hand and ran him through part of the checkpoint. Through all the chaos and noise, he found his young three or four-year old son walking around crying by himself.

As they were reunited, the father grabbed and picked up his son and was spinning in circles crying holding his young son.

"Thank you, thank you, thank you," he screamed in his broken English.

"Allah Akbar, Allah Akbar," he cried as he hugged the lieutenant and me.

The lieutenant gasping for breath and looking relieved said, "I'm not sure how I knew that kid belonged to him, but something inside me told me he did."

As we walked away, the sergeant from the other platoon in a whiny voice said, "Sir, you shouldn't have done that, we were ordered to keep the checkpoint closed, nobody goes in or out."

This sergeant was actually a nice guy talking to him but still everybody hated him. During our first deployment in Ramadi, he was of course part of Echo Company and he abandoned one of his men behind enemy lines after he was shot four times on April 6. This young Marine was all alone in the middle of a combat zone surrounded by hostile forces fighting for his life trying not to get captured. Fortunately for him, he managed to survive.

"Shut the fuck up," our lieutenant growled. Even after the sergeant witnessed a father and son being reunited, how could he say something so stupid? I walked away with a grin on my face knowing that our lieutenant was a really awesome guy and under his command, we would make it OK.

I will tell you a little about our lieutenant. We didn't follow his orders because he was an officer and we had to, we followed him because we wanted to. That is what made him the best officer I ever served with, and that's all you need to know about him.

Taking my gear off back at the Playboy Mansion, I was drained from the stress of what I just witnessed, I knew that none of us would ever be the same. We would now have two empty beds at the Playboy Mansion. The missions would continue with no time for grieving because there was base security that needed to be done. It didn't really matter much anyways. It wasn't who was good or bad, who had the best training, or highest rank.

The sergeant major just like the sergeant major during the Ramadi deployment, was former Force Recon and had over twenty years of service. When I was injured in 2004, I had only nine months in service. It was all about luck. A few hours before, I was standing in the same spot where the sergeant major was killed. The suicide bomber or his spotter saw me no doubt standing at the checkpoint while he was doing reconnaissance of the target and decided not to blow himself up, but rather wait for a better opportunity. I was not as well trained as the sergeant major and probably not a better person than the female Marine, who I spoke to only briefly and still don't know her name, but who left a lasting impact on my life.

I was just lucky.

I wish that all of the suffering that day could've ended over the last few pages. Secrets of that day still need to be revealed. Secrets that have been hidden because others have deemed them to be insignificant or of no importance. I am not one of those people. When it is an open secret where everybody in our company knows why this tragedy potentially happened and nobody has said a word, that's a problem. When people die and lose limbs because of stupidity and failure, then there is a problem and secrets must be revealed. I am here now, and the secret of what happened that day will be no longer.

The events leading up to that fateful moment will be revealed now.

Complacency Kills

This lesson was driven into us like a hammer pounding into a nail. We were reminded of it wherever we went. It was an echo in the back of our minds, a constant reminder that the second we let our guard down, our friends would be killed because of us. Close your eyes on post, somebody will get their neck slit open and you have to write a letter home to their parents explaining why you fell asleep on post allowing the enemy to infiltrate the base because you were complacent and thought they would never attack.

Everywhere we went they would even have signs posted that said "Complacency Kills" in big letters. You enter the chow hall and clear your weapon before entering; there was that damn sign again. You wake up to take a piss at night, that damn sign was staring at you. It is easy to understand how that lesson could vibrate and pound deep into your soul forever. How could it not? Unfortunately, the people in charge of us seemed to forget that basic lesson. Their complacency got men killed and yet nobody but me seems to care or notice.

Part of surviving in combat is to make yourself a hard target. Never exposing yourself too long in open space and finding cover and concealment are perfect examples of this. There are many things you can do to mitigate the risks against you but some are impossible to hide. The enemy decides who is most important and who is not the same way the Marines or any traditional military would. Just because they don't use tanks or jets doesn't mean they would rather kill a young Marine over a general. The enemy is not stupid and if you don't believe me, you can visit the tombstones of all the people I know who died.

Nobody can hide their age. If you look older than a teenager, let's say in your late thirties, that means you are important because you have a high rank. If you are using shiny rank which signifies you are an officer, that means you are important. To mitigate that risk, officers in combat use a blacked-out version of their rank as to not draw extra attention. The radioman with his big antenna is of course a big target because communication between us is so vital, from calling in grid coordinates, airstrikes, or a MEDEVAC. There is no hiding that big antenna sticking out of the backpack.

Anybody reading a map is a greater target for the enemy and when necessary, try and go inside a vehicle or even a house to read the map to make sure no one in the street sees you. Young Marines probably will not be reading a map on their patrols so only the most important squad members would. These little precautions can help you avoid getting targeted by the enemy. Is it a perfect system? Of course not, but if it may prevent you from getting hurt or killed, these extra things are well worth the little extra effort.

Another safety precaution is that nobody bunches up and everyone keeps a good distance from each other. During the day this distance is much greater than at night. During the day, we would also be at a much higher risk of attack. The distance between us should be great enough so that one order can't be heard by everyone. It should be passed down in order to keep the distance between everyone. It would be catastrophic losing more people than necessary if an RPG or IED went off.

After returning to the Playboy Mansion after the massive suicide bombing, our platoon was in absolute shock. People couldn't control their emotions. Some had to throw up from the gravity of what just happened. Besides the sergeant major, two of our guys in our platoon were gravely injured.

I sat alone for a while trying to gather my thoughts and kept thinking how lucky I was. On any other day, my two best friends could've been killed and I would've needed to send the letter I was carrying for the Big Guy to his family. The sadness overtook us as darkness began to set in on the Barwanah horizon. Our house could have been abandoned it was so silent.

After composing myself, my first worry was to try and comfort our new guys who had never witnessed any destruction like they had a few hours previously. I knew this gut wrenching feeling from my first deployment and the feeling of emptiness. Sitting there wondering why you made it while the others didn't was always the hardest part. I could do nothing but hug the guys and ask how they were doing knowing that at first you just want to be left alone. I told them that if they want to talk and although it didn't seem like they ever would want to, eventually they would and I would be there for them.

As I returned that day from my squad's initial patrol, I saw around forty men ready to start patrolling. Besides the thirteen men from 3rd squad, the commanding officer, sergeant major, and a warrant officer also joined them. Each of them had their own security and in this new massive patrol, there was at least five radios. It is easy to notice when there are certain people being protected and that they are also not teenagers.

A few paragraphs above, I detailed certain steps you can take to avoid making yourself a target. How many of those simple common-sense steps were broken on that patrol? Almost every one of them was broken before the patrol even began. The suicide bomber must have thanked the heavens when he saw that group of forty men patrolling towards the checkpoint.

The question that everyone is still wondering, which I haven't answered yet, is why? What was the point of this patrol? Why now? The answers that everyone deserves to find out are some of the most tragic and difficult things that I have ever needed to write about.

I actually started writing this part when I first started this book but these events when recalling them were too difficult to write about. I would get angry and start pacing back and forth recalling these events and after all these years, still cannot believe that everything I am about to say is 100% true. I hope after writing about these events once and for all, I can finally forget about them and maybe have a good night sleep.

It was for a reenlistment ceremony in the middle of a combat zone.

Where do I begin? Do I write this when I'm angry or maybe at 2am when I can't sleep?

Let us do some basic math first. With the higher-ranking people on patrol, there was close to eighty years of Marine Corps experience. All the other guys had less than four years of experience. Upon reaching the checkpoint, the majority of the Marines there also had less than four years of experience.

At the checkpoint there was the captain, first sergeant, and gunny. Between them there was easily forty years of experience. Between the leadership arriving to the checkpoint and the leadership already there, there was at least one hundred twenty years of experience.

One person with some authority should have said that having a reenlistment ceremony was a bad idea. Someone should have reminded the person with power and said something to the effect of,

"Remember the signs we walk by every day and are constantly reminded of before every patrol? The ones that say complacency kills. Isn't this the definition of complacency what we are doing now?"

In all fairness and thankfully that inside the checkpoint some of my fellow Marines who I knew for my whole time in, had a little common sense and they are alive because of it. The squad leader of 3rd was the New Yorker who along with Tommy was my first roommate, sent part of his team on a roof to provide overwatch for the checkpoint. The Big Guy was one of these men thankfully.

Tommy decided he had enough and took his whole squad away from the checkpoint onto a hill far enough away from where the explosion would be. He didn't even want to stay for the ceremony and even begged our captain and I repeat begged our captain to shut the checkpoint down for this ceremony.

The captain's logic and I agree with it in principle was simple. Closing off this vital checkpoint to the city disrupted the lives of the local Iraqi population we were trying to help. Closing off this checkpoint did nothing to help them and would only make them late coming or going from work. There are a million possibilities how closing this checkpoint would negatively affect their lives. In this crazy world we were in, it was best to try and make as few enemies as possible. Disrupting the daily lives of the population is an easy way to make unnecessary enemies.

Now the best and simplest course of action would have been to have this ceremony in the safety of the house that 1st and 3rd platoon stayed in every night. The battalion leadership could have taken vehicles to that house and the ceremony would've have happened without any disruption at the checkpoint and no risks would have been taken.

Reflecting back on that day for many years of my life, it is impossible to know if the suicide bomber blew himself up then for a specific reason or if it was just coincidence. No one can ever know that answer. In theory, I could've a few hours before waved to the bomber or his spotter like I always did to everyone. He could've thought that there was nothing worth blowing up at that given moment and decided to wait for a better opportunity. He could've have seen me and thought,

"Well, maybe I'll wait to blow myself up so that one day this small guy waving at me with a shitty mustache can become an author of a book."

Two hours later, when this incredible target of opportunity came, a spotter or the bomber himself decided that this was the perfect time to strike. All those important people walking around being seen at the same spot in open public was a once in a lifetime opportunity to do serious damage.

It could also have been a complete coincidence. The bomber could have planned it for this time no matter what and after a few prayers, he blew himself up. Unfortunately, we will never know. This is why making yourself a hard target is so critical. All the things I spoke about earlier, like never reading a map in public or never having important people travel together really does matter.

The most important question remains. Why would so many people with so much experience do something so stupid?

The answer can only be explained as pure stupidity and damn arrogance. They showed no respect for the potential enemy and disregarded every lesson of war ever taught. There are Marines with one day of experience who know better than that. There are people who sit on a couch and play video games like Modern Warfare, who know better than that. Everybody in the world knows better than that, except somehow the group of people with over one hundred twenty years of experience. The people I cared about most were let down by the people whose responsibility it was to protect us. It was their responsibility to lead us and make decisions that allowed us to do our jobs with the least amount of danger possible given the circumstances.

I know a lot of heroes from that day. All the ones I knew were less than twenty-four-years old and cashed paychecks that were less than $2,000 a month. All those people knew that arrogance gets you killed and disrespecting the enemy in their own country, is an open invitation to get you sent home missing your legs or buried six feet in the ground.

In the aftermath of this attack, there was no investigation as to why this happened. No investigation as to any of it. The careers of these people continued without any questions as to why such blatant complacency could take place in a combat zone. I am convinced that many people will find this all very offensive and I don't understand why and I don't care. People hate the truth and would rather believe a lie. This is not the type of person I am and this is not a book about lies. The truth about that awful day needs to be told.

I was told recently by a friend who was there during the explosion, that whenever it's quiet and he closes his eyes, he can still smell the burnt flesh and see the missing body parts. If you are reading this and are in the military or thinking about joining, I want you to remember something. Your lives are the most important things in the world to both me and your family. Never ever forget this:

Complacency kills.

After the attack, we did what Marines always do and carried on. We no longer had vehicles which was a good omen. Nothing changed for us; the routine of patrolling was always the same. What was strange about Barwanah, was how little we felt this city changed for us. The attack seemed like a one-off incident and we didn't sense any hostility from the people towards us. I never even found out if intelligence learned anything about the suicide bomber in the aftermath. Honestly, who would even care? He was already dead.

In the next few days, we got a glimmer of good news. The man in our platoon who lost his legs was expected to live. It was a miracle after all the injuries he took.

After the suicide bombing on February 7, there was no action. In the months that followed, the deployment was as straightforward as could possibly be. We were all getting very anxious walking around with a rifle all day never being able to shoot it.

Surrounded by months on end with so little to do, Marines start to go crazy. Boredom is the root of all evil among young men with too much testosterone in them. Boredom causes rumors to be spread, smoke endless amounts of cigarettes, and do the strangest things to pass the time.

The Big Guy, was the king of passing boredom. We would love laughing at the dumb things he would do. Whether it was making a costume and running around in his underwear with no care in the world or showing us his balls for no reason. Stupid things like this, keep you sane when you are going insane.

March came and went without incident as did most of April. Before we knew it, the time was getting close to start the journey that would eventually take us home.

A Plan is Formed

As the deployment grew longer and longer and we kept on getting extended, the original idea of watching a European soccer game in April slowly started to fade from reality. Instead of being back in early April, it looked like returning home in May would be a real possibility. We were then told that once getting home, our post deployment leave would take a long time to happen and with the timing issues there wouldn't be any time left to watch any matches in Europe.

I needed to develop a plan, a great plan, a plan that would involve certain parts skill, certain parts cunning, and a whole hell of a lot of luck. Fortunately for me, I had in myself a pretty clever person who was motivated to accomplish a dream of watching a professional European soccer match. I needed a plan that was believable enough that people wouldn't think twice about it being a lie. I would use how Marines love believing rumors and how even the smallest whisper would spread like a spark that causes a wildfire. I had an idea and it was now time to execute it.

The captain would not grant any early leave requests and by the time the unit would be on their post deployment leave, I would not be able to leave because I would be starting the checkout process to get out of the military. I would need to use that window where nobody would be allowed to leave and somehow get the captain to let me go.

I told my father over email, that the plan would be that he was getting married in Europe and that I was the best man and needed to go. Since I knew that the military didn't really care about personal issues, they would just tell me that my dad would need to reschedule the wedding if it was so important. Since now I had my plan, I needed to set the spark and basically tell everyone how excited I was for my dad to get married.

After being told we would be extended, I told everyone that my dad had to cancel the wedding because we wouldn't be coming home in April anymore and my dad wouldn't have the wedding without me. I pretended to be depressed as I told every single person I spoke to. I told the gunny, the first sergeant, my own team, squad leader, and platoon sergeant. I probably even told the Iraqis as I walked by waving to them.

The rumor I created slowly made its way through my company and people even started asking me where the wedding was. I had to make sure that my lie was always the same so nobody would think twice about it. My parents would be getting married in Lake Como, Italy. They already cancelled once and had changed the date to a May time frame.

This trip I wanted to plan was becoming more and more complicated and I was running out of time in the season to have any games to watch. The longer the deployment lasted, the less time I would also have back home to get used to the idea of being in the civilian world once again. I wanted to have time to decompress before starting a new phase in my life. The longer the deployment lasted, the less time to acclimate I would have. Imagine the feeling of being in the military for four years and having just a month back at home before starting a new chapter in your life. It is a mix of excitement and terror to say the least.

The Last of Everything

The countdown had finally begun. We received word when we would go back to the Al Asad Airbase and would just need to make it one more week. The days came and went and the patrols and guard shifts continued. The clock never stopped and before I knew it, there was just one more patrol left. I didn't need to pack much because we were living out of our sea bags. I remembered how my dad always told me to stay focused and for one more patrol of my career, I could do it.

I put my gear on and tightened the laces on my boots as I prepared for one more patrol in the cold. This would be our farewell tour where we would be going to many houses and saying goodbye to the many people we met during the deployment. The first house we stopped at was a man whose wife was expecting their first child. We would regularly go to this house and show support to his family and see how his wife was doing.

On one patrol, we even brought in the Navy doctor to examine her and make sure everything was going as planned during her pregnancy. The man and his wife were in tears as we told them that this would be the last time that we would ever see them. Our lieutenant told him through our interpreter that we would tell the Marines replacing us about his family, so they could be there to look after them.

Families like this were the reason we were proud to be Marines. This family made the patrols and the hardships worth it sometimes. They had respect for our sacrifices coming so far from home to try and help their country out. Of course, in the big picture it wasn't like this, but in our small world, it was. We cared about the people in this small town more than they could ever know. This was not Ramadi in the heart of the Al Anbar province. This was a farming village where we recognized everyone. The kids knew I was good at soccer and would kick the ball at me so I could do tricks for them. There was no rock throwing or pro-Saddam Hussein chants as we patrolled down the street. Besides the IED the third day we were in Iraq and the suicide bombing, there was actually no violence of any kind. I never even fired my rifle. It was as boring of a deployment as a Marine infantry platoon could expect.

Leaving the family with tears in their eyes I really hoped the future would treat them well. Iraq was too big and complicated to think of as a whole. If I could break the whole country into just this family, I hoped we really made a difference. I saw sadness in the father's eyes as he gave everyone one last hug.

We said our last goodbyes and departed into the night.

I crossed back into the Playboy Mansion as a huge sense of relief overcame me. I was done. I would never go on another patrol in my whole life. I would never experience anything like this again. It was a mix of emotions. I was jubilated that it was all over and happy to have survived. Packed and ready within five minutes, I would just need to sleep one more night at this place and then the next day we would work our way back to Al Asad.

The next morning came slowly because I couldn't sleep. I watched the sunrise from out the front door hoping it would calm my nerves. The clock slowly ticked and ticked as I agonized over every second. After waiting for what seemed like an eternity, transportation had finally arrived to take us to the "Pretty Shitty Base" which was renamed after our fallen sergeant major. We threw our sea bags in one 7-ton and then we all got into the other vehicles.

Driving away from our home of so many months, I said my last goodbye to the Playboy Mansion. Twenty minutes later, the "Pretty Shitty Base" appeared in the distance. We still weren't finished and after dismounting, we would have to wait under the glaring sun for helicopters to pick us up for the last stage in our journey. Waiting and waiting, I sat there watching our numbers drop as one helicopter would pick up a group of Marines and leave. A few hours later, it was my squad's turn to go. This was my first time flying in a helicopter since being injured. The first time was June 14, 2004, while I was clinging to life.

I buckled in and the helicopter took off. I got the sensation of floating in the air as my chest seemed to go into my throat. The sound was loud and it was impossible to hear anyone speaking. The sound of the helicopter relaxed my nerves as we got closer and closer to the base. I felt the helicopter start descending and I knew we were close. The HELO landed with a thud.

We got off the chopper and double checked to make sure we had all of our gear. We walked in single file away from the propeller blades until we were safely out of the danger area of the bird. It was over. Hundreds maybe even a thousand patrols I did in my career and it was finally over. I kissed the Al Asad ground as me and a few others in my squad punched the sky in joy.

I saw the Big Guy a few minutes later and we embraced exhausted by the weight of the last few years.

Now back at Al Asad, we did nothing but eat and rest. It felt great to have almost unlimited free time as the battalion was organizing our flight back to Kuwait. We got lucky in one more respect as well.

At the phone center near the big tents where we were sleeping, a guy from a completely different unit than ours was in a rush and seemed stressed wanting to use the phone really badly. Corporal Lopedog, who was one of the Marines in my squad could tell that he was really agitated and offered him the phone.

After the quick phone call ended, this unknown Marine grabbed his rifle and without hesitation shot himself in the head. There was complete chaos as people were running out while medics were trying to run in. There was nothing anyone could do as he was killed instantly. We were fortunate the Marine didn't take his gun and start shooting anyone else in the phone center before taking his own life. Most likely he took his own life because he suspected his wife or girlfriend was cheating on him while he was so vulnerable so far from home. Maybe she was or maybe she wasn't, but I know Marines well and the only way a Marine would kill himself in that situation, would be over a woman.

Packing for Kuwait, I remembered the letter I had written to my dad in case I was killed in action. Since I didn't need it anymore, I threw it in the burn pit with its words forever gone, except in my memories.

I left my blood, sweat, and tears in you. Goodbye Iraq.

The Last Sail Home

We got on a C-130 and made the short flight back to Kuwait where we were no longer in a combat zone. We stayed at the same base where we arrived after getting off the ships in the middle of October. We again did nothing but relax and eat, where I probably gained five pounds between Al Asad and here.

After we got back on ship, we received official word when we would be returning home. I asked to speak to the first sergeant and explained my situation. My father had already postponed the wedding and I needed special permission to go on leave earlier than the rest of the company. I told him it was very expensive to change wedding dates and to do it again would be unfathomable. He told me he would pass my request up to the captain and we would see from there.

In my mind, there was no way I could be turned down. Let us break down the math of my military career to see if I deserved or didn't deserve the captain granting me an early leave request. Let us not forget that everyone thought I was telling the truth about the whole marriage thing. This is how I calculated my military service:

1) I was about to complete my four-year military service contract.

2) Three months of boot camp, followed by three months of infantry school.

3) Seven-month deployment to Iraq which I did four because I was critically wounded by a machine gun.

4) Seven-month deployment to Okinawa. No combat but lots of training far from home.

5) Seven-month deployment, again with a good amount of time spent in Iraq.

6) Before these deployments there were also lots of workups, which prepare you for the deployment. Near the beginning of a deployment, you are gone doing the workup, which is working up towards the deployment.

7) In my four-year contract, I would easily say that I was deployed or in some type of training for over three years.

8) After being injured, if I really wanted to get out and really pushed for it, I'm sure I could have been discharged medically. I didn't and completed my contract.

Verdict: I would let me go on leave early for my dad's wedding.

We started the long sail back to San Diego. The journey would begin in Kuwait then sail to Perth, Australia, where we would have five days of fun. After that great time, we sailed to Hawaii where we stayed for three days. The final sail home from Hawaii to San Diego would take five days.

The days on ship with even less to do than on the sail towards Iraq went slower than ever. There were no classes to give because most of us would be getting out of the military soon and frankly I didn't care anymore. We gave our junior Marines the run of the company and let them start taking the responsibility for little things. We had a great group of junior Marines and I'm sure that they did an excellent job on their following deployments.

Soon after, word came down that the captain approved my special leave request and I would be able to go to my father's wedding. Once my staff sergeant told me, I pumped my arms in jubilation and couldn't wait to tell my dad the great news. The word was official and because we had an official date we would be coming home, my dad and I could now start planning when and where we would go. All I would need to do was keep my mouth shut and not tell anyone that my lie worked. If I could just celebrate on the inside, all would turn out well.

Although the ships would be going to port in San Diego, the Marines would be getting off at Camp Pendleton. Our company was put in our Amphibious Assault Vehicles and we took off from the back of the ship and splashed into the ocean. Here is a funny fact. Golf Company which was the AAV company, never used these vehicles in combat nor did we even see them. The first time we used them during the deployment were the last ten minutes of it to land at Camp Pendleton. Not once during my Iraq deployment did I ever see the tracks that we trained with constantly over and over before the deployment started. The AAVs drove us to the beach and dropped us off in some parking lot where we would load onto buses.

The Last Ride Home

The buses were late of course and we just sat there waiting. We knew that our families were awaiting our return at our camp at the 62 Area. The buses appeared in all their glory and like a mechanized unit, I swear we put everybody's packs and sea bags inside and were seated in less than ten minutes. It was a glorious symphony of men wanting to go home and see their families.

The buses turned on their engines and we all roared and started cheering. We would have a thirty-five-minute ride to our camp as the minutes again started to count down. I missed the first homecoming because I was injured and watched as my battalion came home. On our return from Okinawa, the celebration was great but not the same because there was no combat involved. This would be my first return home from a combat deployment and the nerves kept growing and growing.

We turned the corner and drove up the big hill. We were greeted by the all too familiar sign, "Welcome to the 62 Area, Home of the Fighting 5th Marines." Families were waving and cheering at us with many of them holding up signs of support and love.

Some of the signs were more interesting than the others. One that really got my attention was one that said, "Juan let's make a baby." Poor guy whoever he was, he probably just wanted a beer and his wife was already talking about making a child.

We parked outside the armory and as usual had to turn in all of our serialized gear. This took forever. I had a scope, rifle, night vision, and a knife to turn in and have my cards returned to me. Each piece of gear had a card you would get once you returned your serialized gear to the armory.

An hour later it was all over and we got into our company formation and marched to the 62 Area parade deck. Left right, left right, left right. Closer and closer, every step we got closer, until we were in sight of the parade deck and all our awaiting family and friends.

Company halt. One hundred fifty men halted in position. Left face. We all left faced, snapping our heels together sounding like thunder.

Golf Company dismissed!

There was a thunderous scream from the parade deck as the deployment was finally over. It was chaotic with family looking for their sons and husbands; Marines looking for their wives and girlfriends, if they still had them after so long. I couldn't find my parents. There was too much pandemonium and too many people who looked alike.

My dad and I found each other and we ran into each other's arms and hugged like never before. It was over, it was finally over. I looked over to my right and I saw my captain looking at us.

"Captain, this is my dad Sergio."

"Your son did a fine job out there."

"Thank you sir, I'm happy to hear that," my dad proudly stated.

The captain added, "Congratulations by the way on your upcoming wedding in Europe."

"Oh fuck," I thought to myself. I imagined myself getting thrown in military jail for falsifying a leave request. I wasn't sure if my dad even remembered our little plan. I hadn't mentioned it to him for a while and after getting my leave approved, I didn't see the need to bring it up.

What were the odds that the captain with his own family to see for the first time in months, would mention the wedding to my dad during all this happiness and joy that we were surrounded by.

My dad looked at the captain and with a twinkle in his eye said, "Thank you sir, we really love Europe."

I was in shock as the visions of me going to jail faded away. How the hell did my dad remember about my plan during all this pandemonium?

"I can't believe it," I screamed as my dad and I embraced once more and started hugging and jumping in circles.

The deployment was over, but my life was just getting started.

Thanks for Serving

It all came to a quick end as I saw our eighteen-year old replacements waiting for us on the parade deck. They were fresh out of infantry school and it was amazing how fast the four years went by. That's actually a lie, they went by really slow sometimes. I felt like I was looking at myself seeing the new boots terrified that the rest of the battalion had arrived home. They would now be yelled at constantly and never be allowed to pass their room inspections.

Since we were getting out soon and no longer needed, we were sent to the barracks down the road far from our company. They were affectionately known as the Crack Houses. Nobody knew exactly when they were built but I would guess sometime during the 1960s. These barracks were absolutely disgusting and not meant for humans anymore. They were in need of major repairs and still had communal showers. Each room was meant for four guys and had rats running around everywhere. Usually the Marines that failed their drug tests were sent to the Crack Houses, so they would be segregated from the rest of the Marines and not to badly influence the Marines who hadn't done drugs, or hadn't been caught at least.

After coming back from Europe, I had about thirty days left in my contract and they would be dedicated to the long process of checking out and getting two wisdom teeth pulled. I would need to go to parts of the base I had never been to before to get signatures from places I had never heard of. The command didn't want anything to do with us and we had all the free time in the world we wanted. They never even took accountability if we were on the base. If somebody asked what unit we were in, we would still say 2/4 but in reality, we were on our own program.

I started growing my hair and could finally as the expression goes "drop my pack." Actually, I started doing that on the way back on the ship. Of course, since the Marine Corps never makes anything easy or explains to you anything, I almost wasn't able to get out of the military on my contract end date.

One of the requirements for checking out was taking TAP classes, which were designed to teach you about all the benefits you were entitled to and how to get them. These classes would also teach you how to be a civilized person again. Apparently in the civilian world, it isn't customary or normal to say things like, fuck, shit, bitch, or cunt every other word. These words can get you fired very quickly from a job instead of encouraged while in the Marines.

Showing up for this class with a week left in my contract, I had no idea what to expect. By this time, our battalion was on vacation and there was nobody left that I could ask any questions to. I just showed up to the class and was preparing to enter the classroom. The guy who was giving the class asked me If I had a certain type of paper that would be needed so I could get it signed once the class was completed.

I told him I had no idea about this paper and there was nobody in my command left to tell me these things. I was told that the reenlistment sergeant in my battalion was responsible for giving me this paper. I told him that was impossible because he was on vacation as was everybody else in my battalion. There just simply wasn't anybody around.

He then started being an asshole and telling me that I could've taken this class up to a year before my contract ended. I tried telling him that I just came back from a seven-month deployment. He then told me that

I should've taken the class before I deployed. He suggested I go talk to his boss to see if he could help me.

This idiot actually thought that in the Marines you get to tell your command when you get to take classes so you can get out of the Marine Corps. My command would never in a million years let me miss pre-deployment training to go attend TAP classes. This asshole actually had the balls to make it sound like it was my fault. I don't know what kind of Marines usually attended his classes, probably like admin or some other jobs that I never heard of before, but never would any infantry battalion let you take classes a year before you needed to; specially to get out of an organization where they wanted you to stay in.

I stepped into his boss's office a bit angered at how the class instructor spoke to me earlier. He was such an asshole and I wished I was momentarily back in Iraq where you didn't have to take shit from anyone. His boss was the complete opposite of him and an incredibly caring man. I told him my situation and that I was running around like a chicken with my head cut off. I just got back from Iraq and my whole battalion was on leave. That was the reason I didn't have the paper for the TAP class. I was just running around the base getting my required signatures and thought I just showed up and I get a signature somewhere on the paper and that was it. Once he found out I was the infantry, he agreed to help me.

We chatted all day long and he told me about all the benefits I would receive and how to go about getting them. He was a great storyteller in the sense that he was giving me all this great information but it wasn't like it was in a classroom. I would just listen to him speak and soak up all the information and just listen to his stories fighting in the Vietnam War. I could tell the memories were still painful because tears would swell up in his eyes talking about all the friends he lost during these horrible battles in the jungle. After all day speaking with me, he took the TAP paper I needed and stamped it. I did three days of classes in just a few hours.

One signature left until I was out of the Marine Corps.

The one signature I needed was the Marine whose job it was to convince other Marines to reenlist and sign another contract. Since our company reenlistment guy was on vacation I did the next best thing. Yes, I did consider forging his signature but being so close to getting out why risk it. I went to the regimental reenlistment Marine so I could get his signature.

It is no coincidence that talking to these guys is part of the sign out process. This is their last chance to get you to sign a new contract and they would put on the pressure I knew it.

I entered his office and explained that my battalion was on vacation and I needed his signature to get out. The Marine told me that before he would sign my paper, he wanted me to talk to the regimental colonel. I wasn't sure what the colonel could tell me about the benefits of me reenlisting. I never met the guy before and maybe the sergeant thought that speaking to a colonel would put the pressure on me to sign another contract. Still under contract, I couldn't just tell him to shut up and sign my paper. I had to be respectful and listen to his bullshit telling me how special I was.

The sergeant didn't know me for shit, yet he tried to make me feel so important. If this guy knew me, he would have known that I wasn't really that great of a Marine. Hell, I wasn't even that good of a Marine. In fact, I was probably a barely average Marine. I was a terrible hiker, average shooter, and most importantly, I was really lazy. In fact, the only thing I was good at was eating and sleeping. Ever since that day in October 2004, when our company hired private contractors to do the work on the company headquarters that they humiliated us injured Marines with, I lost all motivation for the Marine Corps. I knew that whatever job that needed to be done would be done regardless. I would just put in average effort in any situation that wasn't combat related. I just honestly didn't give a shit after the way we were treated.

I left his office telling him I would speak to the colonel. I went to grab lunch instead then took a nap. Waking up, I cleaned myself up a little before going to see the sergeant again. I told him that the colonel and I had a great talk and if he could please sign my paper once and for all. With a look of dissatisfaction on his face, he reluctantly took the paper and signed it. It was now official, I would just need to turn in my paper to the administration department down the road and I would be out of the Marine Corps.

I had a few days left till the end of my contract so I went to my room at the Crack Houses and passed out and did whatever I wanted until the magical day happened.

Those last few days passed slowly counting down the minutes until I would turn in my papers and get discharged. I walked into the admin building and sat down waiting to be helped. There were a few people in front of me and the wait was agonizing. I just needed to turn in the damn paper and I was out of the Marines. I was called up to the desk and gave them my check out sheet with all the required signatures. The Marine looked it over and put a few more stamps on it. He looked up from checking over the paper and said,

"You're a lucky guy, I wish I was getting out too, but I have two years left of this shit."

I smiled and nodded to the Marine,

"You'll be there soon."

Just like that my career was over. Four years had come and gone. Walking towards my car down the road, I still got a dose of Marine Corps reality. I saw a staff sergeant from my company who must have come back early from vacation. For some reason, he never seemed to like me even though I never really talked to him before and tried to avoid him.

Getting close to my car and freedom, the staff sergeant saw me from down the road and yelled out, "Rosman, looks like you need a haircut."

This was my chance to finally not give a fuck because I was no longer a Marine and I honestly couldn't stand the guy.

"Bro, take your haircut and shove it up your fucking ass. See this paper right here? This means I don't give a flying fuck about you or your fucking haircut. I'm out motherfucker."

I got in my car, turned on the ignition and sped away driving out of the gate. There is a tradition once leaving the Marine Corps, to stop outside the gate and throw your boots over the power lines. I didn't stop and I just wanted to get as far from the base as possible.

Where can I start to describe these four years? It was grueling and painful for large parts of it. A majority of the time, I would dread waking up and wished it was all a nightmare.

Other times looking back, I am happy that I did what I set out to do. It is impossible to know if I would've loved the Marines or not unless I did it. Being a Marine was something I wanted to do since I was a young kid and if I never did it, I would've lived the rest of my life full of regret.

There is usually a moment in every sports game when you are facing a difficult opponent and the stakes are at their highest, that's when you can see and feel it. There is a certain intensity and you can't lose your focus for even a second because the other team might win.

Then, when you look into your teammates' eyes you feel this incredible connection with them. This connection feels like you're all in it together and whatever it takes to win, you will do it for them.

That is the closest feeling you will ever get to what being in combat is like, without the fighting. In combat, you are locked in and focused and the brotherhood you feel knowing that everyone is in it together sacrificing for one another is incredible. The friendships and that feeling of comradery you have in the most intense of moments, is what I miss most.

July 13, 2007, was my last day in the Marine Corps.

Where Are They Now

My friend Richey Baby was buried at the Woodlawn Funeral Home in Nashville, Tennessee. He was twenty-two-years old.

Our fallen sergeant major was buried in Arlington National Cemetery, with full military honors, as a hero like him should. I visited his gravesite and there are no words that can describe what it's like seeing so many tombstones all in one field in a row.

Mark Doddridge works for his father's jewelry company in Orange County, California, and is still the coolest dude I know.

Danny McGuigan still drinks and is still a womanizer.

The Big Guy is still big and is currently married. At first, he couldn't afford a ring because he chose to buy an awesome TV instead. As good as always with his hands, he made a ring by himself. He bought a piece of wood and shaved it down in the shape of a ring. He then bought his wife's birthstone and fastened it in, making it look like an incredible piece of handmade jewelry. He still has the wife, the TV, and a real diamond ring now.

The Big Guy works in the oil service industry doing inspection work in refineries in the Houston area. He has a great job and he is doing well for himself. He and his wife are planning to buy a house and start a family. We have been best friends since we were eighteen-years old and we will always be.

Richard Cantu is in a long-term relationship with the Big Guy's sister. They have two daughters together. He works in the same company as the Big Guy and has recently relocated back to Texas. He has a great job and seems to be doing very well. I am very proud of him. After living in Texas for a year, I no longer have any problems understanding his cowboy accent.

Brian Lenhart has returned to the greater D.C. area and spent the years since in various police agencies. He is now a marshal and is part of the Special Reaction Team. I saw him a few years ago and he is doing great. He is married with two kids.

Charles Shepherd is currently living in Indianapolis, Indiana, and I'm not sure why this "California Kid" even knows why. He currently works for the Veterans Administration and is married to his lovely wife. He is no longer an asshole. Even though he treated me like shit and I hated him, I knew he was a good guy at heart. He became a good friend of mine and we speak on a regular basis.

Sergeant America is currently living in Moldova. He has a daughter and is the co-owner of a company that works with governments all over the world supporting various missions. I visited him recently and he is doing great. He is an even cooler guy than I imagined and is still a badass. Even though he is older now, he could still easily kill me in four seconds instead of three when we were both younger.

Chris "Tommy" Thompson didn't take my advice and reenlisted in the Marine Corps. After spending time at Division Schools training other Marines, he was deployed to Afghanistan with a platoon in charge of protecting a general. On one mission, his vehicle was hit by a massive IED and he had to be MEDEVACED. He suffered a horrible knee injury, a severely broken nose, and a bad concussion. Because of the explosion, he ruptured his eardrum for the second time. He has no cartilage in his knees and is partially deaf. After getting medically discharged, he returned to St. Louis, and is going to college for computer programing. He has a beautiful daughter and has been divorced twice, both while in the Marines.

After disappearing off the face of the Earth for four years, he finally reappeared and I got in contact with him immediately. I was angry that he could just disappear with no trace even from the people who cared about him the most. I searched and searched and asked everyone that knew him if they knew what happened to him. Unfortunately, nobody did. He had a lot of personal things going on in his life and just wanted to get away from everyone and get his life straightened out. As it was when we met when we were eighteen-years old or now, I will always be there for him, anytime anyplace. It looks like he has turned a corner in his life.

We are forever held together by a bond that can't be broken. When faced with the worst of all possible humanity, the bonds you make aren't the same as the ones you make in school. When we see each other, we don't even need to speak, but can just nod our heads. We all share the lost innocence of our youth that was left somewhere in the desert all those years ago.

The night patrols, the day patrols, the long guard shifts, the marketplace, the battles, and the friends lost, are all memories of a life I will never know again.

As for me, my future is still being written. Stay tuned…

The End

is the Beginning

The Future

I hadn't felt this kind of fear since Iraq. I was too scared to look behind me, even though looking would've probably been the smartest thing to do. I instead turned my head to the man running next to me and looked into his eyes. They weren't normal size but had the look of fear, the look of a man being chased by a bull in Pamplona, Spain.

I felt my life was in danger and turned my head to see for myself. I saw him in the newspaper that morning and I thought he was almost cute, cute until he was close to me. His name was Chupado, and he was a big grey, one thousand-pound Spanish fighting bull, and he was charging towards me.

This next adventure is a story for another day.

About the Author

Jason was born in Southern California and is currently living everywhere and nowhere. At seventeen-years old, he joined the Marine Corps and deployed three times. In 2004, he deployed to Ramadi, Iraq, and was part of the Battle of Ramadi. In 2005, he deployed to Japan as part of the 31st MEU. In 2006, he again deployed to Iraq with the 15th MEU to the Haditha Triangle.

Some of Jason's decorations are the Purple Heart, Combat Action Ribbon, and Good Conduct Medal. He is most proud of coming home alive.

After being honorably discharged, he enrolled in the University of Nevada Las Vegas, where he received a Bachelor's degree in International Business and Spanish.

In 2015, Jason had an idea to become more artistic but didn't know what this would entail or how he would even start. Without realizing it, he accomplished this by writing a book and learning how to dance Zouk. In order to complete his artistic journey, Jason wants to learn how to play the piano and start contemporary dance training.

Jason is an avid traveler and would like to visit every country in the world. He has currently been to fifty-three countries and has lived in Australia, Argentina, Brazil, and Spain.

For more information and photos please visit his website at: Ishouldhavegonetocollege.com

Facebook page: I Should Have Gone to College

Email: Ishouldhavegonetocollege@gmail.com

Made in the USA
San Bernardino, CA
29 May 2018